NOW FOR THE CONTEST

GREAT CAMPAIGNS OF THE CIVIL WAR

SERIES EDITORS

Anne J. Bailey
Georgia College & State University

Brooks D. Simpson
Arizona State University

WILLIAM H. ROBERTS

Now for the Contest

Coastal and Oceanic Naval Operations in the Civil War

University of Nebraska Press
Lincoln and London

Library of Congress Cataloging-in-Publication Data
Roberts, William H., 1950–
Now for the contest : coastal and oceanic naval
operations in the Civil War / William H. Roberts.
p. cm.—(Great campaigns of the Civil War)
Includes bibliographical references and index.
ISBN 0-8032-3861-4 (cloth : alk. paper)—ISBN
0-8032-0475-2 (electronic : alk. paper)
1. United States—History—Civil War,
1861–1865—Naval operations.
I. Title. II. Series.
E591.R635 2004
973.7'5—dc22
2004005362
Set in Plantin by Kim Essman.
Designed by Debra Turner.
Printed by Thomson-Shore, Inc.

To Peg and Judy

Contents

Illustrations

Charts

Series Editors' Introduction

Americans remain fascinated by the Civil War. Movies, television, and video—even computer software—have augmented the ever-expanding list of books on the war. Although it stands to reason that a large portion of recent work concentrates on military aspects of the conflict, historians have expanded our scope of inquiry to include civilians, especially women; the destruction of slavery and the evolving understanding of what freedom meant to millions of former slaves; and an even greater emphasis on the experiences of the common soldier on both sides. Other studies have demonstrated the interrelationships of war, politics, and policy and how civilians' concerns back home influenced both soldiers and politicians. Although one cannot fully comprehend this central event in American history without understanding that military operations were fundamental in determining the course and outcome of the war, it is time for students of battles and campaigns to incorporate nonmilitary themes in their accounts. The most pressing challenge facing Civil War scholarship today is the integration of various perspectives and emphases into a new narrative that explains not only what happened, why, and how, but also why it mattered.

The series Great Campaigns of the Civil War offers readers concise syntheses of the major campaigns of the war, reflecting the findings of recent scholarship. The series points to new ways of viewing military campaigns by looking beyond the battlefield and the headquarters tent to the wider political and social context within which these campaigns unfolded; it also shows how campaigns and battles left their imprint on many Americans, from presidents and generals down to privates and civilians. The ends and means of waging war reflect larger political objectives and priorities as well as social values. Historians may continue to debate among themselves as to which of these campaigns constituted true turning points, but each of the campaigns treated in this series contributed to shaping the course of the conflict, opening opportunities, and eliminating alternatives.

William H. Roberts's examination of the naval conflict reminds us of the need to temper notions of the American Civil War as the first modern war. Both sides embraced innovation in different areas, with the Union surpassing the Confederacy when it came to the construction of ironclads, while the Confederates excelled in underwater warfare. Yet innovation wrestled with tradition, suggesting the transitional nature of the conflict in the evolution of naval warfare; many of the gains realized by the war would erode soon afterward. Roberts restates the case for the importance of the Union blockade, a subject of some controversy in recent scholarship, by highlighting how it constricted Confederate commerce and restricted the Confederacy's ability to import materials, machines, and munitions essential to waging war. While the Union's efforts at challenging Confederate control of the coast yielded mixed results, its riverine flotillas proved invaluable as Union armies penetrated southward along the Tennessee, Cumberland, and Mississippi Rivers; the capture of New Orleans in April 1862 marked a major Union triumph. The Union's efforts to fend off Confederate commerce raiding largely nullified the impact made by the css *Florida, Alabama, Shenandoah,* and other commerce raiders. Nevertheless, the Confederacy made good use of some of its opportunities, applying technological innovation in the form of submarines and mines to fend off the invaders. Roberts reminds us of the important role played by the Confederate army in defending the coast, and notes how Robert E. Lee's decision to deploy a defense in depth along the south Atlantic coast contained Union encroachments. Finally, he argues that the civilian and military leadership of the Union navy outperformed its Confederate counterpart, despite the dashing exploits of a handful of grayclad commanders: David G. Farragut's colorful language overshadowed the accomplishments of several of his comrades, notably David D. Porter and Samuel Du Pont, much as the clash between the *Monitor* and the *Virginia* seized center stage in the imaginations of many observers then and now. Often cast in the background of the ground conflict, the war on the waters receives its due in this volume.

Preface

The presidential election of 1860 was over. Few Southerners had voted for the winner, Republican candidate Abraham Lincoln, and his overwhelming majority in the Electoral College came entirely from Northern states. Southerners saw the eventual demise of slavery in Lincoln's election, and in December 1860, South Carolina made good on decades of threats by voting to withdraw from the United States. "The Union," read a Charleston handbill, "is dissolved!"

The navy of 1860 was poorly prepared for the roles that would soon be thrust upon it. Accustomed to the peacetime routine of "showing the flag" and protecting commerce on distant stations, it was an amalgam of old and new. Most of its 7,600 enlisted men were seamen, but the force included mechanics and firemen. Some of its 1,550 officers had fought in the War of 1812, and younger officers had distinguished themselves in the Mexican War and in antislavery operations and hydrographic expeditions. Steam engineers, a growing minority, understood the latest technology even though their service could not afford to implement it fully.

The navy's ships showed similar contrasts of old and new. They ranged from antique sailing line-of-battleships to modern steam frigates. Most were deep-water vessels, intended for oceanic operations, although a few shallow draft vessels formed the legacy of efforts by Southern congressmen to further Southern aspirations in Central and South America. Steam technology had brought a new way to propel ships, and with it the beginning of new ways to build and outfit them as well.

This volume is inescapably more about the Union navy than the Confederate. The Union navy at its peak encompassed over fifty thousand men and nearly seven hundred ships; operationally, as Lincoln put it, everywhere the ground was a little damp, "Uncle Sam's web-feet" made their mark. The Confederate navy was far smaller, never exceeding some five thousand men, and its ships numbered in the tens rather than the hundreds. Yet it, too, made its mark, embracing innovation in everything from ironclad warships to underwater explosives and scoring some inspiring successes. In this work as in the Civil War itself, the Confederacy's "technology strategy" and its overseas programs form the main counterweight to the Union's numerical preponderance.

Both innovation and asymmetry shaped the naval war. The Civil War brought the widespread use of steam propulsion, iron armor, underwater mines and torpedoes, rifled cannon, and instant communications. It saw the first steps toward submarine warfare, centralized control of naval operations, and industrial mobilization for naval purposes. Although both sides embraced innovation, asymmetry was the order of the day, from the resources and strategic objectives of the belligerent nations to the size, composition, and employment of their naval forces.

The Civil War's many modern aspects can mislead, however, and to understand the war's context, the reader must be wary of assumptions. The common caution about things appearing more clearly in hindsight is certainly valid, but we must delve deeper in a number of areas. Modern technology, for example, may skew the reader's appreciation of the options available to the historical actors—navigating Charleston Harbor today with radar and fathometer is not without hazard, but the experience belies the difficulties of moving up Rebellion Roads under fire in a monitor. The accumulation of "operational art" also skews our perception, as we view amphibious operations through the lens of Normandy and Inchon rather than through the lens of Veracruz.

A more important factor is our changed view of society and social organization. Civil War America, North and South, was a much "looser" society, and that looseness had important consequences. Popularism, the idea that civilian leaders would automatically be good military leaders, was strongly entrenched and widely approved. Most real power had been held at the state and local levels, and extensions of national power were strongly resisted. During the war state governors North and South openly defied their national governments.

Even within the national governments, as one author understated it, "Modern concepts of administrative unity do not apply to the Civil War." On both sides, cabinet officers did not routinely coordinate with each other, and rather than make joint plans, army and navy officers were likely to proceed independently or even to conceal their intentions from their counterparts. Union or Confederate, army or navy or civilian, no group held a monopoly on stiff-necked insistence upon minutiae and prerogative at the expense of larger goals.

The oceanic naval war involved three major campaigns: the blockade, the commerce raiders, and the projection of power ashore. After discussing the improvised navies of 1861–62, this work examines the development of these three campaigns in the early years of the war. Thematic chapters on the blockade and the commerce raiders are followed by a discussion of the late war period and a summary of the naval war's lessons and effects.

Secession split the service and created two navies from one, and the circumstances of civil war led the two on differing paths. In the end, innovation met innovation, courage and skill met equal courage and skill.

NOW FOR THE CONTEST

CHAPTER ONE

Secession at Sea

After South Carolina seceded, President James Buchanan watched and waited while the other Deep South states followed. Although Buchanan's policy of conciliation and delay offered the only hope of preserving the Union and avoiding war, his execution of that policy appears timid and blundering.

On January 5, 1861, the steamer *Star of the West* left New York City for Charleston, South Carolina. She carried reinforcements and supplies for Maj. Robert Anderson's garrison, which had recently moved from Fort Moultrie to the more defensible Fort Sumter. When the vessel arrived at Charleston four days later, South Carolina troops occupying Fort Moultrie fired upon her. Unarmed and unescorted, *Star of the West* returned to New York without reinforcing Anderson's troops.

Other recently seceded states had already begun to join South Carolina in flexing their muscles. Alabama militiamen seized Fort Morgan at Mobile, Alabama, on the same day that *Star of the West* left New York. Louisiana troops took over Forts Jackson and St. Philip on the Mississippi on January 10, and Alabama and Florida units occupied Fort Barrancas and the Pensacola Navy Yard at Pensacola, Florida, on January 12. Hoping to avoid confrontation, Buchanan vacillated between the desire to strengthen Federal positions and the desire to not alarm Southerners or precipitate an armed conflict. His weak stance and unwillingness to dismiss openly pro-secession men from his cabinet encouraged other secessionists to think he would make no forcible effort to maintain the Union. Secessionists were further emboldened by local "nonaggression pacts" like the one concluded at Pensacola at the end of January 1861 between Florida officials and Capt. William S. Walker. Walker, acting under orders from Secretary of the Navy Isaac Toucey, agreed not to land troops to reinforce Pensacola's Fort Pickens if Florida agreed not to attack the fort.

When Abraham Lincoln took office as president on March 4, 1861, his goal differed from Buchanan's in one crucial way: Buchanan wanted to preserve the Union without war whereas Lincoln wanted to preserve the Union. Even within Lincoln's cabinet, reasonable men differed in their opinions as to how to hold the Union together. Buchanan had done nothing to prepare the navy for conflict, but Lincoln's avowed policy of conciliation and his urgent desire not to commit an overt act of war against the new Confederacy became a handicap almost as big as Buchanan's inaction. Lincoln believed that a mild policy would hold the border states and the Upper South in the Union and encourage the seceded states of the Deep South to return. On the Southern side, Confederate leaders read Lincoln's conciliatory policy as evidence of weakness; the Northerners—materialistic, divided, and lacking honor—would back down.

Although willing to compromise on many points to restore the Union, there was one issue upon which Lincoln stood firm: the containment of slavery. The men leading the Republicans had been working toward this end since the Free Soil Party was established in 1847, before the Republican Party itself was formed. After a dozen years of effort they had fairly and squarely elected a "containment" administration. Lincoln could not and would not ask them to go back and start over—containment was nonnegotiable.

From the Southern point of view, containment was similarly nonnegotiable. Even if the Republican Party ultimately did not come out for abolition, slavery was a fragile institution that required wholehearted control and constant attention from all levels of government. Were a Republican administration to fill Federal offices in the South with men who were lukewarm to slavery, they could gradually build Southern loyalty to the Republican Party; if contained, slavery would collapse of its own weight. Southern elites perceived Lincoln's election as a direct threat to the economic, political, and social fabric of the South.

The chief actors in the new administrations were the presidents. Jefferson Davis had a long history of public service. An 1828 graduate of West Point and a veteran of seven years of frontier duty, he had returned to the army to serve as commander of a Mississippi regiment in the Mexican War. After four years as secretary of war in the Pierce administration, Davis was elected to the Senate in 1857, a seat he left when Mississippi seceded early in 1861. On February 9, 1861, Davis was elected provisional president of the Confederate States of America. Sam Houston once characterized the wealthy Davis as "cold as a lizard and ambitious as Lucifer." Recent scholarship casts Davis in a more flattering light, but it is difficult to argue with the contention that his remarkably erratic judgment of people and his resistance to changing his mind after making a decision undoubtedly hurt the fortunes of the Confederacy.

Abraham Lincoln was far less polished. Mostly self-educated, Lincoln served but saw no combat as a militia captain in the Black Hawk War of 1832. The young Whig lawyer served four terms in the Illinois legislature and one term as a U.S. congressman. He ran unsuccessfully for the Senate in 1855, and joined the new Republican Party in 1856. Lincoln gained national recognition in 1858 during his unsuccessful Senate campaign against Stephen Douglas. When the Republican Party turned away from William H. Seward for being too controversial, Lincoln became the party's compromise candidate for president in 1860. Many found him rough and uncouth, but he learned quickly on the job.

The presidents' chief subordinates were likewise quite different. Gideon Welles was Lincoln's secretary of the navy, chosen in part because of the geographic balance he gave the cabinet. The Connecticut newspaper editor, a Jacksonian Democrat turned Republican, fit the traditional mold of a secretary of the navy in that he had never been a seafarer. He did have solid experience with naval administration, having served as the chief of the Bureau of Provisions and Clothing from 1845 to 1849, and he would prove to be an astute observer, a prolific diarist, and a tireless worker. Welles would need all his energy to meet the challenges facing the Union navy.

On the Confederate side, Stephen R. Mallory faced even more daunting problems. Mallory, an attorney and customs official from Key West, had seen military service as a Florida militia officer in the Second Seminole War. His acquaintance with the navy, however, came primarily from his ten years as a senator. As a member and later chairman of the Senate Naval Affairs Committee, he obtained a good policy-level view of the navy, but his administrative abilities had not been tested. Mallory, whose appointment also reflected the perceived need for a geographically balanced cabinet, took office on February 21, 1861, one day after the Confederate States Navy Department was established.

Although Mallory's problems mirrored those of other departments of the new Confederate States government, he and his colleagues in Davis's cabinet had reasons for optimism. Northerners were divided, and Northern "mudsills," they thought, would not fight for the Union. Should Lincoln's "Black Republican" government force a war, the border states and Upper South would provide a defensible buffer zone, "Southron" valor would be irresistible, and European powers would quickly intervene to maintain their vital supply of cotton.

The "short war" idea was central to most early Confederate thinking. The North was little stronger than the South, and if the war did not last long, the South's weaknesses might not matter. But the longer the war, the more difficult the Confederacy's task would become. With few ships and seamen at the outset, Mallory faced other areas in which the Confederacy's potential strength was lacking.

Financially, the South mixed strength and weakness. The Southern economy was overwhelmingly based on the export of agricultural staples, predominantly cotton, and those exports earned much of the foreign exchange of the United States. The nation's primary capital markets remained in the Northeast, however, and the exchange earned by Southern products usually passed through Northern banks.[1] The South's export trade would be a significant advantage if the Confederacy could take it over and keep it going, but building an army and navy from nothing would take every cent and more.

In population, the long-term balance was less favorable to the South. In 1860 the Northern states and territories boasted a population of nearly nineteen million, to three million in the slaveholding border states and nine million in the Confederacy. Of the aggregate twelve million people in all the slaveholding states, however, only eight million were free.[2] The slaves could be a significant economic asset, but the specter of a slave rising had haunted Southerners for decades, and the departure of many white males for military service could make slavery a long-term domestic liability. When the war began, however, the size of the opposing armies was limited not by the number of men available but by the difficulties of arming, equipping, and maintaining them. Initially, those difficulties were not much greater for the Confederacy than for the Union.

The least favorable balance in the long term was industrial. The Census of 1860 counted 1,173 "manufactories," of which only 115 were in the South. The region produced about 10 percent of the country's bituminous coal, 5 percent of its refined iron and railroad rails, and none of its anthracite. The South was also woefully weak in "tools to make tools," because not one of the seventeen factories that built machinists' tools was in the Southern states.[3] In 1861, however, very little industry on either side was actually devoted to arms or munitions; the North's ability to wage industrial war was more potential than actual. Again, a short war would favor the South, because it would take time for the North to mobilize.

The proximate cause of war turned out to be the issue that Buchanan had dodged: Federal property in the seceded states. As long as Federal troops occupied Federal forts in Confederate States territory, the Confederate claim of sovereignty was a sham. Confederate leaders wanted the forts; Lincoln, who saw that giving up the forts would be tantamount to recognizing the Confederacy as a separate nation, promised to "hold, occupy, and possess" the government's property. In early April, he authorized an expedition to reinforce and reprovision Fort Sumter in Charleston Harbor, and he sent Lt. John L. Worden overland to Pensacola with orders to land the reinforcements that Buchanan had sent to Fort Pickens.

The naval aspects of the Sumter expedition and the competing expedition to Pickens remain murky. Gustavus Vasa Fox, a former naval officer turned businessman, had proposed the expedition to reinforce and reprovision Sumter. After Fox reconnoitered Charleston in person in late March, Lincoln approved the plan, which would involve several small vessels covered by the warships *Powhatan*, *Pawnee*, and *Pocahontas* and the revenue cutter *Harriet Lane*. Seward, now secretary of state, may have had his own informal agreements with Southern authorities, and he supported the Pensacola expedition over the Charleston effort. Taking advantage of Lincoln's trust and the president's heavy workload during the early days of his administration, Seward bypassed the secretary of the navy to have Lt. David D. Porter placed in command of the steamer *Powhatan* and to have that powerful ship diverted from Charleston to Pensacola.

Welles was not the man to allow such interference to pass unchallenged. He believed strongly that cabinet officers should consult freely with each other but should not try to run each other's departments. When he discovered Seward's meddling, he insisted upon an immediate meeting with Lincoln.

At the meeting on April 6, Seward admitted that he should not have interfered, and he sent a telegram to Porter instructing him to return the *Powhatan* to her regular commanding officer. Whether by accident or design, though, Seward signed his own name to the telegram. Porter, claiming that his original orders had come from the president and that therefore only the president could countermand them, refused to turn over the ship and steamed off for Pensacola. Porter's willful action crippled the Charleston expedition before it began.[4]

The expedition had another major problem. Despite Welles's attempts to maintain operational secrecy, the Confederates knew all about it. Seward had maintained unofficial but close contact with representatives of the Confederate government and may have deliberately informed them, either directly or through an intermediary, but official Washington was so notoriously leaky that there was no real need to construct any conspiracies. The Confederate government had plenty of warning and plenty of time to consider what to do.

Hoping to engage the fence-sitting Upper South as well as to wrest the fort from the Union, Confederate authorities ordered Gen. Pierre G. T. Beauregard, commanding at Charleston, to demand Fort Sumter's evacuation. Beauregard did so on April 11, 1861.[5] When Major Anderson refused his demand, Confederate forces began to shell Fort Sumter on April 12. The fort surrendered after a day's bombardment while Fox's relief force, weakened by the diversion of the *Powhatan*, stood impotently off the harbor.[6]

On April 15, Lincoln's call for seventy-five thousand volunteers showed that he meant what he said about using force to hold the Union together. The prospect of coercion triggered the departure of the states of the Upper South (Virginia, North Carolina, Tennessee, and Arkansas), albeit with substantial Unionist minorities.[7] War had begun, and the time for naval temporizing had passed.

The nation's naval potential vastly exceeded its strength, but in 1861 both were divided unequally between the combatants. Almost all of the U.S. Navy's enlisted personnel remained with the Union, and the North's pool of merchant seamen was six times the size of that of the South and the border states combined.[8] Officers were less unevenly divided, and a substantial minority "went South" during the secession crisis or soon after war began. Others sought distant assignments, hoping to wait out the crisis without having to commit themselves decisively.[9] When war began in April, a combination of administrative inexperience, uncertainty, and the disloyalty, opportunism, or confusion of some officers hobbled the U.S. Navy Department's ability to act.

The loss of the Gosport (Norfolk) Navy Yard provides a prime example. Fearing that the state of Virginia would secede, in early April Welles dispatched officers to take charge of the steam frigate *Merrimack*, then under repair at the Gosport yard. Chief Engineer Benjamin Franklin Isherwood performed near-miracles to reassemble *Merrimack*'s engines, but Commodore Charles F. McCauley, the shipyard's aged and vacillating commandant, negated his efforts.[10] McCauley, a veteran of the War of 1812, was confused by the pace of events. Deterred by the counsel of his junior officers, many of whom were Confederate sympathizers, and fearing to precipitate violence, McCauley would not allow the repaired *Merrimack* to depart.

Welles sent Capt. Hiram Paulding to relieve McCauley, but by the time Paulding reached the shipyard, Virginia state troops were massing nearby. Paulding and his men burned and destroyed what they could, but their time was short and the destruction far from complete.[11] When the Confederates captured the yard on April 20, 1861, they got not only the salvageable *Merrimack* and the yard's drydock and shops but also more than 760 heavy cannon and 140 tons of powder for them. Captured cannon from Norfolk armed many of the coastal defenses the Confederacy built during the first year of the war.[12]

Beyond such overt manifestations, Southerners occupied positions throughout the federal bureaucracy. Especially at first, it was difficult to determine who was loyal to the Union and who was not.[13] Welles wrote that many secessionists in the Navy Department, military and civilian, had resigned, sparing him the need to remove them. This pleased the secretary, since the subject required delicate treatment.[14] Questioning an officer's loyalty and integrity was a grave matter, but a disloyal officer might do great harm, perhaps by turning his ship over to the Confederacy.[15] The officers and employees who resigned identified themselves unequivocally, but a few sympathizers appear to have thought to aid the Confederacy from within the U.S. Navy. The most visible was Capt. Samuel Barron.

On April 1, 1861, Welles received an unexpected order from President Lincoln that instructed him to place Barron in charge of the Bureau of Detail, with an expanded mandate that extended from officer assignments to recruiting and naval discipline. When Welles went to remonstrate with the president, he found that Secretary of State Seward had handed the letter to Lincoln and Lincoln had signed it without reading it. Lincoln told Welles to disregard the order, and in their conversation it emerged that Lieutenant Porter and army Capt. Montgomery C. Meigs had drafted the missive.[16] Barron's home state, Virginia, seceded on April 17, and

Barron resigned from the U.S. Navy on April 22. Exemplifying the hard-line policy applied after the war began, Welles refused to accept Barron's resignation and instead dismissed him from the service.[17] The captain promptly joined the Virginia Navy and later the Confederate States Navy.

Unlike Welles, Mallory could at least count on the fidelity of his officers, all of whom had committed themselves irrevocably by entering Confederate service. Yet for all his troubles, Welles inherited a functioning naval bureaucracy, a pool of ships and seafaring men from which to increase his navy, and an undeveloped but substantial industrial base. Mallory had to start from scratch, simultaneously developing everything from an administrative organization to ropewalks, biscuit bakeries, and shipyards. Beyond the 373 U.S. Navy officers and midshipmen who "went South," he had a handful of seized and purchased ships and the inadequately destroyed Norfolk Navy Yard. The South's maritime weakness was profound, and the relative positions of the two combatants helped to shape their initial strategies.

When war began in 1861, the Union's war aim was to restore political responsiveness in the South without losing support in the North. The Lincoln administration had to move cautiously, since even after Sumter, some Northerners had reservations about forcing Southern states back into the Union. Of those who were willing to apply coercion, the vast majority wanted to restore the status quo rather than to undertake experiments in social reform—they wanted a war for Union, not a war for abolition.

The North based its initial strategy on the idea, strong in Republican circles, of the "slave power conspiracy"—the concept that a slaveholding aristocracy (the "slave power") controlled the South and was trying to control the entire Union. Lincoln and many others thought a minority of Southerners had hoodwinked the rest into leaving the Union; since the "slave power" couldn't control the Union anymore, slaveholders had decided to leave. His conciliatory policy and his initial war-fighting strategy were based upon what John Shy would later call "triangularity of struggle." In Lincoln's view, the war involved not two parties but three: the United States, the Confederate leadership, and the Southern people. The North's best policy would be to separate the perceived Unionist majority of Southerners from the slaveholding leadership.

The North's initial strategies reflected both its conservative war aim and its belief in the "slave power" theory. In May 1861, General in Chief Winfield Scott enunciated a strategy to isolate the South economically.[18]

His scheme, referred to by detractors as the "Anaconda Plan" because it was intended to constrict the South, made economic isolation on the seaboard the job of the navy. The army would gain control of the Mississippi River, simultaneously opening that artery to Northern trade and blocking it to Southern trade. Economic pressure would bring out latent Unionism, Scott hoped, but his plan would also avert bloodshed— bloodshed that would harden attitudes both North and South and make reconciliation impossible.[19]

Scott, however, envisioned taking six months to build and train an army for the Mississippi expedition, during which the South would be able to consolidate its position. Others could not accept such a delay. Like Scott, Lincoln hoped for reconciliation, but unlike the general, the president believed it was vital to crush the rebellion quickly before disunionist attitudes could solidify. Accepting the blockade and the need to control the Mississippi River, Lincoln combined these elements with a ground offensive to take the new Southern capital at Richmond, Virginia, in a short military campaign. Quick military victories and increasing economic pressure would combine to cause Southern Unionists to rally to the old flag, and a conciliatory attitude would help to reestablish "the Union as it was."[20]

On the navy side, the Union had three major strategic concepts that would have to be embodied in operational campaigns. Welles enumerated them late in 1861 in his annual report:

> 1. The closing of all the insurgent ports . . . in the form and under the exacting regulations of an international blockade. . . .
> 2. The organization of combined naval and military expeditions to operate in force against various points of the southern coast. . . .
> 3. The active pursuit of the piratical cruisers.[21]

The opening of the Mississippi, it should be noted, was not a navy objective. Following the logic of Scott's plan, the War Department took responsibility for the Mississippi campaign, and the navy initially provided only a few naval officers and naval constructors to help the army convert and build gunboats. Welles's willingness to back away from the Mississippi force appears to have had two major roots. For one thing, the Navy Department had challenges enough on the coasts. For another, "brown water" riverine navigation and warfare were not part of the "blue water" navy's professional repertoire.

Strategically, that repertoire involved a reasonably well developed concept of aggressive wartime naval operations. As Cdr. Samuel F. Du Pont articulated the concept in his 1852 *Report on the National Defences*, however, it was based upon the attack and defense of trade. Du Pont argued that the navy should "contend for the mastery of the seas, where alone it can be obtained, on the sea itself." It would obtain this mastery by sweeping away foreign commerce, by fighting the foreign warships and fleets that tried to protect it, and by protecting its own commerce. In addition, the navy's function as the "sword of the state" would include short but highly destructive surprise raids against enemy cities and naval facilities, "the kind of warfare we must look to, and which we must carry on ourselves." To mid-nineteenth-century U.S. naval officers, and to the Confederate officers who shared the identical strategic heritage, mastery of the sea meant commerce destruction and commerce protection, not sustained amphibious campaigns and climactic fleet actions. We must be cautious about measuring the Civil War navies' "mastery of the seas" against an anachronistic version of "command of the sea."[22]

Certain aspects of this naval paradigm were more familiar than others. One reason was that for most of the navy's existence, it had been weaker than its potential adversaries, and its "service culture" was shaped by an underdog's view of sea warfare. The War of 1812 remained a defining experience for the navy of 1860—many of its veterans were still on active duty—but objectively, in that war, the United States had been bested. The victories on the Great Lakes marked the only American strategic successes. The navy's minor achievements in commerce raiding had been counterbalanced by an almost hopeless record in commerce protection, and the "raids from the sea" fell mainly upon the Americans. The "glorious" single ship actions mattered primarily for their psychological effect in building the young U.S. Navy's confidence; they had almost no practical impact on the Royal Navy. In terms of drawing lessons from experience, as the underdogs the Confederacy's naval leaders would be on much surer ground.

Another reason stemmed from the operations of the Mexican War. The navy had landed General Scott's army over the beach at Veracruz, kept it supplied for three weeks by the same route, and supported its siege of the city. Although this gave American naval officers an opportunity to develop more than theoretical knowledge of "mastery of the seas," it seems to have been an episode rather than a campaign. On the Gulf coast, the navy's role stressed blockading and raiding, while in California, raids and direct support of troops were most important. Du Pont's own experience in command of the *Cyane* highlighted incursions rather than invasions, and his *Report* stresses raids and offensive action against commerce.[23]

The first formal enunciation of naval strategy came from the Federal side, where on April 19, 1861, President Lincoln proclaimed a blockade of the ports of South Carolina, Georgia, Alabama, Florida, Mississippi, Louisiana, and Texas as part of his policy of economic isolation. Another proclamation on April 27 extended the blockade to Virginia and North Carolina.[24] Secretary Welles grumbled that a blockade would elevate the insurgents to "the dignity of nationality" and would replace U.S. domestic law by "the law of nations, as expounded by British Admirals."[25] Welles argued that Lincoln should have closed the Southern ports by decree, but hindsight shows that Lincoln and Seward made the correct decision. Although the term "blockade" implicitly granted the Confederacy de facto status as a belligerent nation, it also carried connotations that European powers could not ignore.[26] Great Britain worried especially about establishing precedents, since a strong British defense of neutral rights in the "American war" might well boomerang in some future conflict.

At the operational level, increasing the fleet and establishing a blockade had considerable historical precedent. Both could be begun without much discussion, but once they had been initiated, thought would be required as to what to do next. On May 30, 1861, Welles instructed the chiefs of the Navy Department bureaus to consider how to supply the blockading squadrons. Welles saw the Gulf of Mexico squadron, farthest from Northern ports, as the most difficult challenge.[27]

Supplying a blockading fleet was not a new problem, but in the days of sail, the blockaders' main needs had been infrequent supplies of provisions and water, with perhaps a few havens in which ships could take refuge against storms and conduct occasional refits. The steam machinery that had revolutionized blockade tactics and naval construction had also revolutionized naval logistics. To maintain their ships on station, the blockading squadrons would need not only provisions but also frequent repairs and constant supplies of coal.

Unfortunately for the Federals, the few Southern outposts that remained to them could not support a blockade. On the Gulf coast, Union troops held Fort Pickens at Pensacola, Florida, but the Confederates had captured the Pensacola Navy Yard and Fort Barrancas across the bay, so there were no repair facilities. Key West, Florida, had remained in Union hands, but it also lacked repair facilities. Between Key West and

Hampton Roads, Virginia, Union ships had no place to go for supplies or storm avoidance; for major repairs, ships had to go even farther north than Hampton Roads.[28] Unless the Union could establish logistics facilities close to the theater of operations, a blockade would require too many ships to be practicable—more ships would be occupied in traveling between their bases and the blockaded ports than would actually be present on station.

Welles recognized the broadening scope of the blockade support problem, but he also recognized that the bureau chiefs, who already had full-time jobs, were not the best men to address it. At the instigation of Professor Alexander D. Bache, the superintendent of the U.S. Coast Survey, Welles decided to form a board to combine all the information available to the government about the Southern coast. In addition to Bache himself, loaned from the Treasury Department, the group included Maj. John G. Barnard, USA, and Cdr. Charles H. Davis. Welles appointed Capt. Samuel F. Du Pont as the senior member. The conference (also called the Blockade Strategy Board and the Committee of Conference), which Du Pont thought would involve a week of his time, convened on June 27, 1861, for what became three months' work.[29]

Welles told Du Pont that the navy needed to capture at least two points on the Atlantic Coast and at least one on the Gulf of Mexico. Du Pont was to survey the information available to the government and report any that would bear on the "contemplated movement" to seize blockading bases on the Atlantic coast. The conference went beyond that, again apparently at Bache's instigation, to produce "mémoires" with broader implications.[30]

The reports of the conference show that the conferees carefully distinguished between "a purely military expedition" and the establishment of bases "for promoting the efficiency of the blockade." The military expeditions they had in mind corresponded roughly to a modern amphibious campaign, in which troops use the mobility conferred by seaborne transport to begin a land campaign from an advantageous location or employ planned sequential landings to turn enemy defenses. Such a campaign requires the invader to select landing locations that allow good communication with the interior, both to prevent the troops from being bottled up near the landing site and to facilitate supplying large forces.

For a blockade base, however, the most desirable sites were those that combined adequate harbors with defensibility against attacks from landward, rather than sites that offered easy access to the interior for an invading army. The conferees' first report proposed Fernandina, Florida, as the best site on the Confederacy's Atlantic coast; its second report added Bull's Bay, Saint Helena Sound, and Port Royal Sound, all in South Carolina. The conferees ranked Bull's Bay and Saint Helena above Port Royal, explicitly noting that Port Royal's fine harbor and other advantages would be offset by the need for more defensive troops and fortifications. This theme of defensibility carried through all of the Conference reports dealing with the Atlantic coast.

The Conference issued its last report on September 19, 1861, and its members turned or returned to other duties. Despite Bache's desire to establish an "advisory council, to determine military proceedings and operations along the coast," no organizational successor appeared after the Conference disbanded.[31] Contrary to assertions that it was a "proto–Joint Chiefs of Staff" that provided ongoing strategic direction, the Committee of Conference was merely a temporary study group. The conference's reports, limited as they were, did greatly influence Union naval strategy. On August 3, 1861, Welles told Du Pont that the "invasion and occupation of the seacoasts of the States in rebellion, as proposed by the Navy Department," had been accepted by the government. The War Department had agreed to an expedition to seize a blockade base, with troops to be commanded by Brig. Gen. Thomas W. Sherman, and Welles appointed Du Pont to command its navy component.[32]

Opponents of Scott's "Anaconda Plan" clamored for a more active strategy that would produce results more quickly. Public opinion or no, the "Anaconda" initially became more than a constrictor because the navy needed to support and tighten the blockade. The logistics of steam compelled the snake to develop fangs, but the navy's commitment to the offensive use of naval power against the Confederacy's coasts never wavered.

Early Southern policy was similarly affected by perception. Northern leaders perceived that most ordinary Southerners were loyal to the Union, whereas Southern leaders perceived that most ordinary Northerners would not fight for it. Even if some did fight, "Southron" manliness and virtue would quickly overcome Northern avarice and dishonor. Leroy P. Walker, later the Confederacy's first secretary of war, expressed a common opinion when he offered to mop up all the blood that would be spilled over secession with his handkerchief.

Secession left the Confederacy facing a simpler strategic problem than that which confronted the Union. Like the colonials in the American Revolution, the Confederates began the war with de facto control of the government of their territory—in a word, independent. To undo this fait accompli, the North would have to conquer the seceded states. To maintain their independence, the Southerners needed to hold what they had and to outlast the North. On the face of it, the situation seemed to call for a defensive stance.

As one author has pointed out, however, Confederate war aims were in fact threefold: independence, territorial integrity, and the union of all the slave states and territories.[33] De jure independence was the only aim of the three that could be gained by standing purely on the defensive. The latter two required offensive action, first to expel Federal forces from the South and then to incorporate the border slave states and the territories of the Southwest. Given its disadvantages in men, resources, and geography, the South could not afford to cede the initiative to the North. Moreover, the goal of territorial integrity and the expectation of a short war contributed to the Confederacy's decision to defend its entire border.

This decision has been criticized on military grounds, but there were valid arguments in its favor. Psychological reasons for forward defense abounded; in addition to public clamor, one of the Confederacy's most cherished contentions was that it was a real nation, a going concern, and that real nations defended their borders. Practically, both military and economic factors favored forward defense. Militarily, in the short term the Confederacy was about as strong as the Union and had the advantage of interior lines. Economically, the loss of territory meant the loss of its resources of material and manpower, and much of the Confederacy's industry was located near its borders. Also practically, despite the Union's early-war insistence that it did not want to interfere with slavery, the "peculiar institution" would never be the same if Federal armies could enter Southern territory with impunity.

The equation changed, however, as one neared the shoreline. The Confederacy was far from equaling the Union's naval strength, and the disparity was increasing almost daily. On the coasts, the mobility advantage lay not with interior lines but with sea power, and perimeter defense thus meant defeat in detail. Prewar U.S. planning for coastal defense had recognized the need to concentrate, envisioning a scheme based on four pillars: "fixed defenses, a navy, a professional army supplemented by a well-organized militia, and an efficient system of interior land and water transportation and communication."[34] The navy was to attack an invading force at sea and force it to remain concentrated. Once the attacker landed, the permanent fortifications and the standing army would fight a delaying action until the militia could assemble and drive the invaders into the sea. For a nation averse to standing armies, the system was theoretically sound, although the deterioration of the militia by the 1830s rendered it decidedly questionable in practice.

When war began, the Confederacy had to make adjustments, not least because the Confederate navy could not make the defensive contribution that prewar planning had assumed. Yet the most significant adjustment recognized political necessity at the expense of military prudence. Public pressure forced the South to adopt perimeter defense of its coast, with results that will be discussed in chapter 3.

At sea, the Confederacy initially sought to implement the "coast defense and commerce raiding" strategy and to counter the Federal blockade. The Confederate navy's initial defensive contribution was essentially nil, but the desire to "break the blockade" helped to drive Mallory's choice of a technologically based strategy, and the first Confederate ironclads were intended to open the Confederacy's ports.[35] Attacking Union shipping, Mallory thought, would also cause the Federals to pull ships from the blockade to chase the Confederate cruisers.

In the "commerce raiding" portion of the "coast defense and commerce raiding" strategy, the asymmetry of Confederate and Union sea power favored the Confederacy. The South had no merchant marine of its own, so it could attack Northern merchant ships without fear of direct Federal retaliation. Unfortunately for the Confederacy, the resources available for such attacks on commerce were correspondingly slim. The South adopted a time-honored way of increasing them when on April 17, 1861, President Jefferson Davis proclaimed that the Confederate government would issue letters of marque to privately owned vessels, allowing them to capture U.S. ships as prizes.[36] Northern commercial interests promptly panicked at the prospect of attacks by hundreds of "piratical" cruisers, a panic that remained more or less in effect throughout the war despite the small number of privateers and the few prizes they took. Du Pont was correct when he wrote in July 1861 that the privateers would be short-lived, but "we must remember those Navy officers South are bone of our bone and could not sit along shore and devise nothing."[37]

Soon after the Confederate announcement came the British government's proclamation of neutrality, excoriated by Northerners as pro-Southern because it recognized the Confederacy de facto as a belligerent power. Mature reflection, however, would have shown that there was much for the North to applaud, most significantly Britain's refusal to permit the entry of privateersmen's prizes into British and colonial ports. The decision gave the British the practical benefits of noninvolvement and advanced Britain's long-held desire to outlaw privateering altogether.

Privateering was not the only way that the Confederates planned to attack Union shipping, and the British prohibition on the entry of prizes may have increased Confederate efforts to fit out and commission naval vessels for commerce raiding. The reason turned on maritime law: After a privateer captured an enemy vessel, he had to obtain a court's ruling that the capture was legitimate, or his action was mere piracy. Privateering involved taking the property of enemy civilians, and as such, it could not be reduced to simple capture and destruction. In contrast, a warship acting on behalf of a government could, if necessary, legally destroy the vessels she captured. The Confederates began to convert merchant ships into commerce raiders shortly after the outbreak of war, and the first such cruiser, css *Sumter*, left New Orleans on June 30, 1861, under the command of Raphael Semmes. Meanwhile, Mallory had dispatched agents to Great Britain to buy or build cruising ships, but this effort would take time to bear fruit.

Both Federals and Confederates developed their strategy with an eye toward Europe. The principal powers, Britain and France, developed a reasonably well coordinated response to the "American question," a task perhaps eased by the recognition that disunion could cripple a potential rival. Yet their policies of neutrality, superficially similar, masked differing national interests and differing ways of making political decisions. The French, interested in protecting their Mexican adventure, were initially more willing than the British to help the Confederate States. In addition, given France's governmental structure, Emperor Napoleon III's whims and calculations could provide a highly elastic interpretation of even the most clearly expressed policy. Britain's concern for British North America made her more sensitive to the United States, but the maritime role of neutrality was unusual for the British. Taking up the cudgels for neutral rights could set precedents that would likely injure British interests in the longer term. Further complicating the issue, making and implementing policy was a more public process in Britain than in France, and both belligerents tried hard to influence the process.

By mid-1861, then, both Union and Confederate leaders had established strategies to govern their conduct of the war. The North would use its maritime superiority to interdict the South's commerce and raid the Southern coast, while the South would try to protect its coastline and to render the blockade ineffective. To execute their strategies, however, each would need far more naval force than either had readily available. Improvisation would be essential on both sides.

CHAPTER TWO

Improvised Navies

When war began in April 1861, the U.S. Navy boasted fewer than seventy usable vessels—thirty-four steamers and thirty-five sailing ships—and rapid expansion of the fleet became a top priority. This expansion took two forms, purchase and construction, and the navy began building gunboats and buying merchant vessels that could be converted into blockaders (see figure 1).

The navy entered the commercial shipping marketplace with stumbling steps. Line officers, naval constructors, and engineers received the responsibility of buying merchant ships, but their lack of experience as shipbrokers quickly became evident. Shipowners took advantage of the opportunity to unload almost anything that would float—at excessive prices. To cope with the problem, Welles combined the personal and the professional by appointing George D. Morgan, his brother-in-law, and John M. Forbes as purchasing agents in New York and Boston, respectively.

Morgan made excellent bargains, purchasing eighty-nine vessels for $3.5 million and saving the navy about $900,000 in the process. Those bargains, however, enraged many New York shipowners, and Morgan's receipt of $70,000 worth of commissions on the purchases gave Welles's political enemies a convenient opening to charge the secretary with nepotism.[1] Welles may have been politically injudicious in granting Morgan a shipbroker's percentage instead of paying him a salary, but Morgan gave Welles what the navy needed: quality ships at excellent prices at a time when fraud and profiteering were rampant.

Once purchased, the ships had to be converted for naval service. This was not conceptually difficult, since the vessels were not expected to fight other warships. Relatively few changes were required, and those were predominantly connected with mounting a few pieces of heavy ordnance, such as strengthening the decks and building magazines. The difference between theory and practice, however, was greater in practice than in theory. Converting one ship would have been simple, but converting many in a short time was much more difficult, and the program quickly bogged down. To manage the process, Welles chose to decentralize it. In July 1861 he recalled Capt. Francis Hoyt Gregory from retirement and appointed him to supervise the construction and conversion of gunboats in the New York City area.[2]

Gregory's appointment roughly coincided with the commencement of the first large class of purpose-built warships, the Unadilla class of wooden-hulled screw gunboats. The twenty-three "ninety-day gunboats," small but heavily armed for their size, were begun in early July 1861, and the *Unadilla* was in fact commissioned just ninety-three days after her builders received the contract for her. The Navy Department pushed gunboat construction hard enough that four of the class participated in combat at Port Royal in early November 1861 and seventeen had been completed by year's end. The ninety-day gunboats reflected both Welles's sense of urgency and his willingness to take risks. Congress had not authorized the ships, but Welles began them anyway, reasoning correctly that he would receive approval after the fact.

The year 1861 saw much more new construction. Seven steam screw sloops authorized in February 1861 were begun in May as the Ossipee class. Six "fast screw steamers," deep-water vessels capable of up to 13 knots, were laid down late in 1861. Most peculiar were the twelve "double-enders" begun in autumn 1861. These side-wheelers were designed for work in narrow waters where they would be unable to turn around.[3] The navy encountered few technical or contractual problems in any of these programs, but steam propulsion, of itself, was no longer high technology (see figure 2).

Because of the magnitude of the effort, most of the new ships were built by contractors. The navy had always preferred to build ships in its own shipyards, where it had complete control of design and construction, but the prewar navy yards of the 1850s could not build steam engines and boilers. To integrate private contractors without losing control, the navy evolved "carrot and stick" contracts. First, to encourage timeliness and relieve contractors of financial burdens, the navy made progress payments at certain construction milestones. Second, each contract included a performance guarantee. The navy would "reserve"—that is, withhold—final payment until the ship performed successfully at sea.[4] The Union's early efforts seemed to show that the system could work in wartime. Not until 1862 would it begin to break down under the twin pressures of urgency and technology.

By the end of the summer of 1861, then, the U.S. Navy's expansion was well begun. As poorly equipped as the Union navy was, it still far outstripped its opponent. In February 1861, the Confederate States Navy boasted four seized revenue cutters, three small steamers, a captured slaver, and a creaky U.S. Navy side-wheeler that had been laid up in Pensacola.[5] The Confederates followed the same pattern as the Federals, buying and building ships as best they could, but it was evident that the Confederacy could neither outbuild nor outpurchase the Union.[6] If the Confederates chose to build wooden ships, Mallory wrote, they would have to build several at once or risk being "easy prey" for the more numerous Union vessels.[7] Since maritime and industrial weakness made a symmetrical force-on-force strategy impractical, Mallory had to find another way to defend the new nation.

As one recent historian has convincingly argued, Mallory chose technology as his counter to Union material preponderance, and ironclad warships became the first manifestation of this technology policy.[8] Southern congressmen had urged the construction of ironclads as early as February 1861. During the second week in May, Mallory told the chairman of the House Committee on Naval Affairs that invulnerability could make up for unequal numbers, and in response, the Confederate Congress approved $2 million to purchase ironclads in Europe.[9]

Although Mallory wanted to obtain an ironclad as quickly as possible, and even directed an agent in Europe to investigate purchasing one of the existing French Gloire class, he also began to assess the South's resources for construction at home. The reports he received were not encouraging—only the Tredegar Iron Works in Richmond could make the heavy plates that an ironclad would need. Nonetheless, by late June Mallory had decided to build seagoing ironclads in the Confederacy.

The first project Mallory approved was developed by Lt. John M. Brooke and naval constructor John L. Porter. An otherwise unsuccessful search for engines and boilers to use in an ironclad led to the machinery of the sunken *Merrimack* and then to a proposal to use the existing hull as well. In late June or early July, Mallory ordered the Gosport Navy Yard to begin converting the *Merrimack* into an ironclad, which would become CSS *Virginia*.[10] Brooke's vessel would have a broadside battery behind a sloping armored casemate. Notwithstanding the submerged bow and stern that were an integral part of Brooke's scheme of protection, Mallory expected a seagoing vessel to emerge.

New construction vessels followed closely in the wake of the *Merrimack* conversion. In August, Mallory approved the construction of two ironclads in Memphis and one in New Orleans, and in September he contracted for another at New Orleans. The converted *Merrimack* and the four new construction ships were intended to go to sea; besides keeping the Union out of Southern waters, the ironclads would ultimately "contest with [the Federals] the possession of [their] own."[11]

Mallory also planned to contest Federal waters with ships built overseas. The Confederate navy had begun to look for ships in Europe soon after war broke out, sending James D. Bulloch and James H. North to England as special agents under the authority of a secret act that the Confederate Congress passed in May. Bulloch, a former U.S. Navy lieutenant who had resigned in 1853, was to procure cruising ships, while North, who had resigned his U.S. Navy lieutenancy during the secession crisis in January 1861, was to obtain ironclads.[12] Bulloch, an energetic and highly capable officer, set to work immediately and by August 1861 had placed contracts with British builders for the ships that would become the commerce raiders CSS *Florida* and CSS *Alabama*. North, operating with far less of a sense of urgency, did not contract for an ironclad until May 1862.

The second major element in Mallory's "technology strategy" was the torpedo, which we would now call a mine.[13] The South began to experiment with torpedoes soon after the war began, and in June 1861, Matthew Fontaine Maury demonstrated the possibilities of submarine explosions to a group of Virginia state and Confederate officials. He soon became the leader of the Confederate navy's torpedo efforts, in charge of the navy's "Bureau of Special Service."[14] Others of like mind were also at work, including former U.S. Navy lieutenants Beverly Kennon and Isaac N. Brown. Kennon appears to have been responsible for the first operational torpedoes, encountered by the USS *Resolute* and USS *Pawnee* in the Potomac River on July 7, 1861.[15] Brown, meanwhile, was sent west to assist Maj. Gen. Leonidas K. Polk on the Mississippi and its tributaries.[16] Maury was not content to lead from the laboratory, either, and personally commanded a attempt to torpedo Federal ships in Hampton Roads in July 1861. Later that year, he took charge of submarine defenses in the James River, for which he developed electrically controlled torpedoes that could be exploded by an observer ashore. Maury supervised the navy's torpedo effort until he was sent overseas in 1862, when he was relieved by Lt. Hunter S. Davidson.[17]

The Confederate navy thus placed its faith in advanced technology because it had few other choices, but the decision had its drawbacks. The elements needed for successful torpedo warfare were still laboratory curiosities, and much experimentation would be required to develop reliable, effective weapons. Similarly, although the Confederacy began the "ironclad race," it was constrained by its limited engineering and industrial resources to choose a very simple type of ironclad (the armored casemate ram). On the Union side, greater resources permitted more design freedom, but with increased options came more complex interactions, both technical and nontechnical.

On May 30, 1861, Secretary Welles had instructed the chiefs of the Navy Department bureaus to consider how to supply the blockading squadrons, especially in the Gulf. The board of bureau chiefs met the same day and quickly determined that special supply steamers would sail from the North to the Gulf and back by way of Key West, with a similar plan for the squadron on the Atlantic side. More recommendations followed, but by the third day of its meetings, the board had expanded its scope to discuss shipbuilding policy and "mail clad steam floating batter[ies]."[18]

Based on the bureau chiefs' recommendations, Welles prepared legislation to authorize ironclad construction, and on August 3, 1861, the U.S. Congress appropriated $1.5 million to build ironclads. Four days later the navy advertised for proposals, eventually receiving seventeen that ranged from a 90-ton iron gunboat to a "shot-proof vessel" of 6,520 tons. An evaluation board reviewed the proposals and selected three of the seventeen to build.[19]

The ironclad board's choices varied widely. One proposal, which would become the *Galena*, had a conventional hull and broadside battery covered with a novel system of interlocking armor strips. The second, which would be called *New Ironsides*, was a fully rigged, high-freeboard ship with solid armor and a broadside battery. The third was John Ericsson's proposal for a single-turreted, low-freeboard "Impregnable Floating Battery," which became the *Monitor*. In making their decisions, the board members showed their support for unconventional ideas; both *Galena* and *Monitor* were novel designs, and *Monitor* offered the shallowest draft and the shortest building time of any of the three ships.[20]

At the same time, the board understood that ironclads were the high technology of their era. By 1861 the British and French navies had built successful ironclad vessels, but opinions on ironclad design varied widely. Ironclad technology had advanced beyond the ability of theory to explain it; it offered both great promise of success and significant risk of failure. As the board members clearly saw, the nation dared not risk everything on a single variation—if it failed, the consequences would be grave. To hedge their bets, the members selected a range of designs, from the conservative *New Ironsides* to the radical *Monitor*. Ericsson's quick-to-build design offered a large potential payoff, while the *New Ironsides* traded higher cost and longer construction time for low technological risk and greater assurance of effectiveness. The immediacy of the naval threat made time the single most important driving factor. When the board made its report on September 16, 1861, the conversion of the *Merrimack* was known to be well under way.

In fact, if one were to characterize the Union ironclad program with a single word, that word would be "urgency." Urgency kept the navy from meeting the rigid testing schedules mandated by its 1850s-style contracts. Urgency prevented the navy from taking time to resolve technical ambiguities in advance. Urgency drove the navy to make production decisions in a partial vacuum, committing itself to produce several similar classes of ships before "lessons learned" from the first vessels were available, and urgency rendered the navy vulnerable to political pressure in its acquisition decisions. The theme of the first two years of the war was urgency, first, last, and always. Under such pressure, the prewar ship acquisition system began to break down.

The urgency was not confined to the Navy Department. Word of the Confederates' Memphis and New Orleans ironclads had probably reached official Washington, but the Mississippi theater was initially the responsibility of the War Department. The navy only provided the army with advisors, sending Cdr. John Rodgers and naval constructor Samuel M. Pook to Cincinnati in mid-May 1861. Rodgers purchased the riverboats *Lexington*, *Conestoga*, and *A. O. Tyler* in early June, and he and Pook managed their rough conversion into "timberclad" gunboats quickly enough that they could fight their first action against a Confederate gunboat on September 4, 1861. Pook meanwhile designed the vessels that became the seven "city" class ironclads, for which James B. Eads of St. Louis received a contract in August 1861.[21] Pook completed all seven ships in January 1862, but the Union's riverine construction and conversion program continued through 1865, eventually producing more than twenty ironclad vessels. Even after the river flotilla was transferred to the navy on October 1, 1862, riverine construction continued to be managed independently of shipbuilding on the Atlantic coast. Although it began earlier, the riverine ironclad program never approached the level of industrial effort expended on the coastal ironclads.[22]

On the coast, Welles also moved promptly, and by mid-October all three first-generation oceanic ironclads were on the stocks. Counting the army's riverine efforts, by that date the United States had eleven ironclads built or building, compared with seven in the Confederacy. Despite their not unequal numbers and their head start, the Confederates had to cut their coats to fit their very limited cloth, and shortages had already begun to retard construction. Both Welles and Mallory faced significant obstacles to increased ironclad production. The Confederates' domestic ironclad program was handicapped by shortages of material (especially machinery and armor), of skilled labor, and of cash, and their overseas building efforts needed constant infusions of hard currency and skillful diplomacy. The North had plenty of resources, so the Union's problems were less technical or logistical than political.[23]

Even before the contracts for the North's first three oceanic ironclads were let, the U.S. Navy was planning follow-on ships. Chief Constructor John Lenthall and Chief Engineer Benjamin Franklin Isherwood developed a design that in essence combined *Monitor*'s shallow draft, low freeboard, and turret-mounted guns with *New Ironsides*'s solid armor, and added twin screw propulsion for maneuverability. With this design in hand, Welles in December 1861 asked Congress for authority to build twenty more ironclad vessels. Fearing that the navy's in-house design would compete too heavily with Ericsson's proposed "improved *Monitors*," the inventor's influential backers stalled the "twenty ironclads" bill in the Senate. After six weeks of delay, Welles broke the logjam by promising to forsake the Lenthall-Isherwood design, and the "twenty ironclads" legislation passed the Senate within hours. Further delay was inevitable, however, since Welles also had to agree that the navy would wait until *Monitor* was tested before contracting for any of the twenty vessels.[24]

The winter of 1861–62 saw both Union and Confederate shipbuilders working hard on ironclad vessels, and both sides began to consider how they would use the ships once they had them. Confederate policy appears to have passed through two stages. When the first Confederate ironclads were approved in July 1861, Secretary Mallory appears to have intended to use them to break the Union blockade. As late as March 1862,

Mallory urged Commodore Franklin Buchanan, commanding the iron-clad *Virginia*, to break the blockade in Hampton Roads and put to sea to attack and burn New York City, saying that this would "strike a blow from which the enemy could never recover."[25]

The Union, facing different strategic challenges, planned different employment for its ships. The Union's first three ironclads were built to counter the Confederate vessels that were already under construction, but the ships of the follow-on "twenty ironclads" program were conceived with other priorities in mind. One of them was defending the United States from Great Britain; the other was offensive action against the Confederacy.

The need for oceanic defense seemed acute, since the country was then embroiled with the British over the *Trent* affair. Charles Wilkes, commanding the steamer USS *San Jacinto*, had received intelligence that two Confederate diplomats, James M. Mason and John Slidell, would take passage from Havana in the British mail packet *Trent*. On November 8, 1861, Wilkes stopped the *Trent* at sea and removed the Confederates, inflaming public opinion in Britain and causing a major crisis.

The episode ended in an American apology and the return of the prisoners, a legacy of bad feeling—and the sense in the Lincoln administration that war with England must be avoided for the time being, "for the plain reason that *now* we are unable to meet it."[26] The "twenty ironclads" would both bolster the nation's defense against Great Britain and allow the navy to take the offensive against the Confederacy. In a February 1862 letter to John P. Hale, chairman of the Senate Naval Affairs Committee, Welles made the navy's offensive policy explicit: the ironclads, he wrote, were "to reduce all the fortified seaports of the enemy and open their harbors to the union armies."[27]

An offensive ironclad policy, however, would have to wait until the ironclads were built, and that would not be soon. Ericsson's powerful backers had forced Welles to agree not to order more ironclads until "Ericsson's battery" was tested, and *Monitor*'s construction had stretched well beyond the contracted one hundred days. At the beginning of March 1862, the Union still had only three ironclad ships under construction.

The situation changed dramatically during the second week in March. The newly completed *Virginia* attacked Federal ships in Hampton Roads on March 8, destroying the sailing frigates USS *Congress* and *Cumberland*. The news sent the North into panic, with even cabinet officers verging on hysterical fear. *Monitor* and her exhausted crew arrived from New

York that evening, after nearly foundering during the passage. She fought *Virginia* to a draw on March 9, 1862, transmuting the North's fear into euphoria. Ericsson's prestige soared.

Assistant Secretary Fox witnessed the battle and came away an ardent admirer of Ericsson and of the monitor design. If "timing is everything," *Monitor* had great timing—Ericsson's vessel had dramatically retrieved a naval disaster and scored a tremendous public relations success for the navy. Fox's enthusiasm was understandable, but it caused him to overlook *Monitor*'s faults and accept uncritically the popular assessment of victory. Fox became a true-believer "monitor man," giving Ericsson's design the "most potent countenance of the Navy Department."[28] Welles, too, jumped on the monitor bandwagon. Within a week after Hampton Roads, he ordered six identical "improved *Monitors*" from Ericsson, which were soon joined by four more copies from other builders. They were only the first of many.

By the end of the first year of war, then, both navies had embarked on major shipbuilding programs. The ships, however, would do little good without crews to man them. In 1861, the U.S. Navy expanded its enlisted force threefold, from 7,600 to 22,000 men. During this era there was no recruit training system, so most men went directly to ships to learn as best they could.[29] The officer corps, already depleted by the departure of officers to join the Confederacy, posed a more difficult challenge.

The U.S. Naval Academy provided excellent training, but the navy needed officers immediately rather than years in the future. To meet the need, Welles began in March 1861 to appoint "acting" officers, although the practice was not sanctioned by law until late July 1861. The initial legislation allowed the appointment of acting officers up to the grade of lieutenant. Later laws expanded the secretary's authority to allow acting appointments up to the grade of commander, although none were made to that relatively high rank.[30]

The secretary could draw from several sources, including former officers and midshipmen who had resigned before the war, former navy enlisted men, and men with experience on inland waters. As might be expected, though, the largest supplier of acting officers was the merchant marine.[31]

John Mayhew Butler was in many ways typical of the volunteer officers. Butler, born on Martha's Vineyard, was a veteran of whaling and merchant voyages when he enlisted in Chicago in May 1861 and was sent to the

USS *Michigan* as a clerk. His sea experience earned him a transfer to the Washington Navy Yard for gunnery instruction, an appointment as mate in January 1862, and a commission as acting master in May 1862. Butler soon joined the ironclad *New Ironsides*, then building in Philadelphia, as a gunnery division officer.[32] During the course of the war, the Union commissioned about seventy-five hundred volunteer naval officers.

In some respects the Union navy and the Union army faced similar difficulties, but the officer procurement policies they followed in their expansions quickly diverged. The army accepted volunteer units formed by state governments, which came complete with their own officers. Most such officers had no military experience, but whatever their professional shortcomings, their initial state commissions made potent political and recruiting incentives in the hands of state governors. In addition, the army eventually allowed its regular officers to serve with volunteer units at increased rank and made wide use of brevet (temporary) promotions for both regular and volunteer officers. Volunteer commissions and brevet appointments also smoothed the return of former officers who had resigned before the war.

By contrast, Welles worked hard to keep the navy a national service rather than a state service, so there were no volunteer units in which regular navy officers could serve at increased rank.[33] Volunteer officers commissioned from civilian life rarely reached even the grade of lieutenant commander. While promotions came more quickly than in peacetime, the navy did not follow the army's practice of granting brevet ranks. Despite its tenfold expansion, the navy required few officers of high rank compared with the army, and the unquestioned need for nautical expertise prevented the appointment of "political admirals" to match the army's "political generals." The war did loosen the stranglehold of seniority at the higher levels, but even a court favorite like John Dahlgren had over thirty-eight years of naval service when he was promoted to rear admiral.[34]

The navy's restrictions also complicated the return of former officers. A proposal to restore them to their former positions on the navy list caused considerable service controversy, especially among those who had remained on active duty and over whom some of the returnees would take precedence. Former officers lobbied hard to be reappointed with their former dates of rank, arguing that the earlier appointment should be honored. Their peers, and especially their juniors, objected—they could not see why men who had left the navy for several years should be preferred over men with more active naval service. Because naval officers advanced by seniority, those years were crucial. In almost every case, former officers were reappointed to more junior ranks than they had held or to their old ranks but with new (and thus more junior) dates of rank.[35]

Relations between volunteers and regular navy officers were not always smooth.[36] Many volunteers thought that the regulars were inefficient or lacked zeal in their efforts to put down the rebellion or that the regulars were more concerned about their careers than about winning the war. Acting Master Butler complained, "Who cares whether a man knows his duty or not as long as he is a regular," and asserted that the regulars "do not like the Acting men to go ahead."[37] Not everyone shared Butler's opinion of the relative merits of volunteers; enlisted man Charles Post claimed that hotel hallboys were "generally far more intelligent and agreeable than the average 'acting officer.' "[38] Sailmaker Nicholas Lynch agreed, writing disparagingly of acting masters who had been "boarding house runners, Cape Cod fishermen, and blubber hunters."[39]

The Confederate navy faced somewhat different challenges. For one thing, the Confederacy was at first better provided with officers relative to the size of its force, so Mallory had less need to expand the Confederate officer corps than Welles had to expand the Union one. For another, almost all of the Confederacy's line officers had previously served in the U.S. Navy. The Confederate structure, however, suffered severely from top-heaviness: Not only did it have too many senior officers for its size, but its assignment policies were more strictly controlled by seniority than were the Union navy's. As a result, Confederate officers spent much of their time wrangling about who should be senior to whom, and each chief of the Office of Orders and Detail appears to have used his office primarily to angle for orders to an operational command.[40] John M. Brooke wrote that the "system of making no promotions" and filling positions "with men according to their age" left to the younger officers "the task of mending bad work."[41]

After trying for two years to circumvent these difficulties, Mallory finally obtained a law creating a "provisional navy," in which seniority would be less influential. He planned to make operational assignments based upon provisional navy, rather than regular navy, ranks, but it was another year before all physically qualified officers were assigned to the provisional navy.[42] In this respect as in others, the Confederate navy's institutional focus on the long view seems to have overlooked the South's overriding need to prevail in the short term, and Mallory's inability to control backbiting and jealousy in the officer corps was clearly detrimental.[43] Similarly, the Confederates were less successful than the Federals in unifying their naval efforts, although most of the state organizations were eventually absorbed into the provisional navy.[44]

On the enlisted side, the Confederacy's requirements were considerably smaller than the Union's, but Southern manpower resources were extremely sparse. Few prewar Southerners were seafarers, and in the South, as in the North, laws governing enlistments and conscription favored the army. The service's initial authorization of 500 men had been filled by July 1861, and Mallory had to ask Congress for 500 more. Further increases followed, and the Confederate navy appears to have peaked in the spring of 1864 at some 4,460 men, of whom "about 500" were then serving overseas.[45]

At any given time over the course of the war, from 80 to almost 90 percent of Confederate navy enlisted men were serving in home waters. Few Southerners served in the crews of the commerce raiders because most of these ships were built and manned overseas. It was difficult enough to assemble a ship's complement of officers discreetly in a foreign port, and it would have been prohibitively difficult and expensive to transport an entire crew from the South to meet a new ship. The commerce raiders' pattern of Southern officers and predominantly foreign sailors held true to the end of the war.

Although many average, undistinguished, or superannuated officers "went South," the Confederate navy's rolls also included a number of top-notch men, and the South clearly received its fair share of the prewar navy's line officer talent. In the key area of naval engineering, though, it was seriously shortchanged. Less than 17 percent of the navy's prewar engineers went South, compared with almost 24 percent of commissioned line officers, and few of the engineers were among the front-runners in their corps.[46] The lack was crippling.

The shortage of naval engineers required both sides to recruit them from civilian life, but the South was also distinctly short of civilian engineers and mechanics from which it could draw experts for the navy. Although the North had a far larger pool of civilian engineers from which to draw, the massive naval buildup, concentrated on steam-propelled ships, demanded a similarly massive expansion of the Engineer Corps. At the beginning of 1861, the U.S. Navy had a total of 192 engineers, all of them regulars. By the end of 1861 the regular U.S. Navy Engineer Corps had grown to 404, and by January 1865, to 474. During the same period, however, the number of volunteer engineers rose from zero to 1,803.[47]

Although the standards for appointment to the regular service were not noticeably relaxed during the war, little examination was required of volunteers, and many marginally qualified or inexperienced men were appointed as acting engineers. It took time to weed out the hopeless cases and train the others.

Both sides found that even men who were competent operating engineers in other environments had difficulties at sea. Boilers ashore and on the rivers, for example, made their steam from fresh water; boilers at sea used salt water, which caused increased fouling, scaling, and corrosion. Engines ashore were solidly bedded on unmoving ground, or like locomotives were small enough to be self-contained, while engineering plants at sea suffered from the stresses and misalignments caused by ship's motion. Even civilian marine engineers found differences: Unlike seagoing merchant ships or river steamers, naval vessels often had to be at instant readiness for full power for weeks or months at a time. For an engineer trained on steamboats on the inland waters, a seagoing engineering plant would have many technical and operational surprises.

Chief Engineer Benjamin Franklin Isherwood, the man in charge of the Union navy's engineering expansion, did his best to minimize those surprises. Appointed engineer in chief in 1861 over several more senior men, he became the head of the Bureau of Steam Engineering when it was created in 1862. Isherwood's emphasis on practicality placed him at odds with many in his profession, and his blunt, combative manner helped to make him a controversial figure. The engineering plants he designed received constant criticism for being too large and heavy, but Isherwood understood what his critics did not: in wartime, durability and reliability trumped technical elegance. Peacetime machinery, operated by experts, could be designed for maximum efficiency; Isherwood's machinery, operated largely by amateurs, had instead to be designed for effectiveness. His conservative designs continued to work when other machinery broke down or wore out.

In contrast, the Confederate navy did not even have an engineer in chief until after a year of war. William P. Williamson had been the most senior engineer in the prewar U.S. Navy, but had been passed over by Isherwood's appointment as engineer in chief. Unlike Isherwood, Williamson left his subordinates to their own devices. Isherwood attacked the problem of inexperienced engineers by concentrating on simple designs and by prescribing technically conservative instructions, regulations, and operating procedures. Williamson never addressed the issue. Instead, he busied himself designing ineffective machinery for nonexistent vessels.[48] Start to finish, engineering would be a key Confederate weakness.

This weakness was reflected in the organization of the Confederate Navy Department. The Confederate structure included four offices (the equivalent of the U.S. Navy's bureaus): Orders and Detail, Ordnance and Hydrography, Provisions and Clothing, and Medicine and Surgery. Given that Mallory had espoused technology as the "equalizer" between his David and the Union Goliath, it is surprising that the Confederacy made no clear organizational provision for building or repairing ships and engines. Not until April 1862 did Mallory appoint Williamson as acting engineer in chief, and there was no central construction and repair organization until 1863.[49] The Confederate navy officially appointed only three naval constructors—John L. Porter, the chief constructor, and two acting constructors—and Porter did not receive his appointment until late 1862.[50] Although this lack of emphasis probably reflects the lack of emphasis that the service's uniformed leaders placed on engineering and material issues, Mallory was ultimately responsible for the organization of his department. His failure to act decisively in such a critical area bespeaks a failure of leadership or of perception.

Both Mallory and Welles, however, correctly perceived the need for haste. Neither navy was adequate to its task, and the war would not wait until either had been expanded and perfected. The navies would begin their operations with what they had, while their shore establishments strained to provide more ships, more guns, and more men.

CHAPTER THREE

Early Operations

Execution of the opposing strategies began long before they were fully articulated. In the North, the blockade had first call on naval resources; in the South, coastal defense and commerce raiding were the top priorities.

Lincoln had proclaimed the blockade of the Southern coast in April 1861, leaving Welles and the navy scrambling to support it. Welles immediately began to purchase and arm merchant steamers and to enlist men to supplement the ships, officers, and crews he had, but at first his force was totally inadequate. On May 1, 1861, Flag Officer Silas H. Stringham was appointed to command the newly formed Coast Blockading Squadron and directed to blockade all the ports east of Key West. Stringham arrived at Hampton Roads to find he would have to cover the coasts of Virginia and North Carolina, and the entire Chesapeake Bay, with his flagship *Minnesota*, the sailing frigate *Cumberland*, three steamers, and two steam tugboats. Other portions of the Atlantic coast were equally barren: A single vessel blockaded Charleston, South Carolina, for example, and there were no ships available to close Savannah, Georgia.[1] Stringham's shortage of ships presented both a practical and a legal problem. Specifically, legal scholars of the time agreed that a "paper blockade—that is to say a blockade by mere proclamation, without ships, or with but an inadequate force of ships,—is entitled to no deference from neutrals."[2]

Commodore William Mervine was in a like predicament. In early May, Welles appointed him to blockade all the ports from Key West through Texas and gave him ten steamers and a sailing sloop with which to do it.[3] In the first of several reorganizations that affected the navy's forces afloat, on May 17, 1861, Mervine's command was officially named the Gulf Blockading Squadron. Simultaneously, Stringham's force was renamed the Atlantic Blockading Squadron, and Flag Officer Garret J. Pendergrast's Home Squadron was redesignated as the West Indies Squadron (chart I).

More descriptive names did not change the underlying problem of inadequate force, nor did Welles's attempts to respond to intelligence of specific blockade-runners and cargoes by shifting forces from one port to another under centralized direction.[4] Because the intelligence was vague and general, communications were slow, and the chances of successful interception were low, this practice increased the flag officers' difficulties in stationing and supplying their ships without conferring any benefit. As the blockade began to stabilize later in the year, the Navy Department learned to content itself with passing intelligence about known and suspected blockade-runners to the on-scene commanders.

The commanders' resources, although still far too thin to enforce even a reasonably porous blockade, were at least increasing. By the end of June, Stringham's squadron could boast eighteen steamers and seven sailing vessels. The navy's frantic efforts in Northern ports were beginning to show results, albeit somewhat mixed results: Of the twenty-five ships Stringham listed, six were suited only for the relatively calm waters of the Chesapeake and four were under repair.[5]

The British government, at first skeptical, had by November 1861 privately accepted that the blockade was effective; by the spring of 1862, Lord Russell stated publicly that a blockade that created "evident danger" of entering or leaving port was legally effective even if some ships escaped capture. It was very much in Britain's long-term interest not to "question too closely . . . lest precedents be set which could one day be used against Britain."[6]

The blockaders, especially at first, concentrated on the South's major seaports. The low-lying Southern coast featured many inlets, bays, and rivers, but poor interior connections meant that few ports were of much use outside their local trading areas. The best connected Confederate ports were New Orleans, Norfolk, Pensacola, Mobile, Charleston, Savannah, and Wilmington, North Carolina. In the prewar economy, however, where free access to riverine and coastwise shipping dominated the poorly developed Southern transportation system, connections did not always mean commercial success.

In 1860, the most successful Southern port was New Orleans, second nationally only to New York City. Besides shipping almost half of the South's raw cotton, New Orleans was a major outlet for the produce of

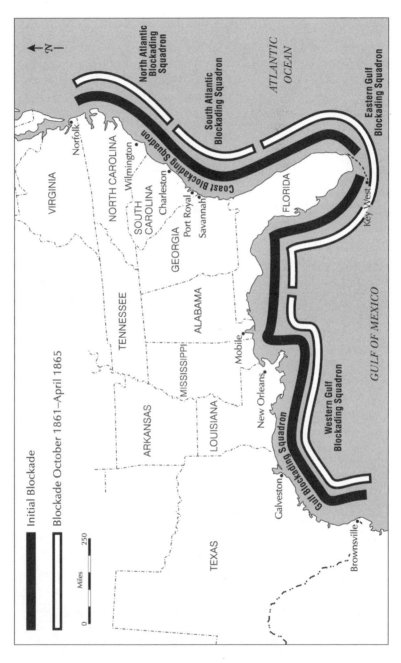

1. The Southern Coast and the Federal Blockade.

the upper Mississippi, and the Crescent City's domestic exports of nearly $108 million dwarfed Mobile's $39 million and Charleston's $21 million. Savannah rounded out the national top five at $18 million. Even Richmond, distant from the sea but well situated on the James River, exported $5 million in 1860. Despite their seemingly favorable locations, Wilmington's business amounted to $650,000 and Norfolk's only $480,000.[7]

The Union's blockading tactics were complicated by the Confederate defenses that kept the blockaders at arm's length and offered ports of refuge for blockade-runners. Almost all of the major Confederate ports were protected by prewar fortifications. Most belonged to the so-called Third System, built of stone or brick, with guns mounted in multitiered casemates for concentrated firepower. Hampton Roads, Charleston, Savannah, Mobile, and New Orleans boasted such defenses, designed by U.S. Army engineers and built over the decades with as much vigor as congressional appropriations permitted. Although prewar Corps of Engineers planning envisioned an elaborate scheme of defenses with nearly two hundred forts, relatively few were ever built. For armament, the prewar forts predominantly carried 42-pounders and 8- and 10-inch columbiads, all smoothbore weapons, and Congress's slow pace usually left a gap of several years between the time a work was ready for its armament and the time the guns were available.[8]

The fortifications were intended to operate as part of a system that included naval forces, fixed defenses, the standing army and militia, and good interior communications. Because seaborne mobility gave an invader the advantages of surprise and concentration, the prewar coastal defense plan that the Confederacy inherited called for concentrating the defenders as well. It focused on the most important points and left the rest undefended, which did not sit well with citizens who wanted protection. The Confederates found themselves expanding their defenses to cover the new nation's entire perimeter.

The expansion was not, strictly speaking, government policy. As one author phrased it, early Confederate coastal defense "policy" was the "sum total of actions of local commanders under the loose supervision of the Secretary of War."[9] Local politicians responded to public pressure by demanding protection for every town, river, and bay, and the Confederacy's dependence upon local resources meant that they generally got their way. During the first months of the war, small earthwork batteries sprouted all along the Confederate coast, and each locality besieged the central government for heavy guns and trained artillerymen, which the central government could not provide.

The amphibious operations that Confederate citizens so feared ranged from hit-and-run raids to more elaborate operations intended to take and hold small areas.[10] Amphibious operations gained the Union its most important blockade base, Port Royal, and helped to close Charleston, Savannah, and Hatteras Inlet. Despite these successes, the Union never attempted an amphibious operation to begin or support a land campaign against the enemy.

Especially in this respect, analyses of Civil War amphibious operations suffer considerably from hindsight. Viewing the Civil War through the lens of Normandy or Inchon, it is easy to assume that the war could have been dramatically changed if only the commanders had seen the possibilities of an amphibious campaign. Certainly there were unrecognized possibilities, but more than strategic blindness was at work. Amphibious operations were limited by very real strategic and technological problems.

Strategically, the blockade bases were ill-suited to support land campaigns. The Committee of Conference deliberately recommended sites for blockade bases that were poorly accessible by land. This made the bases easier to defend, reducing the number of troops needed for defense and increasing the chances that the army would agree to provide them. Yet the site selection cut two ways: the same remoteness and inaccessibility that helped to protect the Federal enclaves made them unsuitable as bases for large armies operating in the interior.

Technologically, several issues combined to make amphibious campaigns difficult. Chief among them was tactical mobility, which in Civil War armies depended upon animal power. Men were relatively easy to transport and land over a beach, but horses and mules tolerated shipboard life poorly, and offloading and landing them was difficult. Invading armies, once ashore, would be poorly provided with artillery, cavalry, and logistical support.[11] The lack of tactical mobility magnified the effect of defending forces, because if the defenses included fortifications or a field army, the invaders would have to land some distance from their objective. The only significant American amphibious experience, Winfield Scott's Mexican War campaign against Vera Cruz, bore out these points, and its success had been due more to Santa Anna's mistakes than to Scott's vision.[12]

Because technology limited both the pace at which the invader could build up combat power ashore and the size of the army he could support over the beach, attackers and defenders alike knew that the initial objective of an amphibious campaign had to be a seaport. Both sides also knew that railroads and telegraphy had markedly increased the ability of the defenders to concentrate against an invasion. A would-be invader thus faced a dilemma. An amphibious campaign required landing in an area with good landward communications, but good landward communications improved the defenders' ability to expel the invaders in both relative and absolute terms.

Another realm in which modern experience fails is in interservice cooperation. Although the practice is often less tidy than the theory, modern amphibious operations involve unified forces, subject to the orders of a single commander. During the Civil War, however, command was far from unified. Successful operations depended far more upon the personal qualities of the commanders involved than they did upon any formal structure.

The problem was common to both belligerents. Although the Confederacy had fewer opportunities for coordinated offensive action than did the Union, unified defensive commands would have made considerable sense in places such as Wilmington, Charleston, and Savannah. Yet at Wilmington, for example, the Confederate army and navy defenders were the antithesis of unified. In March 1864, a dispute over the blockade-runner *Hansa* led Flag Officer William F. Lynch to seize the ship. Maj. Gen. W. H. C. Whiting evicted Lynch's marines from the *Hansa* and set guards to prevent the navy's sailors from boarding their own ships. Lynch then moved the ironclad *North Carolina* into position to shell the *Hansa* and advised Whiting that he would use force "in the last resort" to retake the ship. No blood was shed, but the secretaries of war and of the navy had to intervene to resolve the matter.[13]

On the Union side, several factors hindered interservice cooperation. One was a common feeling in the navy that the army "never do us justice."[14] Naval officers received little reward, Capt. Louis Goldsborough complained, whereas if an army officer mounted his horse and rode a few miles, he was "forthwith elevated in rank."[15] Rear Adm. David Dixon Porter asserted in 1862, "The Brigadier Generals will flourish when we are all forgotten."[16]

Much of this perception stemmed from differing needs and personnel policies in the services. As previously noted, the army gave Federal commissions to the officers appointed by state authorities and needed far more high-ranking officers than did the navy. It took more than thirty-seven years of service for John Dahlgren to reach the grade of captain in the U.S. Navy; his son, cavalryman Ulric Dahlgren, attained the equivalent grade of colonel before the age of twenty-one. Ulysses S. Grant and Cornelius Van Alstine left the regular services in 1854 and 1859, respectively, at the equivalent grades of army captain and navy lieutenant. When war broke out, Grant returned to the army as a colonel, a three-step promotion; Van Alstine rejoined the navy as a master, a one-step demotion.

Exacerbating this problem, many army officers assumed that superior rank in itself entitled them to direct their naval counterparts. The difficulty was especially acute early in the war, when the most senior naval officers were captains and commanders. Those grades ranked with army colonels and lieutenant colonels, respectively, small potatoes indeed given the profusion of brigadier and major generals. Similarly, the growth of the fleet brought afloat command to navy lieutenants, the equivalent of army captains. In an environment where every colonel of a regiment wanted his own gunboat, naval officers who did not strongly maintain their independence would find themselves whipsawed by conflicting orders.

For their part, army officers resented the prize system. Under the law, army officers would be court-martialed for the same acts of "lawful looting" for which naval officers were rewarded.[17] Loose interpretation of the prize laws certainly led to temptation at all levels, from Rear Admiral Porter, accused of paying too much attention to cotton during the Red River campaign, to Acting Master A. S. Gardner, who surreptitiously shipped contraband cotton from Port Royal.[18]

The Union war effort provided a number of examples of successful interservice cooperation, including Grant and Rear Adm. Andrew H. Foote, Grant and Porter, Rear Adm. Samuel F. Du Pont and Brig. Gen. Thomas W. Sherman, Rear Adm. David G. Farragut and Maj. Gen. Edward R. S. Canby, and Porter and Brig. Gen. Alfred H. Terry. Unfortunately, these successes depended much more upon the circumstances and the personalities and "chemistry" of the officers involved than upon any established doctrine. When the chemistry was bad, as it was between Du Pont and Maj. Gen. David Hunter, between Dahlgren and Maj. Gen. Quincy A. Gillmore, or between Maj. Gen. Benjamin F. Butler and just about everyone, the commanders spent more energy fighting each other than they did fighting the Confederates.

Even when it existed in the field, joint cooperation dissipated before reaching the level of national planning. In the Confederacy, the overwhelming predominance of the army practically eliminated the need, but in the Union, one factor was the lack of corresponding elements between the military and the naval command structure. In the War Department, below the civilian secretary of war came the general in chief. Although the office did not fulfill its promise until Grant ascended to it in 1864, its existence recognized the need for a military officer who would be responsible for planning the war as a whole.

The Navy Department had no counterpart to the general in chief. Each of the navy's admirals was concerned about his own squadron and theater; none had the responsibility of examining the "big picture." Assistant Secretary Fox tended to take the lead in operational planning, but those who see him as the prototype of a mid-twentieth-century chief of naval operations make far too much of his role. Just as the navy had no "admiral in chief" to work with the general in chief, the army had no "operationally oriented" assistant secretary to work with Fox. If cooperative planning were to occur, it would have to take place at the cabinet level, between the secretary of war and the secretary of the navy.

Cabinet-level cooperation was notably absent. Welles's initial counterpart was Pennsylvania senator Simon Cameron, who became secretary of war when Lincoln reluctantly honored a promise his campaign managers had made. The appointment quickly proved to be a mistake. As Welles opined, Cameron lacked the "grasp, power, energy [and] comprehension" needed for his post, and Cameron's efforts appear to have gone primarily into advancing his personal interests.[19] His administration of the War Department was marked by blatant corruption, and the scandals finally became so public that in January 1862, Lincoln removed him. His replacement as secretary of war was Edwin M. Stanton, who had served as attorney general during the last four months of Buchanan's term.

Stanton's appointment caused an immediate downturn in army-navy relations. Cameron had generally ignored the navy; Stanton saw it as an adjunct to the army and tried to treat Welles as a subordinate. Welles stood firm, Stanton moderated his tone, and Welles decided that Stanton would take advantage of men who allowed themselves to be intimidated.[20] Welles successfully established the principle that the navy would cooperate with the army as an equal, but Stanton continued to work to expand his own influence, and he made the most of any circumstance in which his fellow cabinet officers had to ask something of him.

Stanton's biographers justly characterize him as an actor, not a thinker, who combined vast energy and personal loyalty to Lincoln with impulse, prejudice, and reluctance to admit error. Interested only in the success of the army, he displayed little breadth of vision. Distrusting strategy as the resource of "generals afraid to fight," he wrote that the army had to "boldly pursu[e] and strik[e] the foe."[21] His narrowness and his belief that wars could be won only by fighting combined to preclude any significant amphibious effort. Similarly, his estimate of the costs and benefits of supporting the blockade caused him to refuse to commit more than a minimal number of troops. A division sent to close Wilmington in 1862 or 1863 might have influenced the struggle more than a corps or an army anywhere else, but Stanton refused to supply troops for operations that he considered to be diversions. Not until Grant became general in chief did Union army eyes turn to the Army of Northern Virginia's long overseas supply line.

Lincoln, the one man who could have forcibly broadened Stanton's view, did not do so. The president allowed his subordinates great leeway and, as a later author noted, "never really tried to run his cabinet in a single harness."[22] A contemporary compared Stanton's position as secretary of war to that of a lawyer who could "abuse his client as much as he chose, provided he won his case."[23] In such a climate, interservice cooperation suffered.

Valid strategic differences compounded the structural and personal deficiencies. The army strongly resisted efforts to divert troops from "important" theaters for navy sideshows. Maj. Gen. George B. McClellan clearly evinced the attitude when he refused to provide additional troops to the Port Royal expedition, writing, "I need far more [troops] than I now have to save this country. . . . It is the task of the Army of the Potomac to decide the question at issue. No outside expedition can effect the result."[24] The same attitude prevailed even after McClellan's departure, as shown by the general reluctance to move troops from the supposedly decisive Virginia theater, where a high ratio of force to space made for deadlock, to the west, where low force to space ratios offered better prospects for maneuver.

Army leaders met similar problems when they sought support from the navy. In 1861, Du Pont warned Fox, "The soldiers will absorb the fleet if I do not look out."[25] Du Pont's Mexican War experience had taught him that the army came to depend on the warships' guns, viewing them as mobile heavy artillery and becoming reluctant to advance inland beyond their protection. More troops ashore meant more demands for naval support, Du Pont wrote, saying, "Our troops will not fight if gunboats are within their reach."[26] Providing that support would impair the navy's ability to enforce the blockade and deal with Confederate raiders.

Yet despite these difficulties, army-navy operations did succeed. The first significant joint operation occurred in August 1861. The Confederacy had authorized the commissioning of privateers in April 1861, and Hatteras Inlet, North Carolina, quickly became a sally port for them. The small vessels would take shelter in Pamlico Sound in bad weather, venturing out when conditions were good to prey on Union shipping as it rounded Cape Hatteras. A joint expedition, with Butler commanding the troops and Stringham in charge of the naval element, was mounted in August 1861. Although the initial plan was to capture the forts that guarded the inlet, destroy them, and leave, it was immediately recognized that only permanent occupation could suppress the privateers. In addition, the area could serve as a base for raids against the Carolina mainland.[27]

Lacking established doctrine and handicapped by amateur command, the expedition did not begin smoothly. The army conceived its role as limited to providing troops, with all else being up to the navy. Stringham, however, assumed that Butler would arrange for his own transports, and a last-minute flurry resulted.[28] When the expedition reached Hatteras Inlet, the assault on the forts came off somewhat differently than either commander had envisioned. Their plan called for gunfire from the ships to soften up the forts before the troops assaulted them. The navy's two-day bombardment caused the Confederates to surrender, and on August 29, 1861, Butler's men occupied the forts without incident.[29] Butler's self-promoting nature resulted in an unseemly squabble over the public credit for the capture, but within the navy the engagement was taken to show the unexpected effectiveness of gunfire from ships.

Even as the Hatteras force was getting under way, Du Pont was preparing another expedition. This force, with Du Pont as the naval commander and Brig. Gen. Thomas W. Sherman commanding the troops, would implement the recommendation of the Committee of Conference to seize a blockade base. Du Pont began his preparations in August 1861, but despite his energy and enthusiasm, the "Expedition to the Southern Coast" did not sail until October 16. Welles's final instructions listed Fernandina, Bull's Bay, Saint Helena, and Port Royal as potential targets and directed Du Pont to take possession of two of them, to be chosen by Du Pont. Welles emphasized the policy behind the strategy when he stressed the importance of cultivating friendly relations with Southern civilians to return them to allegiance.[30]

Du Pont chose Port Royal as his first objective. Although the Conference had placed Port Royal at the bottom of the list of potential targets, below St. Helena Sound and Bull's Bay, Du Pont appears to have favored it from the beginning. The Conference objected to Port Royal because it would be more difficult to capture and more difficult for ships to navigate its entrance, and it would need a relatively large garrison to protect it after its capture. Du Pont appears to have looked instead at Port Royal's superb natural harbor (chart 2) and the ability of a force based there to control the bays and channels of the South Carolina and Georgia coasts.[31]

Du Pont left New York October 16 and arrived in Hampton Roads October 18. The chartered transports trickled in, but the expedition was delayed awaiting Charles O. Boutelle, a Coast Survey pilot with detailed knowledge of Port Royal. With Boutelle safely aboard, worsening weather delayed the expedition's departure until October 29. November opened with a gale that scattered the fleet, and when Du Pont arrived off Port Royal on November 4 he found only seven of his fifty-five ships in sight. Boutelle and Cdr. John Rodgers set to work to buoy the channel, and when Confederate gunboats under Commodore Josiah Tattnall tried to interfere, Union ships drove them off. As Du Pont began to pass his ships through the bar, more transports straggled in, and by the time he attacked the Confederate defenses on November 7, most of his force had been collected. The original plan for a joint attack was scuttled by the loss of many of the army's surfboats in the storm, and Du Pont and Sherman agreed to try a naval attack.[32]

The entrance to Port Royal Sound was protected on the north by Fort Beauregard on Phillips Island and on the south by Fort Walker on Hilton Head Island. Du Pont's plan was to form his ships in line, enter the channel between the forts, and turn back to concentrate on Fort Walker. Five passes sufficed to cause the Confederates to abandon Fort Walker, and seeing their departure, the less-mauled garrison of Fort Beauregard followed suit. Naval bombardment alone had again driven Confederate troops from their fortifications, which the army could then occupy and garrison without combat. This was fortunate because the army had no small arms ammunition; all of it had been loaded on a single ship, which was late in arriving.[33]

The victory made Du Pont a hero in the North and guaranteed his promotion to rear admiral when that grade was created. The success at Port Royal, however, had papered over several problems. The army's preparation bespoke not only lack of amphibious doctrine but also lack

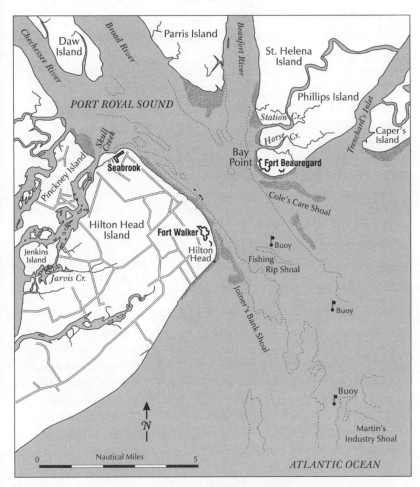

2. Outline Chart of Port Royal, South Carolina. (Redrawn from U.S. Coast Survey chart of 1862, Library of Congress, G3912.P62 1862, at http://hdl.loc.gov/loc.gmd/g3912p.cw0389200)

of thought.[34] Du Pont, although better prepared, had been tactically unimaginative. Several ships followed Capt. Sylvanus Godon out of the battle line to enfilade Fort Walker, and while their fire was the most effective of the battle, it had not been part of Du Pont's plan. Du Pont was enraged at Godon, but it is difficult to credit the commanding officers involved with mass disobedience; it appears more likely that Du Pont had failed to convey his instructions clearly. Neither Du Pont nor Sherman had given much thought or coordination to what they would do after they took Port Royal, and their lack of direction allowed the Confederates to recover from the panic into which the fall of Port Royal had thrown them.[35]

Most damaging in the long term, however, was the tactical conclusion drawn by the Union navy. Combined with the success at Hatteras, Port Royal gave the navy "bombardment fever"—the idea that naval gunfire alone could overwhelm Confederate defenses and allow the army to occupy them without significant fighting.[36] This misconception, seemingly reaffirmed in February 1862 by the capture of Roanoke Island, significantly affected later Federal strategy.

The Confederates, too, changed their strategy as a result of Port Royal. Rumors had circulated widely of the destination of Du Pont's expedition, and in early November, Gen. Robert E. Lee arrived at Richmond simultaneously with the news that the Yankees were at Port Royal. President Davis promptly combined South Carolina, Georgia, and northern Florida into a single military district, appointed Lee its commander, and sent him off the next morning.

Arriving at his new command just in time to hear news of Du Pont's victory, Lee instituted a three-pronged defensive strategy. First, he began to strengthen the defenses of Charleston and Savannah to withstand the sort of bombardment to which Forts Walker and Beauregard had fallen. Second, he ordered the obstruction of waterways to keep Federal ships as far from the vital Charleston and Savannah Railroad as possible. Third, he positioned his meager forces to block the best Federal routes of advance toward the railroad. Within two weeks he had decided to abandon the dispersed "perimeter defense" strategy in favor of concentrating his troops and guns along interior lines, out of reach of the heavy Union naval guns.[37] This disposition would also allow him to counter the Union's seaborne mobility with railborne mobility of his own. During the next months, Lee executed his reconcentration while the Union dispersed to gain footholds on the Georgia and Florida coasts such as Tybee Island and Fernandina.

Lee's promotion had a rough geographical parallel on the Union side. During the interval between Hatteras and Port Royal, Du Pont had become the commander of the South Atlantic Blockading Squadron, responsible for the coasts of South Carolina, Georgia, and northern Florida. The circumstances of his elevation help to illuminate the way in which technology was changing naval operations.

After the capture of Hatteras Inlet at the end of August 1861, Butler and Stringham had raced each other to claim the credit, a race in which the experienced politician held a major advantage over the naval officer. One suspects that Stringham felt entitled to more praise than he received, even from within the navy. In mid-September 1861, Stringham took offense at an official letter from Fox that implicitly criticized Stringham's handling of the blockade and "regretted" some of Stringham's decisions. In response, Stringham asked to be relieved of command of the Atlantic Blockading Squadron.[38]

The Navy Department did not find his request to be unwelcome. As the blockade grew, it had become evident that the entire Atlantic coast of the Confederacy was too much for one squadron commander to manage. Stringham's resignation eased what otherwise would have been the difficult human relations problem of splitting his squadron and diminishing his authority and responsibility. On September 18, 1861, two days after Stringham wrote out his resignation, Welles gave official notice that Atlantic Blockading Squadron was to be divided.[39] Capt. Louis Goldsborough was appointed flag officer and sent to command the North Atlantic Blockading Squadron, responsible for the coast as far south as the border between North and South Carolina, and Du Pont received a similar promotion and an appointment to the South Atlantic Blockading Squadron, responsible for the area from South Carolina to Cape Canaveral, Florida. Both men were elevated over the heads of more senior officers, and as Du Pont wrote, "seniority and rotation [of commands] have seen their last day."[40] The actual division of the squadron's assets took place in October 1861.

Stringham's request for relief points up how naval operations were changing. Before the war, most U.S. naval operations involved peacetime commerce encouragement and "showing the flag" cruises. The slow pace of communications made centralized control of these operations impractical. Although they showed promise, the electrical telegraph networks of the 1850s had not significantly affected the navy's overseas operations; there was no transoceanic cable.[41]

In this decentralized environment, naval officers developed a "command culture" of independence, in which commanders received very general instructions and executed them as they thought best. Most commanders were able to strike a reasonable balance. They clearly understood the career-terminating nature of indecision or apparent cowardice, but they also understood, as John Rodgers wrote, "It was not admissible for any mere casual man-of-war to expound without instructions an interpretation of a formal treaty at the cannon's mouth."[42] The decentralized system produced an embarrassing incident now and then, but diplomats of all nations understood the difficulties and were prepared to disavow an officer's actions or to accept a disavowal if necessary. A commander's tactical decisions were rarely scrutinized.

It soon became clear that Civil War operations would be more centralized. Two reasons stand out. First, the war involved much more than fighting. For the Union especially, complex political questions arose at every level, and it was natural that the government would try to exercise close operational control. Second, the theater of war was close to home; in fact, it was *at* home. War at home had both physical and psychological effects.

Physically, relatively short distances reduced the time it took to communicate. The Mexican War operations at Vera Cruz took place 2,000 miles from New York, and the Baja California theater was over twice as far away. By contrast, Charleston was less than 600 nautical miles from New York and only 327 miles from Hampton Roads. New Orleans was just 881 statute miles from Richmond.

Psychologically, the war's areas of operation were known to leaders on both sides. Although the terrain around Shiloh Church and the waters of Port Royal were in fact no better charted than their counterparts at Chapultepec or Tuxpan, they were perceived to be familiar. Coupling the perception of familiarity with an actual lack of detailed topographic and hydrographic knowledge encouraged second-guessing of the sort usually done on maps scaled 500 miles to the inch.

Proximity and familiarity would have meant little without rapid communications, and technologically the telegraph dominated the war. Telegrams were not yet either ubiquitous or cheap, but American leaders North and South were familiar with them as the "instant messaging" of their day. The land telegraph network covered much of the nation, concentrated in the East; although the Confederacy's portion after secession was less extensive, the Confederate government had the advantage of interior lines. During the course of the war, both governments' appetite for quick communications grew, but the Union's resources allowed it to expand its communications network while the Confederacy's contracted under the pressures of Union raids and aging, overburdened infrastructure.

Then as now, instant communication had its drawbacks. The telegraph combined with well-developed print media to mean that leaders often received war news indirectly through enemy channels before they heard from their own commanders. The problem was especially acute for the

Union navy, operating entirely on exterior lines. Du Pont, for example, attacked Charleston on April 7, 1863. On April 8, Welles expressed his "yearning, craving desire for tidings from Charleston," but it was April 10 before "not wholly reliable rumors" appeared. The first semiofficial report arrived in Washington via an army telegram from Fort Monroe on April 11. Not until April 12 did Du Pont's official report reach the Navy Department.[43]

The telegram came from Fort Monroe because that was the southern terminus of the Federal government's telegraph network on the East Coast. In January 1862, the U.S. Army had run a telegraph line down the Delmarva Peninsula to Cape Charles, across the Chesapeake Bay from Hampton, Virginia. Initially, a dispatch boat carried messages across the bay, but a submarine cable was soon laid to allow direct electrical connection from Fort Monroe to the War Department. Beyond Hampton Roads, orders and information traveled by ship. Routine letters joined the stream of mail carried by the supply vessels, while especially urgent dispatches might warrant a special trip.[44]

The combination of communications technology, political imperative, and geographic proximity provided the "means, motive, and opportunity" for policy makers to enter an arena that had belonged solely to naval officers. Fox, for example, would later prescribe tactics for Du Pont, urging him to enter Charleston harbor, "defiant and disdainful, silent amid the 200 guns, until you arrive at the center of this wicked rebellion."[45] Du Pont, at once less sanguine and more familiar with local hydrography, replied that Fox's grand plan would work, "but, my friend, you have to *get there*."[46] In the end, officers either adapted to the new command climate or were shunted aside.[47]

During the first year of war, Union operations did not focus exclusively on blockade bases and privateers' nests. The Mississippi River had historically been the great commercial artery of the Old Northwest. For this reason, the Lower Northwest, meaning the parts of Ohio, Indiana, Illinois, and Iowa that lay in the Ohio and Missouri River valleys, tended to be aligned toward the South rather than toward the East. Frequent disagreements over national policy and equally frequent threats of secession had strained the region's prewar relations with New England, and after war began there was enough secessionist sentiment to worry Republican leaders.[48]

The Northwest's perceived Southern orientation followed the Ohio River, and Cincinnati, Ohio, was especially well known for its supposed

Southern ties.[49] Careful retrospective analysis shows that these ties had
eroded by 1861, the result of the improved rail connections that had reori-
ented the region's economy from south to east. Yet in widespread contemporary perception, a "Northwest Confederacy" remained a real threat.[50]
Opening the Mississippi would help to reduce that threat. Although the
riverine campaigns are beyond the scope of this volume, a good deal of the
navy's force on the Mississippi sporadically came upriver from the sea.

Looking inland, New Orleans was the first major obstacle to renewed
Federal trade. The Crescent City was also a major commercial port, and
closing it was vital to the Union blockade. Geography both helped and
hurt the Union in blockading New Orleans. About one hundred miles
below the city, the Mississippi River divided into three major channels,
called passes, each of which led to the Gulf of Mexico. Blockading the
individual passes was possible, but the division point, called the Head of
the Passes, controlled all three and the Committee of Conference recommended closing the river there (chart 3). In late July 1861 the Navy
Department ordered Flag Officer William Mervine, then commanding
the Gulf Blockading Squadron, to establish a battery at the Head of the
Passes.[51] Mervine borrowed an army engineer to supervise the construction, but he characteristically did not press forward with the project and,
in early September, cataloged the difficulties in a letter to Welles.[52]

By the time this letter reached Washington, however, Mervine himself
had been replaced, brought down by Welles's perception of his "apparent inactivity and indifference."[53] In the Gulf, as in the Atlantic, Welles
sought commanders with energy, and he did so without being bound by
the strict seniority principle that had governed the peacetime navy. His
appointment of William W. McKean to relieve Mervine reached deep
into the ranks of captains. Du Pont agreed with the relief but opined that
the appointment of an officer so junior would "make a howl and the Department will give in."[54] Mervine did protest, but Welles did not yield.[55]
Combined with Stringham's relief, the action sent a powerful message
that seniority could not make up for inefficiency or lack of energy.

McKean's tenure began with good news. The Committee of Conference had recommended taking Ship Island, in the Gulf between Mobile
and the Mississippi Delta, to serve as a blockading base. Mervine's failure
to do so was a key element in his relief, but on September 17, Confederate forces abandoned Ship Island. A navy detachment occupied the
Confederate fortifications and held them until army troops arrived in
early December.

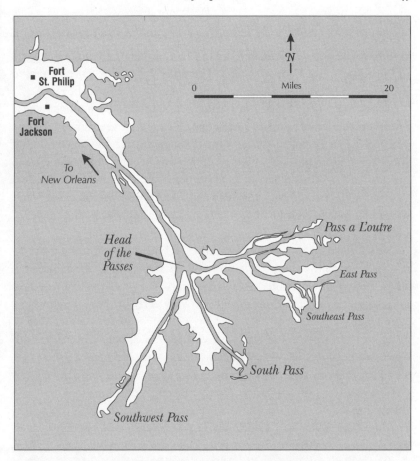

3. Mississippi River Delta. The complexity of the Mississippi Delta forced the Federals to guard three widely separated exits. (Redrawn from U.S. Coast Survey chart, Library of Congress, G3981.S5 1863.U5, at http://hdl.loc.gov/loc.gmd/g3981s.cw0260000)

Bad news quickly followed good, and McKean had barely taken command when he faced his first crisis. Early in the morning of October 12, 1861, Commodore George N. Hollins led the Confederate New Orleans squadron in an attack on the Union warships anchored in the Head of the Passes. The ironclad ram *Manassas* stiffened Hollins's force of gunboats and fire rafts, and the Confederates achieved complete surprise. The shock of their attack counted for more than the physical damage they did, and the Federals fled downstream in some confusion. Two Union ships that grounded were refloated the next day, but the senior officer present, who wrote, "Everyone is in great dread of that infernal ram," nonetheless withdrew to blockading stations outside the passes.[56] McKean did not countermand this decision, and the U.S. Navy did not return to the Head of the Passes until February 1862. The affair appears to have increased the urgency of Welles's search for a more aggressive commander.

Welles chose David Glasgow Farragut, a Southern-born officer whose loyalty to the Union was unquestioned. Farragut, a veteran of fifty-one years of naval service, was appointed to command the Western Gulf Blockading Squadron on January 9, 1862. His primary duty would be to maintain a "vigorous blockade at every point," but Welles also instructed him to "collect such vessels as can be spared from the blockade" and with them to take New Orleans, open the Mississippi River, and "reduce" Mobile.[57]

New Orleans was vulnerable from several directions, but the most direct route, and the only one suitable for heavy ships, was up the Mississippi River. Prewar fortifications covered the approaches, and the Confederates had begun to repair and improve them very early in the war. The most significant were Forts Jackson and St. Philip, located on either side of a bend of the river about sixty-five nautical miles below the city. Both were obsolescent brick works; Fort St. Philip, the older, dated from 1792, and Fort Jackson had been completed in 1832. Most of their weapons were 32- and 42-pounder smoothbore cannon, as obsolescent as the forts themselves.

Maj. Gen. Mansfield Lovell, an 1842 graduate of West Point, commanded at New Orleans. Breveted for gallantry during the Mexican War, the Washington DC native resigned from the U.S. Army in 1854 to work as a civil engineer in New York City. In September 1861 he left New York and accepted a Confederate commission. Arriving in New Orleans in autumn 1861, he promptly began to strengthen the city's defenses.

It seemed to Lovell that the best way to protect the city was to keep the Union fleet from reaching it. The river's hydrography was both help and hindrance. Its swift current would slow Federal ships coming upriver and give Confederate gunners more time to disable them, but the same current would carry a damaged ship quickly downriver and out of range. Both the current and the river's depth, as much as 130 feet in some places, kept the Confederates from emplacing underwater obstructions, so Lovell set his engineers to build a floating obstruction, or boom, below the forts.

This would, he hoped, delay any attacking ships and give time for his relatively light guns to damage them enough to prevent their passage.

Unfortunately for Lovell, the Confederacy's needs in other theaters of war became steadily more urgent. As fast as he scraped together troops, guns, and supplies, the Confederate government ordered them elsewhere. Lovell's pleas for men and heavy guns went unheeded, and in March 1862 he complained that New Orleans had been "drained of everything." He characterized the city as "about defenseless."[58]

The Crescent City's naval defenses were as poor as those ashore. The navy's flotilla included the ironclad ram *Manassas* and the gunboat *MacRae*, veterans of the Head of the Passes action, and the gunboat *Jackson*, while the Louisiana State Navy contributed the gunboats *Governor Moore* and *General Quitman*. The whole force mounted only one gun bigger than a 32-pounder.[59] The Confederate army had taken over a number of riverboats, strengthening them for ramming and giving them one or two guns apiece, and this "River Defense Fleet" operated under nominal army control. Lovell wrote, however, that the River Defense Fleet had "too much 'steamboat' and too little of the 'man of war,' to be effective," and this assessment proved to be accurate.[60]

That left the ironclads *Louisiana* and *Mississippi*. Asa and Nelson Tift, old acquaintances of Mallory from Florida and Georgia, were building the *Mississippi*, while a local man, E. C. Murray, was building the *Louisiana* to a superficially similar design. Both ships were intended only for riverine service, but at 260 feet in length, either would be difficult to maneuver in the relatively narrow river. Both suffered from the Confederacy's inability to build suitable propulsion machinery. The *Mississippi*'s center propeller shaft, salvaged from a wreck, was so big that only the Tredegar Works in Richmond could adapt it to the ironclad, while much of *Louisiana*'s machinery came from a riverboat.[61] Low power to stem the current of the Mississippi would only compound the ships' maneuverability problems.

Neither ship would be stemming the current on schedule, however, and until they were completed their design deficiencies would be of little practical interest. Despite heavy pressure from Mallory and local officials, construction progressed slowly, hampered by shortages of timber, iron, and machinery. The *Louisiana* was launched on February 6, 1862, but the *Mississippi* was not launched until almost two months later.

Even worse than the delay in completing the ironclads, the Mississippi River defeated the engineers sent to obstruct it. Storms and river debris carried away Lovell's first "raft" in late February. Rebuilt in March, the new boom was broken away on April 11. The only replacement available was a group of hulks anchored in the river and connected with chains. The timing was especially bad for the Confederates.[62]

Farragut himself had arrived in the Gulf in February 1862, and he immediately began to collect ships for his attack. Welles had made the flag officer's mission clear, calling it "the most important operation of the war," but did not prescribe how he should accomplish it.[63] At least three plans were in the air. One, proposed by army engineer John G. Barnard, was to take Forts Jackson and St. Philip by siege or assault, supported by "the powerful artillery of the fleet."[64] Another, proposed by Porter, involved reducing the forts to impotence by sustained fire from specialized mortar boats.[65] The third called for the fleet to pass the forts and take New Orleans itself. This third option, Farragut's own favorite, recognized that New Orleans was the objective and that the forts would fall once the city was taken. Delay under fire could be fatal, though, so Farragut acted to increase his chances by allowing Porter to go ahead with the mortar boat scheme in hopes of disabling the forts and by preparing an expedition to break the boom blocking the river.[66]

Farragut's first challenge was to get his heavy ships across the bars and into the river, which took nearly a month of strenuous effort. Meanwhile, Porter's mortar flotilla arrived, and Maj. Gen. Benjamin Butler reported that his troops were ready to support Farragut's effort. On March 27, the Confederates discerned that Farragut's ships were entering the river in force.

The news thoroughly alarmed the city. An ad hoc Committee of Public Safety pressed the shipbuilders to hurry their work. But pressure, however well meaning, could not by itself regain the time lost to inadequate industrial capacity. No amount of driving will or ingenuity could substitute for the steam hammer needed to forge an ironclad's massive propeller shaft. Lovell's regular troops had been ordered away, and by the time he learned of Farragut's arrival in the river, New Orleans was garrisoned only by one company of regulars and three regiments of poorly armed ninety-day state militia.

Porter's mortar flotilla opened fire on Forts Jackson and St. Philip on April 18, and the Confederates' apprehension again increased. On April 20, the still-incomplete *Louisiana* started downriver to the forts, with two tugs to keep her from being swept away by the current. Cdr. John K. Mitchell moored the ship just above Fort St. Philip and brought workmen from New Orleans to complete her. Although the local army commander wanted the ironclad below the forts to attack the mortar boats, Mitchell appreciated the ship's limits and preferred to keep her away from Federal fire while trying to finish her. On April 23, the ship had progressed far enough that Mitchell planned to move her below the forts on the 24th.[67]

Farragut moved first. A boat expedition had partially broken the improvised boom on the night of the 20th, and when reconnaissance on the night of the 23rd confirmed that the Confederates had not repaired it, the flag officer ordered the attack.[68] The fleet's leading ship, the gunboat *Cayuga*, started up the river at 2:00 AM on April 24. The other ships got under way in turn, with Farragut's flagship *Hartford* weighing anchor at 3:30 AM.

The engagement was already well begun by the time the *Hartford* commenced firing on Fort Jackson at 3:55 AM. The narrow gap in the boom (chart 4) required the fleet to advance in single line, and the alert Confederates opened fire on the *Cayuga* soon after she passed the boom. The River Defense Fleet fled, but the other Confederate gunboats and the ram *Manassas* moved to attack the Federals, and a melee ensued. Soon forts, Confederate ships, and Union ships were all firing at each other in the uncertain light of gun flashes and Confederate fire rafts.

In the confines of the river, the fighting dissolved into a series of close-quarters actions. Beverly Kennon, commanding the Louisiana State Navy's gunboat *Governor Moore*, found himself so close to the USS *Varuna* that the Federal ship was hidden by the *Governor Moore*'s bow. Kennon solved the problem by firing right through his own ship's forecastle.[69] Several Confederates, including the *Manassas*, used ramming tactics to make up for their lack of heavy guns.

When the smoke cleared, all but three of Farragut's ships had passed the forts. One Federal ship had been sunk, but almost all of the Confederate vessels had sunk or surrendered. Farragut, leaving the forts behind, pushed on up the Mississippi toward New Orleans. During the morning of April 25, his fleet silenced the batteries that formed the inner defenses, and at noon he anchored off the city. Farragut demanded surrender on pain of bombardment, but Lovell withdrew his troops and left the onus upon the civil authorities, who yielded with bad grace. An uneasy quiet prevailed until April 29, when Farragut received word that the forts downstream had surrendered and that the *Louisiana* had been destroyed to avert her capture. Butler and his troops arrived soon afterward to occupy the city.

The Confederates had done their best to carry off or destroy anything

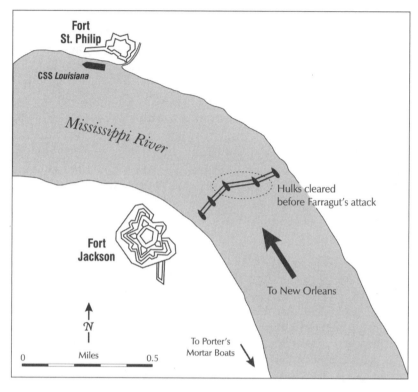

4. *Forts Jackson and St. Philip. The two forts guarded the Mississippi River below New Orleans, but Rear Adm. David Glasgow Farragut ran his ships past them on April 24, 1862. (Redrawn from U.S. Coast Survey chart, Library of Congress, G4014.F685 1862.G4, at http://hdl.loc.gov/loc.gmd/g4014f.cw0235000)*

that might be militarily useful, including steamboats and supplies, and Farragut noted, "Our ingenuity was much taxed to avoid the floating conflagration" drifting down the river.[70] The destruction encompassed the still-incomplete *Mississippi*, launched on April 20. The Confederates tried to tow her upriver but could not muster enough tugs, and she was burned on the 25th as the Union fleet approached the city. Mallory's early start on the *Louisiana* and *Mississippi* had given the Confederates a potential advantage, but slow construction forfeited it.[71]

The fall of New Orleans opened the way for further Federal advances. Farragut sent ships up the river "to keep up the panic," and Baton Rouge and Natchez soon fell to the navy (chart 5). Fox and Welles, however, expected a more extensive movement. By April 1862, Flag Officer Andrew H. Foote's gunboats and Maj. Gen. Ulysses S. Grant's troops had worked their way down the river to Fort Pillow, some eighty miles above Memphis. The Navy Department wanted Farragut's ships to join with Foote's.[72]

Farragut appears to have preferred Mobile as the next objective, since he wrote Fox that when Butler's troops arrived to occupy New Orleans, he would "soon be off for Mobile."[73] On May 12, however, Fox congratulated Farragut on taking New Orleans and reminded him of his earlier instructions to push "a strong force up the river to meet the Western Flotilla." A telegram from Fox soon directed Farragut to "Carry out your instructions of January 20 about ascending the Mississippi River, as it is of the utmost importance." In a personal letter, Fox reiterated the "paramount importance" of clearing the river, writing that the whole coast "sinks into insignificance" by comparison.[74]

By the time he received these instructions, Farragut was back in New Orleans. Assessing the situation at Vicksburg in late May, he determined that the force available could not take the city—the ships' guns could not be elevated far enough to hit the Confederates' defensive batteries, and the 1,500 troops Butler had sent were not sufficient to assault the city by land. Obedient to Welles's orders, Farragut again gathered his ships and started upriver in early June. Several of Porter's mortar vessels accompanied the heavy ships, and the expedition arrived at Vicksburg on June 25. The Confederates had not wasted the intervening weeks, and more batteries had been built on bluffs along the river to oppose the fleet.

Farragut ran his ships upstream past Vicksburg on the night of June 27 to join the riverine force. Butler had sent twice as many troops this time, but they were still far too few for any decisive action, and the joined squadrons above Vicksburg could do no more than the split squadrons above and below. In mid-July the Confederate ram *Arkansas* ran through the Union squadron to reach Vicksburg, embarrassing Farragut no end and evoking a telegram from Welles directing him to destroy the *Arkansas* "at all hazards."[75] Farragut, however, had already followed Welles's orders of July 14 and 21 by retiring down the river before it became too shallow to float his ships.[76] In early August, the *Arkansas* sortied to support a Confederate attack on Baton Rouge, but ran aground due to engine trouble. Threatened by the USS *Essex* and unable to maneuver or fight, *Arkansas* was destroyed by her crew on August 6, 1862. Farragut was able to return his attention to the blockade, but events in the Eastern Theater kept him from receiving the reinforcements Welles had planned to send.

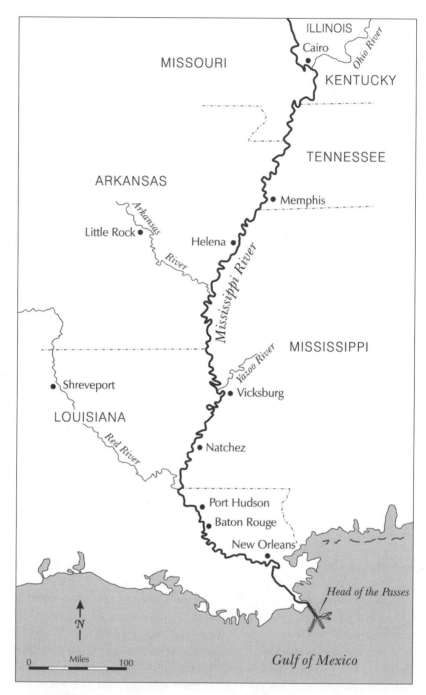

ILLINOIS

Ohio River

Cairo

MISSOURI

KENTUCKY

TENNESSEE

ARKANSAS

Memphis

Arkansas River

Little Rock

Helena

Mississippi River

River

MISSISSIPPI

Yazoo River

Shreveport

Vicksburg

LOUISIANA

Red River

Natchez

Port Hudson

Baton Rouge

New Orleans

Head of the Passes

N

0   Miles   100

Gulf of Mexico

5. *The Mississippi River (Redrawn from U.S. Army Corps of Topographical Engineers map, Library of Congress, G3980 1861.M3CW14.45, at http://hdl.loc.gov/loc.gmd/g3980.cw0014450)*

The capture of New Orleans had certainly been gratifying, but by the time word of Farragut's exploits reached Washington, official attention had already shifted to the Union's "big show" for 1862—McClellan's "peninsular campaign." McClellan, brought from the Ohio Valley in July 1861 to command the Union forces around Washington, had spent months drilling and organizing his army. By 1862 he was under increasing pressure to do something, and Lincoln is reported to have said that if McClellan didn't plan to use the army, Lincoln would like to borrow it. McClellan decided upon a turning movement that would take the Army of the Potomac by water to the Hampton Roads area, whence it would advance on Richmond from the southeast.

As one author has pointed out, McClellan "took for granted the freedom of his army to come and go along the enemy coast. He did not appreciate how the navy secured that freedom, what it cost in ships and effort, and therefore how severely it limited the naval resources available for more immediate tactical support."[77] The navy's job, as the navy and the president understood it as late as mid-March, was to protect the army and its transports from the *Virginia*.[78] McClellan, however, held his service's common view that the navy's highest purpose was to support the army, and he assumed that naval resources would be forthcoming whenever he asked for them. He had already begun moving troops to Fort Monroe when he told Fox that part of his plan "will be the reduction of Yorktown & Gloucester—to effect this rapidly we shall need your help."[79] He did not involve the navy in his planning, nor did he appreciate the navy's other responsibilities.[80]

Fox's private correspondence shows how little McClellan discussed his plans with either Fox in Washington or Goldsborough in Hampton Roads, but it also displays Fox's keen concern about accusations that the navy was not supporting the army. When the Peninsular Campaign stalled in April, Fox saw that "the government and the people call upon us to lift the army of the Potomac out of the mire," and he sent Goldsborough all the ships he could without seriously weakening the blockade.[81]

As Goldsborough pointed out, Yorktown and Gloucester Point were "a great deal stronger than was supposed," with over fifty heavy guns covering the York River, and his wooden ships could only try to destroy the fortifications "at long bowls." In any event, he observed, the idea that the navy would play a major part in capturing Yorktown was "bran [sic] new to me & had it been proposed a few weeks since, I rather think it would have been rejected with indignation by our grand Army."[82] With only the *Monitor* available to guard Hampton Roads against the *Virginia*, he dared not send an ironclad to help. Despite McClellan's concern about the *Virginia* threat, navy appeals to force the *Virginia* out by taking Norfolk fell on deaf ears until Lincoln himself intervened.[83]

The capture of Norfolk on May 10, 1862, caused the Confederates to burn the *Virginia* to keep her from the Union. Along with the city and the wreck of the *Virginia*, the Federals regained the facilities of the Norfolk Navy Yard. The yard, however, displays a microcosm of army-navy relations. When it was recaptured, the navy sent supervisors and workmen to reopen the yard and marines to garrison it. Gen. John E. Wool refused to allow Goldsborough's men into the yard, reasoning that the Confederates around Norfolk had surrendered to the army, not the navy. Welles and Stanton had to intervene, and the need for cabinet-level intervention to allow the navy to reoccupy its own shipyard points up the gulf between Civil War concepts of administrative unity and those that would develop later.[84]

Both army and navy saw possibilities in the *Virginia*'s demise. Upon hearing the news May 11, McClellan immediately urged "most earnestly" that the gunboats and ironclads "be sent as far as possible up the James River without delay."[85] On the same day, Welles instructed Goldsborough to begin preparing for an "immediate" attack on Fort Caswell at Wilmington with "all the force you can spare, including the two iron-clads." Although Welles also directed the flag officer to "Push all the boats you can spare up James River, even to Richmond," he clearly saw this employment as temporary and estimated that the ironclads would be available for Fort Caswell "in a couple of days."[86]

Goldsborough reacted promptly, and on May 15 the *Monitor* joined the *Galena* to attack Fort Darling, at Drewry's Bluff on the James River, six miles below Richmond. The Confederates scarcely harmed *Monitor*, but the ship did little damage in return; the *Galena*, under the redoubtable John Rodgers, was badly damaged. The Confederates had placed obstructions in the river that prevented the ships from ascending further.

Supported by the navy, McClellan's army on the peninsula crawled toward Richmond. A Confederate attack on May 31, 1862, at Fair Oaks had little immediate effect, but in the battle Gen. Joseph E. Johnston was wounded and Robert E. Lee took command of the Army of Northern Virginia. On June 25, Lee initiated what would become known as the Seven Days' Battles. McClellan, convinced that the Confederates outnumbered him when the reverse was actually the case, appealed to Goldsborough on June 27 to "give me all the support you can."[87] The Army of the Potomac, covered by Goldsborough's gunboats, slowly retreated back down the peninsula.

On July 1, McClellan finally made a successful stand at Malvern Hill under the cover of the navy; as John M. Brooke told his wife, "The gunboats always come in to prevent a total rout of the enemy."[88] McClellan's assertion that he had merely changed his base rang hollow on both sides.[89] After a prolonged pause at Harrison's Landing, from August 20 through 26, the Army of the Potomac boarded transports to return to northern Virginia.

Without analyzing McClellan's peninsular operation in detail, it is probably safe to say that its failure put paid to any chance of the Union conducting an amphibious campaign. Although the plan of using seaborne mobility to conduct a strategic turning movement was sound, its faulty execution left both the plan and its author in poor odor. For the navy, it confirmed Du Pont's sentiment that the troops would not fight if gunboats were available.[90] Fox wrote, "The Richmond Engineer said that the first federal officer meeting a navy officer at James River after McClellan's 'strategic move' threw his arms around his neck and said, 'Oh my dear Sir, we ought to have a gunboat in every family!' We shall operate on this text."[91]

The departure of the Army of the Potomac at the end of August led the navy to reallocate most of its James River force to the Potomac Flotilla, but it did not end the navy's involvement on the James. When they evacuated Norfolk, the Confederates were able to save the partially built ironclad *Richmond* and tow her up the James to her namesake city for completion. She was finished in July 1862, but the obstructions that kept Union ironclads from going upriver also prevented the Confederate ironclad from going downriver to attack Union troops or shipping. President Davis, concerned primarily with defending Richmond, refused to permit the Confederate navy to cut a channel through the obstructions. The Federals could not know of Davis's policy decision, so the Confederate ironclad (which they called the "Merrimack #2" or "Virginia #2") remained in their perception a potent threat.

Goldsborough apparently received word of the *Richmond*'s completion in early July, and he promptly began badgering Welles for more ironclads. He had little faith in *Galena*, he wrote, and little more in *Monitor*; specifically, he wanted *New Ironsides*, the only ironclad reinforcement that would be available in the near term.[92] His pleas, coupled with the perceived

Confederate threat to the embarkation of the Army of the Potomac, caused Welles to acquiesce. *New Ironsides* was commissioned on August 21, 1862, in Philadelphia, and she sailed the next day for Hampton Roads and possible action.

The big frigate was already the center of a controversy. Thomas Turner, a captain with thirty-seven years of naval service, had been assigned to take command of the *New Ironsides*, then under construction. His birth in Washington DC raised suspicions among the hypervigilant.[93] Fox later wrote Rear Adm. Samuel P. Lee that Welles had received "so many letters, anonymous and otherwise," warning him against trusting Turner with the *New Ironsides* that it required "strong language on my part to reassure the Secretary." Fox asked Lee to "judge of [Turner's] temper. . . . No Harpers Ferry must occur to us." Turner passed muster and kept his command, but it was clear that even after a year of war the Union was still seeing traitors everywhere.[94] Under the circumstances, it was probably a good thing that Turner's raw crew was not called upon to fight, and after the flurry subsided, the ironclad returned to Philadelphia for post-trial repairs.

Goldsborough and his relief, Lee, tried to keep the ship, but Welles was tired of false alarms and needed ironclads elsewhere.[95] As Fox wrote in early September, "Give us two monitors and the Ironsides, and we will make Jeff Davis unhappy. . . . Every effort should be used to hurry up two or three of these vessels for Charleston."[96] After a taste of glory at New Orleans and a summer of abuse and drudgery supporting the army, the Navy Department wanted to go back on the offensive in the autumn of 1862. The imminent completion of the first Passaic class monitors brought an offensive strategy within reach.

For the Confederates, 1862 also marked a significant change in strategy. In late 1861 and early 1862, Union victories had forcefully underscored the weakness of Confederate coast and harbor defense, while at the same time the hoped-for effect of the "seagoing" ironclads had been negated. The combination appears to have driven Mallory to reevaluate his ironclad program.

This reevaluation came on the heels of Lee's reorganization of coastal defense. It recognized that the Confederacy could not hope to defend every foot of its coastline. As Lee phrased it, "Wherever [the Union] fleet can be brought no opposition to his landing can be made except within range of our fixed batteries."[97] Ashore, Lee's "phase two" had reinstated prewar U.S. defensive policies by concentrating troops and batteries at vulnerable points, leaving less valuable areas undefended, and developing a system that depended upon railroad transportation to exploit the Confederate advantage of interior lines. Afloat, Mallory's "phase two" plan would use technology in the form of ironclads and torpedoes to protect the South from seaborne intrusion. Although the second phase, like the first, included seagoing ironclads to break the blockade and fast cruisers to prey on Union shipping, these second-phase ships would be built in Europe. The home-built ironclads would operate in coastal waters as "moveable forts."

CHAPTER FOUR

Maturing under Fire

We are learning something every day, but it is expensive teaching
for Uncle Sam who has got to pay the bills. – *Gustavus V. Fox to
Cyrus W. Field, March 18, 1863*

By the beginning of 1863, the opposing strategies and technologies had
begun to mature. Strategically, the Union would maintain and tighten
the blockade; the Confederates would defend their coastline and try to
draw off blockaders through commerce raiding. The year saw the peak
of Confederate commerce raiding efforts and the success of the Union's
campaign to open the Mississippi River. Technologically, 1863 marked
the Union's use of ironclads in strength and the elaboration of the Confederacy's underwater defenses.

The year began inauspiciously for the Union. On New Year's Day, two
improvised gunboats filled with Confederate army troops surprised a detachment of the Western Gulf Blockading Squadron at Galveston. The
free-for-all close quarters action cost the Federals the blockaders *Harriet
Lane* and *Westfield*, and the simultaneous land assault recaptured the city
for the Southerners.[1] Almost by the time word of this reached Washington,
the West Gulf squadron had suffered more blows. On January 11, Raphael
Semmes, formerly captain of the css *Sumter*, was off the Texas coast in
the raider css *Alabama*. He had hoped to attack the transports assembled
by Gen. Nathaniel Banks for an expedition deeper into Texas, but found
only warships and correctly surmised that Galveston had been recaptured
by the Confederates. Semmes enticed the blockader *Hatteras* away from
her consorts and sank her in a "sharp and exciting" night action that

lasted only thirteen minutes.[2] Ten days later, the Confederates boarded
and captured two more Federal blockaders, the *Morning Light* and the
Velocity, and temporarily raised the blockade of Sabine Pass, Texas.[3]

Before the month was out, it was the South Atlantic Blockading
Squadron's turn. The Confederates in Charleston boasted two ironclads,
the *Chicora* and the *Palmetto State*. They were feeble, slow, and unseaworthy, but they could still overmatch Du Pont's wooden ships if the sea
were calm enough to allow them to leave Charleston Harbor. Du Pont
had urgently requested ironclads to counter the Confederates, and in
January 1863 the *New Ironsides* was dispatched to him. By the end of the
month the big frigate had reached Port Royal.

The Confederates appear to have known of *New Ironsides*'s arrival and
to have decided to act before she appeared off Charleston. *Chicora* and
Palmetto State got underway the night of January 30, 1863, and crossed
Charleston Bar on January 31. They took the blockaders by surprise at
dawn, and in the ensuing action *Palmetto State* rammed the steamer *Mercedita* and *Chicora* engaged the *Keystone State*. Both *Mercedita* and *Keystone State* surrendered but later escaped.[4] Gen. Pierre G. T. Beauregard,
the Confederate commander at Charleston, proclaimed that the blockade
had been broken, but Federal ships resumed station that afternoon.[5] Du
Pont, stung by the raid, ordered *New Ironsides* to Charleston. One of her
officers predicted, "The Charleston Rams have come out for certain now
for the contest," but *New Ironsides*'s arrival ensured that the Confederates
would not again try to break the Charleston blockade.[6]

The urgency with which Du Pont sent *New Ironsides* to Charleston
rested in part upon the perceived importance of the city. That importance
was political rather than military. Although Charleston was a center for
blockade-running, it was also the "cradle of secession." A naval officer
characterized it as the "cesspool of all infamy," and in June 1862 Fox
wrote, "The fall of Charleston is the fall of Satan's Kingdom."[7] The Navy
Department turned to Du Pont, the victor of Port Royal, to give them
Charleston, and as fast as the monitors were completed during the winter
of 1862–63, Welles sent them south.

Fox demanded that Du Pont mount an all-navy operation, "with the
Army as spectators as we arranged it at Port Royal."[8] In part Fox was
reacting to the army's refusal to supply enough troops for a joint attack,
but his enthusiasm also reflected the unwarranted confidence in the effect
of naval bombardment instilled by the victories of Hatteras, Port Royal,
and Roanoke Island. Never far from Fox's mind was the need to publicize

the navy's contribution to the war effort; the assistant secretary wrote that his duties were, first, to beat the Confederate and, "second, to beat the Army."[9]

Du Pont, the commander on the scene, did not share Fox's enthusiasm for an all-navy attack. Although his initial reaction to the new ironclads had been positive, closer association removed the bloom from the rose.[10] On January 27, 1863, Du Pont sent the newly arrived monitor *Montauk* against Fort McAllister, a Confederate earthwork on the Ogeechee River in Georgia. Although he hoped that the monitor could destroy the privateer *Rattlesnake*, which was lurking above the fort, his primary purpose was to test the monitor against a live but relatively easy target. Neither the fort nor the monitor did much to injure the other during four hours of firing. Du Pont rhetorically asked a friend, "If one ironclad cannot take eight guns, how are five to take 147 guns in Charleston harbor?" He told Welles that the experiment confirmed his opinion that the monitors were defensively excellent but offensively weak.[11]

Du Pont sent the *Montauk* back for another try at the fort on February 1, but even at closer range, the result was inconclusive. *Montauk* returned again on February 28 to find the *Rattlesnake* aground. The monitor destroyed the privateer with little injury from McAllister's guns, but as *Montauk* withdrew down the river, she struck a torpedo (what we would now call a mine). Although the damage was minor, the incident heightened Du Pont's concern about torpedoes.

The admiral apparently used Fort McAllister as a training aid, sending other new monitors there on March 3, 1863. While that gave the monitor crews a taste of action, it did the same for the Confederate garrison, who not only learned from the experience but took heart from their belief that they had driven off a serious attack. Afterwards, Du Pont pinpointed the monitors' major shortcoming when he commented, "Continuity of fire is the thing; twenty-five minutes of the *Wabash*, broadside, would take that fort about three times a day"[12] (see figure 1). The admiral was especially concerned that the Confederates at Charleston would sink and salvage a monitor, "in which case we lose the whole coast, and with it our cause."[13] Fox, clearly in the grip of "bombardment fever," urged Du Pont to simply enter the harbor and demand the surrender of the city. The admiral, who told his wife that Charleston Harbor resembled a porcupine's hide made into a bag with the quills on the inside, reminded Fox that, first, "you have to *get there*."[14] Du Pont had recovered from bombardment fever and monitor mania well before the Navy Department did.

In late January 1863, Welles strongly urged Du Pont to attack the city, but he left the final decision to the admiral.[15] Unfortunately for the Federals, Du Pont had developed a bad case of professional reticence. He had told his superiors of his growing concern about the monitors' lack of offensive capability and hinted that a naval attack on Charleston would fail. However, he never clearly expressed his pessimism, probably because he felt intense pressure from Washington and feared that he would lose his command if he did not yield to it. Welles and Fox, who were used to receiving very direct and forceful correspondence from Du Pont, not surprisingly took his silence as indicating agreement with their plan. Du Pont's delays, combined with his assertion that he wanted all the ironclads the Navy Department could supply, made Welles think the admiral sounded like McClellan.[16]

Du Pont had long felt that joint army-navy action would be needed to take Charleston. The army, he felt, had missed a golden opportunity by failing to take advantage of the panic that followed the occupation of Port Royal.[17] The admiral's hopes for army cooperation were evident as late as February 1863 when a correspondent reported that joint action was planned, but as the year unfolded, it became clear that the army would not provide the needed troops.[18] The pressure from Washington grew steadily, and Du Pont's private letters became gloomier and more pessimistic.[19]

For their part, Welles and Fox did everything they could to strengthen Du Pont's force, giving him all but one of the U.S. Navy's very limited number of ironclads. They further increased their pressure on the shipbuilders and engaged Ericsson to build special obstruction-clearing rafts to be pushed ahead of the monitors. When the monitor *Weehawken* suffered a major engineering casualty in February 1863, they sent Chief Engineer Alban C. Stimers, the technical director of the entire monitor construction program, to Port Royal to supervise the repairs.

Stimers, whom Du Pont called "Ericsson's high priest," was a bona fide monitor enthusiast who had served in the original *Monitor* at the Battle of Hampton Roads.[20] His experience aboard the *Passaic* in the engagement of March 3 changed his impression of the ships, though (see figure 4). While he had earlier told Fox that four monitors would "do up" Charleston, he now told Welles that more guns were needed for success.[21] Du Pont felt that the converted Stimers would have the credibility to make the Navy Department see things Du Pont's way. Although the admiral later suspected that Stimers had changed his tune when he met with Fox,

Welles, and Lincoln, it may have been that the engineer was not as firmly convinced of the monitors' deficiencies as was Du Pont himself.[22]

Stimers, whether more or less reliably converted, returned North in mid-March with ideas for strengthening the monitors. In two weeks he was back in Port Royal with the materials, tools, and workmen to make the alterations. Du Pont, still unwilling to express his misgivings forthrightly, had just about run out of reasons for delay. April 1863 found Du Pont ready to attack—or, at least, fatalistically resigned to it.

The Confederates had taken full advantage of Charleston's tricky hydrography and the Union's delay. Beauregard expanded Charleston's pre-war defenses into a multi-layered system of fortifications, with obstructions to prevent attacking ships from running past the forts as Farragut had done in the Mississippi and range marker buoys to help his artillerymen (chart 6). Beauregard's men had also begun to install torpedoes, and while at this time they were few, the fear of their presence exerted a powerful psychological effect on Union officers and men. When Du Pont's fleet appeared off Charleston Bar on April 5, 1863, Beauregard's command was as ready as it could be. Du Pont would enjoy neither strategic nor tactical surprise.

Du Pont's ironclads crossed Charleston Bar on April 6, but visibility and tide prevented the attack from beginning that day. Early in the afternoon of April 7, the monitor *Weehawken* led six other monitors, the *Keokuk*, and the *New Ironsides* up the Main Ship Channel toward the city of Charleston. Du Pont's offensive plan, poorly communicated to his captains, was to enter the harbor and attack Fort Sumter from behind. Beauregard's defensive plan involved what one Confederate commander characterized as "purely an artillery fight," probably because the Confederate navy's two Charleston-based ironclads would have been ineffective against monitors at long ranges and would have fouled the ranges of the shore-based guns.[23]

The Confederates commenced firing around 3 PM and the ships, advancing slowly against the ebb tide, began to reply soon after. By 4:30 Du Pont ordered his ironclads to withdraw. The slow-firing monitors simply could not produce the volume of fire necessary to suppress the defenses. After receiving the reports of his commanding officers, Du Pont decided that another attempt on Charleston "would have converted a failure into a disaster."[24] He blamed the repulse on the ironclads, calling the monitors "miserable failures where forts are concerned" and characterizing *New Ironsides* as "the greatest *sham* of all."[25] The fate of the badly damaged

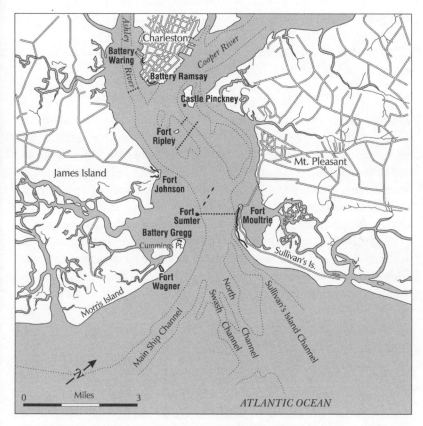

6. *Charleston, South Carolina. Charleston boasted a layered defense and a harbor sown with obstructions and torpedoes. (Redrawn from* ORN, *14:opposite p. 1)*

Keokuk, which sank on April 8, certainly increased Du Pont's pessimism. The monitors soon departed, and *New Ironsides* returned to her blockade station outside of Charleston Bar.

Du Pont's failure to renew the attack did not sit well with the Navy Department. The *Charleston Daily Courier* opined, "It is barely supposable that after two years of preparation the Abolitionists will be satisfied with the result of a two hours bombardment," and the editorialist proved to be right on the mark.[26] Welles and Fox, who were very publicly wedded to the monitor concept, were even less pleased with Du Pont's assignment of blame to the ships. Seeking political cover for the Navy Department's part in the repulse, Welles refused to publish Du Pont's reports because they would "inspire the rebels," and relations between the admiral and his superiors deteriorated quickly.[27]

Meanwhile, Welles and Fox faced the unpalatable fact that the new monitors had failed their first significant combat test. In one sense the ships did well: for the 2,229 shots the Confederates fired, they sank the non-monitor ironclad *Keokuk* and killed one man. Yet the Confederate fire jammed turrets, dismounted guns, knocked the armored roofs off of pilot houses, and broke deck plating. Before Charleston, engagements involving monitors had been few. The lack of battle experience prevented the navy from learning much about monitors, but it also minimized combat-driven changes to the ships. The action at Charleston led to a flurry of alterations, to ships under construction as well as to those already in service, with consequences that will be described in the next chapter.

As Du Pont's war of words with the Navy Department escalated, the war with the Confederates continued. Using the floating shops that Du Pont had established at Port Royal, Chief Engineer Stimers and his mechanics quickly repaired most of the damage from the April 7 engagement, but more than two months elapsed between the Charleston attack and the monitors' next significant action.[28] In June 1863, Du Pont sent the monitors *Weehawken* and *Nahant* to guard the Savannah blockaders from the Confederate ironclad *Atlanta* (see figure 3), and the *Atlanta*'s sortie proved the worth of Ericsson's design in the ship-to-ship action for which he intended it. In an engagement on June 17, 1863, *Weehawken* fired only five rounds, scoring hits with two 15-inch and two 11-inch shot. As Fox had intended, the 15-inch gun was decisive. The first 15-inch shot cracked the *Atlanta*'s armor and knocked down a quarter of her crew, and after fifteen minutes the Confederates surrendered.[29] The victory was gratifying to Du Pont but did nothing to improve his standing in Washington; he had already been officially informed that he was to be relieved of command.

The Navy Department had concentrated its ironclads at Charleston, but doing so had meant making hard choices. For one, Fox had had to shelve his other pet project of taking Wilmington. For another, the threat posed by the Confederate ironclad building program forced Welles to take calculated risks. The squadron commanders, as Fox told Du Pont, had "called for Iron Clads to defend themselves but we have not given them any."[30] Du Pont's failure at Charleston and his subsequent inactivity gave Welles and Fox the impression that they had made considerable sacrifices and received nothing in return.

The concentration under Du Pont meant, for example, that when Farragut ascended the Mississippi for the second time, on March 14, 1863, his force was entirely wooden. The admiral took seven ships up the river to destroy the tin-clad gunboat USS *Indianola*, sunk and captured by the Confederates on the 24th, and to cut off Confederate supplies from the Red River. In passing the Confederate batteries at Port Hudson, Farragut lost the USS *Mississippi* but was able to block the Red River until Porter, who had taken command of the Mississippi River squadron in October 1862, could run vessels downriver past Vicksburg to assist. Farragut returned to New Orleans in May, then moved upriver for a third time later that month to support the siege of Port Hudson.

Port Hudson surrendered in early July, soon after Vicksburg fell to Grant. On August 1, 1863, Porter's Mississippi Squadron assumed responsibility for the entire Mississippi theater, and Farragut's seagoing ships returned to New Orleans and then to the Gulf.

Responsibility for the South Atlantic Blockading Squadron also changed hands. Relations between Du Pont and his superiors had deteriorated rapidly since April, because Du Pont blamed the failure solely on the monitors and thus by extension on the Navy Department, which had so enthusiastically promoted them. When Welles refused to publish his report, Du Pont tried to put his version of the facts on record by court-martialing General Inspector Stimers. Welles knew that the monitors would be in the dock along with Stimers and that a conviction would be a condemnation of the monitors and of the Navy Department. Sensing that Stimers would be "sacrificed" by any court-martial convened by Du Pont, Welles opted for a (less severe) court of inquiry.[31] Several months of proceedings that Stimers characterized as "dignified farce" exonerated the engineer.[32]

Du Pont's private letters show the depth of his bitterness. Writing that he was to be sacrificed to the "ironclad plunderers," Du Pont was especially disdainful of Fox, who was allied by marriage with Du Pont's political enemies.[33] Calling Fox an "upstart . . . swelled out like a toadfish," he dismissed the assistant secretary as "a liar and a scoundrel."[34] It is clear that the Navy Department made Du Pont the goat for the failure at Charleston, but equally clearly Welles could not tolerate such a relationship with one of his principal subordinates. Du Pont would have to go.

To take over the South Atlantic Blockading Squadron, Welles first turned to his close friend Rear Adm. Andrew H. Foote, who had successfully commanded the Mississippi Squadron. Foote, however, became ill and died in June 1863. Welles reluctantly decided to replace Du Pont with John A. Dahlgren.

In doing so, the secretary bowed to heavy pressure from President Lincoln, to whom Dahlgren already owed his admiral's commission. The navy's premier ordnance expert had considerably less seagoing experience than his contemporaries and had not commanded so much as a gunboat at sea during the war. His appointment to a "plum" operational command would be very controversial in the navy, and Welles knew it. Du Pont distilled the thinking of many officers when he wrote that Dahlgren "was licking cream while we were eating dirt," and Welles foresaw "bitter opposition to Dahlgren from some good officers."[35] Nonetheless, Welles yielded to Lincoln and appointed Dahlgren.

Dahlgren took over in early July 1863 and lost no time in beginning the "Siege of Charleston." On July 10, 1863, Brig. Gen. Quincy A. Gillmore's troops attacked Fort Wagner on Morris Island. When the Confederates repulsed the attack, Gillmore besieged the fort, with Dahlgren's ships providing gunfire support for the troops. For the next two months, the monitors and the broadside ironclad *New Ironsides* frequently bombarded the Confederate fortifications.

The siege quickly established a rhythm. The Federals would shell the forts during the day, doing more or less damage, but their failure to maintain control of the harbor at night allowed the Confederates to resupply and repair their works under the cover of darkness.[36] Fort Sumter, reduced to rubble, remained an infantry outpost, and the earthworks of Fort Wagner and Battery Gregg on Cummings Point proved resistant to naval gunfire. The Confederates held Wagner until early September 1863, when a bombardment by the *New Ironsides* killed one hundred of the nine hundred troops there and impelled the garrison to evacuate.[37]

From his Washington experience, Dahlgren knew how urgently the Navy Department yearned to take Charleston, but once on the scene, he found himself facing the same obstacles as Du Pont. In part those obstacles were literal and physical: the obstructions and torpedoes with which the Confederates had blocked the harbor. Du Pont's attack had made it clear that the weight of metal favored the Confederate batteries, and the obstructions pinned the ships right where the Confederate gunners wanted them. To regain the freedom of movement that the ships needed to fight forts successfully, the Federals would have to remove the obstructions. Until then, they could attack only the outer layer of Confederate defenses. Dahlgren sent volunteers in small boats to remove the obstructions at night, but the work was so physically arduous and the area so well covered by Confederate fire that they made little progress.[38] As late as 1865 he had never obtained a complete reconnaissance of the obstructions.

Psychologically, Dahlgren had to deal with the legacy of Du Pont's failure and the lesson it appeared to teach senior officers: better not to act than to act and fail. The lesson appears to have reinforced the inclination Welles noted when he wrote that Dahlgren was a "capable and intelligent" bureaucrat, "but he shuns and evades responsibility. This may be his infirmity in his new position."[39]

Dahlgren also had to deal with the army, and he never succeeded in establishing strategic harmony. Strategically, the army viewed Charleston as a sideshow. Gillmore understood that the plan was to take the south end of Morris Island, reduce Fort Wagner by siege, demolish Sumter, remove the obstructions, and run the ironclads to the city. When Fort Wagner fell on September 7, Gillmore felt that he had completed his part of the campaign.[40] In part this reflected a lack of coordinated strategic direction from Washington—the War Department did not share the Navy Department's focus on Charleston—but it also reflected the lack of detailed consultation between Dahlgren and Gillmore. Dahlgren's last-minute appointment kept him from participating in the discussions among Foote, Welles, Fox and Gillmore, yet he does not seem to have felt it necessary to ensure that he and Gillmore agreed on the plan.[41]

Dahlgren never established good personal relations with his army counterparts, either. In one incident, for example, a party of soldiers from the Provost Guard arrested some civilian carpenters who were building a wharf for the navy. Dahlgren protested to the army commander, Maj. Gen. J. G. Foster, who apologized but refused to court-martial the sergeant in charge or to issue a general order as Dahlgren desired. Rather than accept Foster's assurance that the episode would not be repeated, Dahlgren hashed and rehashed the matter in increasingly querulous tones before he finally let it drop.[42]

Dahlgren's relations with General Gillmore were even worse. He became convinced of Gillmore's hostility, bristling especially at Gillmore's assertions that the navy could have entered the harbor in late August 1863 and that the obstructions could have been removed "with no great delay or difficulty" by troops that Gillmore offered to supply.[43] Dahlgren would later accuse "that 'Ironsides' and Gillmore coalition" of working to have him relieved: "Gillmore, undermining in the papers, and then preparing his book; while [Commodore S. C.] Rowan was ready to take the vacancy!"[44]

Dahlgren's hostility toward Gillmore showed clearly in his arrangements to attack Fort Sumter after Fort Wagner fell. Dahlgren hastily assembled an amphibious force to assault Sumter on the night of September 8, 1863. Gillmore had the same idea, though, and neither Dahlgren nor Gillmore would yield leadership of a joint expedition to the other. The result was an uncoordinated fiasco. The Confederates, warned by the assembly of Union boats and by intercepted messages between Dahlgren and Gillmore, killed 4 of the attackers, wounded 19, and captured 102 more, without loss to themselves.[45] It was one of the few episodes in which a Confederate ironclad engaged Union forces.

New Ironsides's executive officer, George E. Belknap, admired Dahlgren's physical bravery and scientific accomplishments, but found that the failure of the amphibious attack "seemed to paralyze the Admiral" and prevented further offensive action.[46] By October, however, Welles finally began to accept that the game at Charleston was not worth the candle even if Satan's Kingdom had not fallen. Thanks to the capture of Morris Island and Dahlgren's stationing monitors in the harbor mouth, blockade-running dropped from a total of twenty-two transits (in- and outbound) in May 1863 to five in August, one in September, and then none at all until March 1864.[47] With the harbor closed to blockade-runners, Welles wrote, entering Charleston Harbor without troops to support the fleet would be "merely a point of honor." Despite the "excited expectations of our loyal countrymen," the Navy Department "is disinclined to have its only ironclad squadron incur extreme risks when the substantial advantages have already been gained."[48]

The "extreme risks" to which Welles referred stemmed from the Confederacy's increasing mastery of the other maturing technology of 1863, underwater warfare. Obstructions played a key part, and as Fox wrote, "I am afraid all the Southern harbors will be plugged up solid before we can get afloat the next batch of Monitors. The rascals know their only defence is in closing their harbors."[49] In addition to the obstructions that had helped to repulse Du Pont, torpedoes allowed the Confederates to counter the Union's material preponderance with technology.

Originally the Confederate army and navy torpedo programs had been separate. The prewar U.S. Army had been responsible for coastal defense, however, so mining and obstruction of harbors and rivers was a natural extension of the army's protective mission. The programs quickly began to overlap, as evidenced by the work of the navy's Matthew Fontaine Maury and the army's Gabriel J. Rains in the submarine defenses of the James River and the detail of Isaac N. Brown, a Confederate navy officer, to Polk's army command. The unconventional frame of mind that torpedo work required probably encouraged this sort of collaboration, but organizationally, it is difficult to trace the history of the Confederacy's torpedo warfare programs. Besides the "overlap," there are two major reasons.

First, torpedoes were truly "secret weapons"—the less the Union knew about Confederate torpedoes and the men who employed them, the better. The legislation that established the torpedo warfare organizations was deliberately vague and often secret, and much of the expense involved was paid from "incidental and contingent" or other secret accounts. The Confederacy hand-picked the officers involved, and the men who enlisted in the navy's Submarine Battery Service swore an oath never to reveal "anything regarding the methods used for arranging or exploding the submarine batteries."[50] The small size of the torpedo corps aided Confederate efforts to maintain security. Torpedoes were highly specialized weapons whose successful design, construction, and deployment depended upon dedicated experts with special talent and training.

Second, public and service opinion held torpedoes to be repugnant to "civilized" warfare. Critics North and South lambasted the weapons as dishonorable, and even Maury's wife called her husband's work "barbarous."[51] Despite growing Southern acceptance of torpedoes as a way to deal effectively with "brutal" enemies, the debates over whether torpedoes were "proper warfare" continued at least until October 1863.[52] This climate encouraged circumspection, both personal and official.

Maury, his army counterpart Rains, and other inventors faced formidable difficulties. They knew little, for example, of the behavior of underwater explosions. Oversimplifying, if an underwater explosion occurs too close to the surface, much of its energy will be vented to atmosphere instead of transferred to the target. Considerable experimentation was required to find an optimum depth—too shallow, and the torpedo would be ineffective; too deep, and the target might not strike the torpedo at all.

Another handicap was the nature of black gunpowder, a mechanical mixture of saltpeter, sulfur, and charcoal. Black powder does not actually "detonate" but rather burns very rapidly, at a rate that is heavily influenced by the detailed composition of the powder, the size of the powder grains, and the constraints imposed on the burning material. The Confederates quickly and correctly determined that small-grained "rifle" powder was more effective in torpedoes than large-grained "cannon" powder because the small grains released their energy more rapidly. But even fine-grained black powder is inherently a poor underwater explosive.[53]

Beyond these areas in which technology outran theory, the Confederates had to deal with more mundane problems such as waterproofing their work and obtaining the miles of insulated wire needed to install the electrically controlled torpedoes that Maury preferred. Much of the specialized material came from England, but the Confederates also made their own and never missed a chance to salvage anything that would be useful.[54] Even so, the chronic shortage of electrical material impelled the development of sensitive, reliable mechanical fuzes that would do their work upon contact.

In fact, much of the eventual success of the Confederate torpedoes resulted from research focused on improved triggering mechanisms. Waterproofing a mechanical exploder with 1860s techniques was no easy task, and the relatively small "keg" or "soda tank" models that dominated Confederate torpedo production were almost always mechanically fired. Larger torpedoes, containing up to three thousand pounds of powder, and some smaller riverine models were electrically actuated by command from shore, but the scarcity of properly insulated wire limited their use.[55]

The Confederacy made its official endorsement of torpedo warfare manifest in April 1862, when the Confederate Congress ordered a bounty of 50 percent of the value of all Union vessels sunk or destroyed by "any new machine or engine."[56] On October 13 of that year, the Congress expanded the effort by authorizing the formation of "volunteer companies for local defense." This apparently innocuous act provided the legal basis for the official organization of both the War Department Torpedo Bureau, under Rains, and the Navy Submarine Battery Service, under Hunter S. Davidson.[57]

Technical and tactical immaturity dogged Confederate underwater warfare for the first eighteen months of war. Federal reports detail many instances in which torpedoes were recovered or exploded harmlessly, and a Union navy officer observed that these early efforts spread a "feeling of contempt for their originators, and disregard of their possible effects." In late 1862, though, the Confederacy's intense development effort began to pay off. The first Confederate success came in the Western theater, where a torpedo sank the river gunboat *Cairo* in December 1862. The Confederates in the East soon scored as well, damaging the monitor

Montauk in March 1863 and sinking the river gunboat *Baron De Kalb* in July 1863. Confederate torpedoes became "so certain and well devised that the most incredulous and daring began to respect and fear them." By the end of the war torpedoes would sink eighteen ships, including seven ironclads, and damage several others.[58]

In addition to the defensive torpedoes that began to fill Southern rivers and harbors, the Confederates also built torpedo boats to attack the Union fleet directly. The weapon they used was the spar torpedo, essentially a container of explosive on the end of a long pole. A leader in its development was Capt. Francis D. Lee, csa. After an earlier proposal foundered on the rocks of interservice coordination, Beauregard supported Lee's approach to the War Department in October 1862.[59] Lee obtained an unfinished vessel from the Navy Department in November 1862 and immediately set to work to complete it as a "marine torpedo ram." Slowed by lack of materials, lack of funds, and lack of clear authority, Lee pushed the construction of the vessel as hard as he could.[60]

Mallory had apparently blessed Lee's project and ordered the transfer of the incomplete gunboat, but the minimal support the inventor received from the navy seems to have been due as much to indifference as to lack of resources. Although Lee had conceived a vessel armed only with a torpedo, in November 1862 he proposed to add a gun armament, which, he wrote, would bring "the sympathy of those whose co-operation would be invaluable."[61] Delays mounted, primarily due to the lack of iron, and by February 1863 Lee was appealing to Beauregard for help in obtaining it from the avy.[62] By March 1863, Lee had successfully tested his torpedo against a hulk and, at Beauregard's order, he provided torpedo apparatus to the navy for ten small boats. Beauregard, knowing of Du Pont's preparations to attack Charleston, unsuccessfully pressed the War Department for materials, since he considered the torpedo boat to be "much superior" to the Confederate navy's ironclads.[63]

The ironclads did not participate in repelling Du Pont's attack, which gave Beauregard ammunition for his torpedo boat campaign. He continued to support Lee's project and lobbied for torpedo boats to be built abroad, writing that six torpedo boats for Charleston and a dozen for the Mississippi River would be "worth to us a whole fleet and a large army," at much lower cost.[64] Local businessmen also offered to build a torpedo boat in England and wanted Lee to superintend its construction.[65] Beauregard and the War Department approved, but Lee did not go abroad, probably because he was finally making progress on his local project. His torpedo boat was launched on July 13, 1863, and in August the newly named *Torch* was finished and fitted with a spar torpedo.[66] Pilot James Carlin took charge of trying to torpedo the *New Ironsides*. The August 21, 1863, attempt failed, but the Confederates did not give up.[67]

Imperfect as it was, the spar torpedo dramatically changed naval warfare because it gave small ships the ability to destroy big ships and broke the direct relationship between ship size and power that had existed for centuries. As such, it was a natural extension of the Confederacy's technology strategy, and like stationary torpedoes, it was improved over time: the converted *Torch*, roundly condemned by her captain for slow speed and poor handling, was replaced by the css *David*, built expressly for torpedo attack.

On October 5, 1863, the *David*, under Lt. William T. Glassel, csn, attacked the *New Ironsides*, exploding about one hundred pounds of gunpowder against the frigate's starboard side. Although the explosion caused only minor damage, there was at first "considerable excitement on board [*New Ironsides*] to ascertain whether the ship was sinking."[68] The *David* escaped and, as intelligence showed a growing threat, Dahlgren directed anti-torpedo measures for the entire squadron. The patrol boats, extra guards, howitzers, and protective barriers frustrated further attacks that autumn by the *David* and by the "diving torpedo," the hand-powered submarine *Hunley*, but the strain clearly told on Federal crews.[69]

The strain was increased by the living conditions aboard the ironclads. Paymaster William F. Keeler wrote of being shut up in a "close iron box, no ventilation or air, but little light, in an atmosphere at times fairly suffocating, the heat enough to drive out a salamander." Charles Post recorded a monitor commanding officer's observation: "The condensed moisture simply runs in streams from their bulkheads," while a crewman aboard the *Nahant* complained of widespread "physical weakness" among the crew from heat and "extremely bad air below-deck."[70] For the year 1863, sickness rates aboard the monitors averaged over 25 percent.[71]

Much engineering effort went into improving the ventilation of successive classes of monitors, but even with all the Union's resources the problem was never completely solved. A special committee of the U.S. Sanitary Commission investigated the monitors early in 1864, and General Inspector Stimers was clearly defensive about it. Stimers told the doctor who chaired the committee that he had no time to correct all of the doctor's "errors of estimate," but he did challenge a specific remark, asking rudely, "Now how did you arrive at that quantity? Certainly not by any mathematical process." The doctor's presumption in proposing a solution also angered Stimers. "The medical men should state requirements," he wrote, "and leave to the engineer the details by which they are to be met."[72]

Stimers's calculations and improvements eventually had an effect, since an 1865 study by the navy's Bureau of Medicine and Surgery noted that the sick rate aboard the monitors had fallen from over 25 percent in 1863 to just over 5 percent in 1865. However, it took two years to alleviate the "great inconvenience and suffering endured by those who first served on board the monitors."[73] For the most active period of their service, in 1863 and 1864, the monitors' crews required "more than ordinary measures" to keep them healthy.[74]

Confederate ships were at least as physically taxing as their Union counterparts, despite (or perhaps because of) being constantly in port, and the Confederate ironclads routinely reported sick rates of over 20 percent.[75] A crewman described the *Atlanta*'s living quarters as "the most miserable I ever saw." Besides a total lack of ventilation, "if a person were blindfolded and carried below and then turned loose he would imagine himself in a swamp, for the water is trickling in all the time and everything is so damp."[76] Deserters from the Savannah squadron in March 1863 reported that the *Atlanta* and the ironclads *Savannah* and *Georgia* had "no means of ventilation; when the hatches are on they are almost hermetically sealed, the only opening being the ports. There are no blower engines in these vessels."[77] Union officers described the *Tennessee* as being "exceedingly comfortable for an ironclad vessel of her description," but even *Tennessee*'s crew did not live aboard their ship.[78] The Mobile ironclads berthed their crews in warehouses or on barges, and the Savannah Squadron's crews slept ashore or aboard more habitable vessels nearby. In North Carolina, the Wilmington ironclads used tenders, while the *Albemarle*'s crew slept ashore in sheds.[79]

Although such arrangements improved conditions for the Confederate crews, their ability to sleep away from their ships only highlighted the difference between Confederate and Union ironclads. The Confederate ships were pinned in port by their adversaries, their defensive mission, and their own unseaworthiness. The Southern people, however, thought of the ironclads as offensive weapons rather than "moveable forts," and after Hampton Roads, public expectations were high. The inactivity of the ironclads did much to lower the Confederate navy's prestige and to lower the expectations of the Southern press and people.[80]

As 1863 passed, General Beauregard was one whose expectations fell steadily. After the anticlimax of the January 1863 sortie against the blockading fleet, Beauregard grew firmer in his opinion that the Confederate navy's concentration on ironclads wasted resources. As he complained to Congressman Porcher Miles, the three ironclads at Charleston had not fired a single shot during Du Pont's attack, and only once had one of them participated in the defense of Morris Island.[81] Miles forwarded Beauregard's remarks to Mallory, who replied with a spirited defense.[82] Beauregard's frustration was evident when he told Miles that the ironclads were "children of [Mallory's] own creation," and that the secretary could not admit their defects "any more than the owl can admit that its young ones are ugly."[83] Instead of the fast, purpose-built torpedo boats that Beauregard pressed for, navy resources went to the ironclads, and he and Captain Lee had to continue to depend upon "boats and barges" fitted with spar torpedoes.[84]

Dahlgren's Fort Sumter fiasco more than Beauregard's torpedo boats ended the Union's chance of offensive action at Charleston, but Welles's decision to leave the monitors under Dahlgren's command precluded offensive action elsewhere. In the West, Farragut returned to the North in early August 1863 for rest and consultation. He left Commodore H. H. Bell in charge of the Western Gulf Blockading Squadron, with the job of reinvigorating the blockade with ships redeployed from the Mississippi River campaign.

Bell did so, and his success points up what might have happened if Welles had taken Mallory's bait by diverting ships from the blockade to chase commerce raiders. From September 1862 to March 1863, an average of one runner per month had run in or out of Mobile, but during Farragut's riverine effort, from April through July 1863, the average increased to almost nine per month. When Farragut's ships returned from the Mississippi River in August 1863, the average dropped to under two per month through March 1864. Beginning in April 1864, Farragut's preparations to attack Mobile Bay again withdrew ships from the blockade, and from April through July 1864, the average runs rose to nearly seven per month.[85]

Frustration seemed to be the order of the day for both sides in the waning months of 1863. For the Union, Morris Island had fallen, but Charleston was as far out of reach as ever. The raider *Alabama*, somewhere at sea, was still unfindable and the *Florida*, under repair in a French port, was still untouchable (see figure 9). The once-promising monitor construction program had stalled, as will be discussed in chapter 5. Strategically, the blockade continued to improve, but blockading was not as satisfying as offensive action and an offensive against Mobile or Wilmington would require troops for which the army had other uses.

The Confederates faced similar frustrations. Fort Sumter had been held, but Union artillery commanded Charleston Harbor. Federal efforts had sharply tightened the blockade at Charleston and Mobile, and the exploits of the Confederate cruisers had not drawn ships away from the cordon. Torpedoes had begun to score, but equipment was in short supply and torpedo boats had not notably reduced the odds against the Confederates. The British government had seized two ironclads being built for the Confederates in England, but two ironclads and four cruisers were being built in France with the French government's tacit approval. Ironclads protected some Southern ports, but other home-built ships remained unfinished for want of armor and machinery. Both Confederates and Federals had learned a number of lessons and hoped to apply them in the new year.

CHAPTER FIVE

Ironclads in Strength

Without being drawn into the ongoing debates about the "modernity" and "totality" of the American Civil War, it is clear that the war was shaped as much by the economic and industrial resources of the combatants as by their political and strategic thinking. The Union's use of ironclads in quantity was possible only because the navy mobilized Northern industry to build them and evolved a system to manage their construction. The Confederacy, with little industry to mobilize, started at a disadvantage. While improvisation produced some modestly useful vessels, the Confederate navy never developed either a management system for home production nor an overseas procurement system that could deal effectively with the myriad obstacles the Confederacy faced.

Mallory's recognition of the importance of technology had given the Confederacy a slight early lead in the ironclad race, but the Southerners could not maintain the advantage they had taken with the *Virginia* conversion. The Northern industrial base far outstripped that of the South; once the Union reorganized for war production, the Confederacy had no hope of matching either the quantity or the quality of Northern material. Yet organizational problems kept the Confederacy from making the best use of its limited resources. The Confederate Navy Department had no construction and repair organization until 1863, which meant that no one below the secretarial level had the formal responsibility or the authority to coordinate ship design and construction. Despite a casual familiarity with naval construction dating from his years on the Senate Naval Affairs Committee, Mallory was no naval architect, and he had no one of the caliber of Lenthall or Isherwood to assist him.

Mallory's lack of a construction organization drove him to try to break production bottlenecks himself. When the main shaft of the ironclad *Mississippi* was being made, for example, he "visited the Tredegar Works every morning, to see that the work on the shaft was rapidly progressing."[1] Besides the detriment to the secretary's cabinet-level work, the lack of a construction bureau appears to have precluded any serious effort to base Confederate designs on the most critical factor, main propulsion machinery. Bulloch proposed buying critical components such as engines, boilers, and armor plate in Europe and assembling them to wooden hulls built in the Confederacy, but the C.S. Navy Department could not coordinate its designs well enough to make this possible.[2] Instead of tailoring their designs to the available machinery, Confederate constructors tried to adapt the machinery to their designs. Confederate ironclads almost without exception were slow and underpowered, too ambitious for their power plants.

Confederate ironclads bore a superficial family resemblance, since all but two carried an inclined armored casemate atop a low freeboard hull (see figure 3). Beyond that common feature, however, variety ruled. The need to use whatever machinery was available and the need to adapt to local materials and local skills meant that despite later attempts at standardization, each Confederate ironclad was more or less different from every other. Although the Confederacy's ability to build marine engines improved somewhat later in the war, increasing shortages of transportation, iron, and skilled labor combined with operationally driven design evolution to ensure heterogeneity.[3]

In the North, the same industrial resources that allowed design flexibility in the first-generation ironclads also permitted standardization in later vessels. The Battle of Hampton Roads validated the deal that Welles had had to make with Ericsson's backers, but it also marked the end of the Union's experimentation with different ironclad designs. This single, inconclusive action established the monitor design as the basis of the U.S. Navy's ironclad fleet; the de facto parallel development program established by the Ironclad Board report vanished in "Monitor Mania." The Union commenced fifty-six coastal and seagoing ironclads; fifty-two were monitors. The effort to build these vessels evolved into a ship acquisition program of unprecedented size and technological complexity, requiring both a massive industrial mobilization in the North and the development of a flexible, responsive system to manage it.

The experimental nature of ironclad technology complicated matters. Politics and public relations drove the U.S. Navy to select the monitor type of ironclad, but any ironclad was "high technology" for its day. It was difficult enough to get manufacturers to build more copies of proven designs, such as steam engines or small arms. The need to simultaneously develop and deploy a novel technology, in a high-stakes atmosphere of extreme urgency, imposed huge strains upon governmental and economic infrastructures that were not accustomed to large projects or to fast action.

High technology, while necessary, did not itself suffice to enable the Union to create its ironclad fleet—the ideas of the sketchbook and drawing board had to be given physical reality in wood and metal. Traditionally, navy ships were built in navy yards. Steam propulsion had impelled changes, but by the late 1850s the navy had integrated the contractors that built engines and the navy yards that built wooden hulls. Lacking ironworking tools and skills, however, the navy yards of 1862 could not build the ironclads that the navy needed. Since traditional peacetime methods could not produce technologically advanced ironclads in quantity, the navy turned to private contractors to build its ships.

At the same time, the navy experimented with a nontraditional form of shipbuilding management. Although Chief Constructor Lenthall and Chief Engineer Isherwood were by no means opposed to ironclads, they were not nearly as committed to the monitor design as was Fox, and they had responsibilities that went far beyond the ironclad program. To give the monitors the attention Fox felt they deserved, Secretary Welles appointed Capt. Francis H. Gregory to manage the program independently of the existing navy administrative system.[4]

Gregory, recalled from retirement, had been in charge of gunboat construction in New York since July 1861. Although he had no official responsibility for the *Monitor*, he had previously served with Chief Engineer Alban C. Stimers, who supervised the *Monitor*'s construction for the navy. In early May 1862, Gregory became general superintendent of ironclads, responsible for all those built under contract along the East Coast. Two weeks later, Stimers was appointed general inspector of ironclads. Gregory was nominally in charge, but he knew that Stimers had Fox's ear; as he described it, "There came an order stating, very laconically, that Mr. Stimers would have charge of those vessels building on the Ericsson plan, and he took the charge."[5] Stimers's appointment began the process by which the general superintendent's organization evolved into the "monitor bureau," providing desperately needed drive and direction during the critical months of 1862 and 1863.

The Union's ironclad expansion had begun with the ten ships of the

Passaic class, designed by John Ericsson as improved monitors for coastal use, and the Passaics were at the top of the priority list when Stimers assumed his duties in May 1862. Longer and broader than the original *Monitor,* the Passaics were nearly twice as heavy (see figure 4). These ships were to be the first fruits of the "twenty ironclads" legislation for which Welles had waited so long.

Ericsson had begun thinking about a follow-on design even before the *Monitor* was finished.[6] Among other technical improvements, the new ships would carry two 15-inch guns in an 11-inch-thick turret instead of two 11-inch guns behind 8 inches of armor, and the inventor moved the pilot house to the top of the turret for better visibility and less interference with the guns.[7] He worked closely with Fox and Stimers, though, and the ships' characteristics remained under discussion into early April 1862.[8] Although Ericsson and the navy did their best to incorporate the lessons of Hampton Roads, the indecisive battle yielded few lessons in areas that would emerge as vital.[9] The emphasis on improving the monitor design shows that the navy saw the most important issues facing the ironclad program to be technical in nature.

Ericsson's vast prestige caused the navy to insist that other contractors use his drawings for the Passaics instead of developing their own from general plans and specifications.[10] Fox's enthusiasm may have driven the move, but it would give the navy the benefits of a production run of identical units: increased output and decreased delivery time. Both "lead" and "follow" shipyards had mixed reactions. The follow yards avoided expenses that the lead yards had to incur, but from mid-1862, shipyards faced an increasingly intense suppliers' market for materials. The first contractors to order had a big advantage in obtaining materials, and because Ericsson was the designer, Ericsson's group always had that advantage.[11] In addition, the follow yards had nothing beyond Ericsson's assurance that each part would fit. If they did not, the follow yards would have to solve the problems and pay for the rework.

Despite the size of the Passaics relative to the *Monitor,* Ericsson agreed to build four of them in four months and two more in five months. Other contractors would build four more; of the total of ten ships, nine were intended for the eastern theater.[12] Because Ericsson and his partners themselves controlled no shipyards or machine shops, they subcontracted all six vessels. Three went to Ericsson's "first team," the firms that built the *Monitor:* Thomas F. Rowland's Continental Iron Works for the hulls and Cornelius Delamater's Delamater Iron Works for the machinery. Two hulls went to Reaney, Son & Archbold of Chester, Pennsylvania, for which the Philadelphia firm of I. P. Morris & Towne would build engines. The sixth Ericsson subcontract went to the Wilmington, Delaware, firm of Harlan & Hollingsworth.

Ericsson chose machinery or ironworking firms rather than traditional shipbuilders for his subcontracts, in part because most traditional ship-builders had too little capital to take such large contracts, and in any event shipbuilding in wood was already booming. Further, working in iron appealed more to those who already made their living in the metal trades. As one author phrased it, builders of wooden ships "could easily imagine workers in their yards building an iron *ship*. . . . But could they as easily have imagined their men building a *boiler?*"[13]

For the remaining four Passaics, the navy likewise turned to machine shops and ironworks rather than builders of wooden ships. Political agita-tion gave one vessel apiece to two Boston builders, Harrison Loring and Nelson Curtis, each with minimal experience in iron shipbuilding. The last two vessels went to builders with no iron shipbuilding experience at all. Charles A. Secor & Co. included brothers Charles A., James F., and Zeno Secor and, until his death in 1864, their father, Francis Secor. In 1862 the Secors agreed with Joseph Colwell to establish a new ship-yard and machine shop in Jersey City for the express purpose of building monitors. Colwell probably received capital and advice from his father, a wealthy foundry owner, but he had even less shipbuilding experience than the Secors.

The contractors had all agreed to build their monitors in four or five months. That was extremely optimistic, especially since most contrac-tors would have to expand or establish ironworking facilities. The most immediate drawback was the lack of information: without drawings and specifications, the contractors could not order the materials they needed. To further intensify the pressure, the Passaic class was not the navy's only monitor project. Secretary Welles told Congress in March 1862 that the navy wanted monitors with 15-inch guns "for harbor defence and to operate upon the Atlantic coast and in the Gulf of Mexico." Addition-ally, to counter the threat from the British and French, he proposed a monitor "ocean steamer" armed with 20-inch guns.[14] Ericsson provided specifications for the "ocean steamers," twice the size of the Passaics, in late May 1862. In late June, Welles gave Ericsson contracts for two such vessels and the inventor provided the plans within ten days. These ships, later named *Dictator* and *Puritan,* were Ericsson's pets, and he lavished effort upon them.

The effort overburdened Ericsson, who was at the same time producing the detail drawings for the entire Passaic class and directly supervising the shipyard work on six of them. Stimers was at first unable to help; not only did Ericsson object to anyone else designing monitors, but Stimers had quite enough to do in organizing the General Inspectorate, recruiting suitable inspectors, and personally checking the ships under construction.

As the summer of 1862 advanced, the pressure to complete the Passaic class vessels increased. Fox and Welles wanted offensive action, and proposals to attack Wilmington or Charleston were in the air. Wooden ships had taken Hatteras Inlet, Port Royal, and Roanoke Island, but to engage the fortifications at Charleston or Wilmington, the navy needed ironclads. The May 1862 action at Drewry's Bluff in the James River, which showed that the defensively excellent monitor design might not have much offensive potency, merely increased the demand for the new ships.

The first four Passaics should have been completed by July 31, 1862, and all nine East Coast ships should have been in navy hands by September. The shipbuilders could not meet their ambitious commitments, however, and the lead ship, *Passaic* herself, was not even launched until August 30, 1862. Fox knew the ships were far behind schedule, and to speed them up he applied ever-increasing pressure.

The contractors tried their best, but labor and materials shortages, startup and expansion delays, and inexperience had begun to show themselves. In August 1862, Ericsson had to rule out night work because the shipyards were already driving their men as hard as they dared in the warm weather, and there were not enough men available to work separate day and night shifts.[15] In September, Fox told Stimers to add a carrot to the stick of penalties for late delivery by offering overtime payments.[16] By October all the contractors were working days, nights, and Sundays to try to meet Welles's new deadline of November 15.

It was at about this time that the 1850s acquisition system began to show its defects. Looming issues included contract changes, overemphasis on financial controls, and inability to cope with changing economic conditions.

In the 1850s system, contract changes were minimal: in most cases, the contractor built only the machinery, which was unlikely to change much between contract and delivery. Changes to the rest of the ship, built by a navy yard, were "invisible": the navy yard did as it was told by the bureaus, so there were no repercussions outside the navy. Yet with vessels as novel as the monitors, designed and built in great haste, omissions were bound to occur and improvements were certain to suggest themselves. The navy's rudimentary mechanism for dealing with construction changes broke down under the stress. Difficulties included determining the responsibility for the changes, pricing them, and adjusting the construction schedule to account not only for the changes themselves but also for the delay and disruption they caused to other work.

For the Passaics, bigger guns formed the most disruptive change. *Monitor*'s 11-inch guns had damaged the *Virginia*, but Fox wanted decisive results. He directed then-Captain John A. Dahlgren, the navy's premier ordnance expert, to design a 15-inch gun for the "improved *Monitors*." Technical problems abounded, and production began very slowly. At the end of September 1862, when six of the Passaics were to have been delivered, not one 15-inch gun had arrived at a shipyard. To make matters worse, Ericsson had failed to redesign the Passaics' turrets to fit the new weapon, and when the guns arrived, their muzzles would not fit through the gunports. Ericsson had to embark on a crash program to develop a workaround, and the incident displayed the downside of standardization: when one article is wrong, all are wrong. The 1850s contracting system could not deal with such complex interdependency.

The 1850s system also fell short in its emphasis upon gaining leverage by withholding payments to the contractors. Early wartime experiences had reinforced that lesson, and many navy officers had decided that contractors were no more scrupulous than they were forced to be. Navy officials adopted a wary attitude, increased their inspection force, and demanded strict compliance with contracts.

This would not have been so detrimental had it not been for the third major problem: the inability of the contracting system to cope with changing economic conditions. The navy's contracts (what we would now call "fixed price") depended upon two major assumptions: that the articles involved could be described unambiguously, and that prices would not change dramatically during the term of the contract. The two factors combined to give would-be bidders clear standards by which to estimate their costs and profits. Civil War ironclad shipbuilding contracts, on the contrary, suffered from the dual problems of fast-changing specifications and unpredictable changes in costs.

A glance at inflation in the Union wartime economy shows why. Taking 1860 as the base year, by 1862 general prices had risen 21 percent. By the end of 1864 prices were 89 percent higher than 1860 levels.[17] Shipbuilding materials and labor rose far more than the "across the board" averages. Iron armor delivered in Cincinnati, for example, rose from 5 cents a pound in September 1862 to 10.75 cents a pound in September 1864. Brass castings, such as the shipbuilders used for valves or pump bodies, doubled from 35 cents a pound in September 1862 to 70 cents a pound in December 1864. Over the same period, the average shipyard worker's wage rose from $1.42 per day to $3.30 per day.[18]

Even worse, by mid-1862 the Treasury Department could not pay the government's creditors promptly. It was, as Ericsson's biographer pointed out, "hazardous business to estimate upon government work."[19] Although the navy perceived that shipbuilders were profiteering, their profits were in fact shrinking. The navy had learned to react to contractor slowness by withholding payments; the economic climate made withholding payments counterproductive because it starved the shipbuilders of working capital.

Despite the problems, *Passaic*, the class leader, was commissioned November 25, 1862. Two ships followed in December 1862, two in January 1863, and three more in February 1863. The Navy Department maintained the pressure, but Northern shipyards could not concentrate solely on the Passaics. In the late summer of 1862 the Union navy had again increased its already ambitious shipbuilding program.

The Confederates tried valiantly to keep up. In 1861 and early 1862, Mallory had laid down ironclads to break the blockade and to protect major seacoast and river ports, including New Orleans, Memphis, Mobile, Savannah, Charleston, Richmond, and Wilmington. Other vessels, such as the one at Edwards Ferry, North Carolina, were intended to protect broader areas. Yet the Confederacy found it difficult to build its ships fast enough: the *Louisiana*, commenced in September 1861 to defend New Orleans, could function only as a stationary floating battery when Farragut attacked in April 1862, and her companion *Mississippi* could not make even that small contribution. By the time the first of the Savannah ironclads was finished, the Union had already seized Fort Pulaski and sealed the Savannah River. The *Arkansas* escaped the fall of Memphis to reach Vicksburg, but the never-completed *Tennessee*, also built in Memphis, was burned by the retreating Confederates. Under similar pressure, the North completed the *Monitor* in five months and a full-fledged seagoing ironclad in ten months.

The path the South took to mobilize its industry clearly differed from that of the North. Both the Union and the Confederacy initially chose to mobilize through financial incentives—to pay industrialists to produce war materials. In the North, with a sufficiency of industrial capacity, this policy continued throughout the war. In the South, however, mobilization soon took a different course. The initial Confederate navy reliance on civilian contractors had been leavened by a few specialized government facilities, such as the Naval Powder Works and Naval Ordnance Laboratory in Richmond and the Naval Ordnance Works in New Orleans.[20] As the contractors' inability to complete their contracts became evident, the pendulum swung toward government-owned or government-controlled facilities.

Details of the Confederate navy's industrial mobilization are lacking— the Navy Department's records were largely lost in the evacuation of Richmond in 1865, and many of the navy's facilities and records were destroyed by Union raiders or retreating Confederates. However, the outline of the Confederate navy's policy can be discerned. In 1862 the Confederates appear to have realized that only the government had the resources to build what was needed. The spring of 1862 brought the establishment of the Naval Gun Foundry and Naval Ordnance Works at Selma, Alabama, the Naval Ironworks at Columbus, Georgia, and the Richmond Naval Works and the Rocketts and Graves' shipyards at Richmond.[21] Later that year the navy took over the Ettinger & Edmond works in Richmond and merged it with the Naval Ordnance Laboratory to form the Richmond Naval Ordnance Works.[22] As economic conditions worsened and relations between the government and its contractors became more acrimonious, the navy began to build ships at its naval stations and sent naval officers to assist its contractors or assume responsibility for completing contracted vessels.

The Confederates' efforts were handicapped by shortages—of materials, tools, and skilled labor. Raw materials were in short supply; as noted in chapter 1, in 1860 the states of the Confederacy produced only 5 percent of the nation's iron and less than 10 percent of its coal, and Union armies soon occupied areas that had supplied the Confederate states with many valuable resources. Equipment to work the raw materials was even scarcer. The South had not a single factory that built machine tools. Confederate shipbuilders frequently found themselves starting with a vacant lot, like the North Carolina cornfield in which Gilbert Elliott began the *Albemarle* in April 1862 or the "two wharves which served as a navy yard" in Charleston where the *Chicora* was built.[23]

Northern builders had superficially similar difficulties. Alexander Swift, for example, started building two Tippecanoe class monitors in a vacant lot on the Ohio River, while Secor & Co. took contracts for two Passaic class vessels in April 1862 without even that much—the Secor brothers had to lease the vacant lot.[24] As has been shown elsewhere, however, ironclad building differed markedly from traditional shipbuilding, and under the changed circumstances, the Northern builders had two insurmountable advantages. For one, they were relatively well provided with the materials from which to build their shipyards and their ships, and the Northern transportation system could reliably move those materials where they were needed. For another, the Northern industrial economy had tremendous latent capacity that allowed even the least prepared shipbuilder to come up to speed quickly.

The New Jersey–based Secors, operating in the Union's industrial heart, built both a shipyard and a machine shop in a matter of weeks. Swift, who owned an ironworks, partnered with the Niles Works, one of the best-equipped prewar machinery builders in Cincinnati. Although initially the Northern ship's vacant lot may have looked much like the Confederate ship's cornfield, each Northern vessel quickly became the center of a more-or-less well-equipped industrial plant. For the most part, the Confederate cornfields stayed cornfields.

Nathaniel Thom, the construction superintendent for a Cincinnati shipbuilder, found himself arranging for tools in late 1862. He recorded that heavy punches and shears capable of working with armor plate carried four to six weeks of lead time, but he was able to obtain a large planer, boring mill, and engine lathe immediately.[25] In contrast, Catesby ap R. Jones, commanding officer of the Selma Naval Ironworks, wrote, "We have to make the machinery before we can commence the work that is wanted."[26] Building machinery and tools was slow, but ordering from Europe was no faster. It could take months before machinery reached a Confederate port of entry and even longer before it could be transported to the location where it was to be used. Given the erratic nature of the Confederacy's transatlantic exchanges, it might never arrive at all. The January 1863 capture of the blockade-runner *Princess Royal* cost the Confederacy two complete sets of marine engines for ironclads and a specialized machine for making armor-piercing shot.[27]

The Confederacy initially used the prewar facilities it had taken over from the Union, including the navy yards at Pensacola and Norfolk. The Pensacola yard had not been particularly well equipped before the war, and continued Union possession of Fort Pickens left it "useless as a naval establishment."[28] Norfolk, also called the Gosport Navy Yard, was a different story. When Union forces evacuated the yard in April 1861, they destroyed as much of the facility as they could, but the drydock and most of the machinery were saved for the Confederacy's use. By early 1862 the yard had added an ordnance laboratory and purchased a heavy steam hammer to enable it to make the forgings needed for a warship's propulsion machinery.[29]

In March 1862, however, McClellan began his Peninsular Campaign. Mallory, fearing the worst, directed that machinery and stores be removed from the Gosport yard "without attracting special attention or notice."[30] The urgency grew, and on May 1, Mallory told Sydney Smith Lee, the commandant of the navy yard, to send away any machinery that was not in use. On May 3, with the Confederate army's evacuation imminent, Mallory told Cdr. Richard L. Page to find a safe place in North Carolina for the yard's ordnance and machinery.[31] Much of the material was moved to Charlotte, North Carolina, or Richmond before the Union recaptured the yard on May 9, 1862, and many of Gosport's workers followed.[32]

The Confederate navy had used the area at Rocketts Ferry on the James in Richmond as a shipyard since mid-1861, but in March 1862 work began on a second shipyard across the river at Manchester, Virginia, that became known as the "Yard opposite Rocketts" or "Graves' Yard."[33] Richmond's first major project was to finish the ironclad *Richmond,* towed from Norfolk, and the Rocketts yard completed the job in late 1862. Two more ironclads, the *Fredericksburg* at Rocketts and the *Virginia II* at Graves' Yard, were begun in 1863 and completed in 1864. Surviving records indicate that the shipyards themselves worked primarily in wood and that iron and machine work was done in the Richmond Naval Works and at Joseph Anderson's Tredegar Iron Works.

The Confederate navy's shipbuilding aims changed as a result of the general reorientation of Southern defensive strategy in 1862. As recent scholarship has shown, the Union's successful amphibious operations impelled Mallory to focus on making the Confederacy safe from invasion by sea. This "second phase" strategy, like the first, included seagoing ironclads to break the blockade and cruisers to prey on Union shipping, but the second-phase seagoing ships would be European-built. The home-built ironclads were intended only for coast and harbor protection.[34]

European procurement was a fine idea, but in practice it ran up against the Confederacy's lack of funds and James North's lethargy and lack of imagination. Mallory had sent North to Britain in May 1861 specifically to obtain an ironclad, but North showed little of the sense of urgency and ability to improvise displayed by his counterpart, James D. Bulloch, who had been sent to purchase the commerce raiders discussed in chapter 6.[35] It took North a year to order an ironclad, and when he finally did, he showed little appreciation of the Confederacy's needs. Insisting that his instructions mandated an ironclad frigate, North ordered a ship with a 20-foot draft that could not even have approached most Southern ports.[36]

Mallory was concerned at North's slow progress, but took no action to relieve him or to send him imperative instructions until the diplomatic situation had become far less favorable to his mission. Bulloch had traveled back to the Confederacy for consultation in late 1861, and before his return to England in early 1862, Mallory told him to "investigate" the subject of ironclads.[37] Perceiving that shallow draft would be important to any Confederate ironclad, Bulloch promptly consulted shipbuilder John Laird to develop a vessel that combined heavy armor, seaworthiness, and shallow draft. Bulloch had Laird make detailed drawings of his proposed ships, but planned only to send them to Mallory, since by that time North had belatedly arranged for his ironclad and Bulloch himself expected to go to sea in command of one of the cruisers he was building.[38]

After a year, though, Mallory's frustration with North finally moved the secretary to action. In early June 1862, Bulloch received a letter from Mallory ordering him to turn command of the cruisers over to other officers and to take charge of building ironclads.[39] Although disappointed at losing the chance to command at sea, within a few days Bulloch had contracted for two ironclads to his proposed design from Laird, Sons & Co. The vessels, Laird hull numbers 294 and 295, were smaller and shallower than North's ironclad, with turret-mounted armament (see figure 5). Bulloch noted that building the two ships simultaneously in the same shipyard earned him a discount of £1,250 on each vessel, as well as giving more security from "Federal spies, who abound even in this country."[40]

Bulloch had reason to be concerned. At the time, Great Britain was governed by the Foreign Enlistment Act of 1819, which was intended to prevent the use of British neutrality as a cloak for belligerent activities.

It prohibited such overt acts as enlisting soldiers or sailors and forbade British subjects and others in Great Britain to "equip, furnish, fit out, or arm" any ship for a belligerent, or even to attempt to do so.[41] There was considerable room for interpretation, though, since no court decisions under the Act had involved ships. In contracting for the unarmored cruisers laid down in 1861, Bulloch had consulted counsel, who pointed out that as the Act stood, the offense was "not the *building* but the *equipping*" of a ship. As long as he did not "equip" the vessel as a ship of war within British jurisdiction, "any shipbuilder may build any ship in her Majesty's dominions."[42]

In preparing his cruisers, Bulloch kept a low profile and followed the strict letter of the law by maintaining rigid separation between the "building" and the "equipping." Despite Federal fulminations, it seems clear that the cruisers departed British waters as merchantmen, scrupulously free of warlike equipment. Ironclads had their warlike qualities built in from the keel up, but Bulloch's lawyer opined that armor was not "equipment" under the Foreign Enlistment Act, and Laird's solicitor independently reached the same conclusion. On that basis, Bulloch felt "reasonable grounds" to anticipate that his ironclads would be allowed to leave England when they were completed in the spring of 1863.[43]

That assumed, of course, that the Confederate navy would be able to pay for the ships. Because of the informal cotton embargo of 1861–62, Confederate finances in Europe had gotten off to a poor start, and finances at home were little better. The Confederacy's supply of specie was quickly depleted, sent overseas to buy war materials, where the army's needs took precedence over the navy's. By the end of 1861 army purchasing agent Caleb Huse had obligated far more money than he had available or forthcoming to buy small arms, artillery, ammunition, and supplies. The Confederacy continued to print money: by April 1862 the Confederate Congress had increased the Confederate money supply to $250 million, and the lack of sound backing meant that the exchange rate between Confederate dollars and English pounds became steadily less favorable.[44] The year 1862 also saw the first significant shipments of cotton to Europe, but the amount shipped was far below what was required.

By the end of 1862, the Confederacy had determined that its only recourse was to use cotton to get credit, and the first Confederate States cotton certificates were issued in January 1863 to help fund naval construction. These certificates, essentially IOUs backed by the promise of future cotton delivery, called for repayment in cotton at a specified price per pound that was well below the market price. At the same time, however, the Confederates had begun to negotiate a direct loan through the banking firm of Emile Erlanger & Company, and commissioner James Mason forbade the sale of cotton certificates in England for fear of derailing the negotiations.[45] Despite the unfavorable terms of the Erlanger loan, Confederate commissioner John Slidell promoted it because he felt that it would be politically advantageous in France, and the "Erlanger Loan" bonds reached the market in mid-March 1863. If the Confederate government had indeed received the face value of the loan (£3 million, or $15 million gold), the terms would have been harsh but the money would have been a great boon. Half of the money, however, was used to buy back enough bonds to keep the market price up, and in the end the Confederacy realized less than £600,000 ($3 million gold). Money remained Bulloch's and North's number one worry.[46]

The Union, too, was building more ironclads. The Passaic class alone could not meet the Union's needs, and in the early autumn of 1862, Welles commenced another group of monitors. The nine ships of the Tippecanoe class were designed in the summer of 1862, but again, urgency overrode all else, and the design was barely out of the sketchbook stage when the contracts were let in September and October 1862.

The contracts for the Tippecanoe class marked the beginning of an industrial expansion larger and more complex than any previous shipbuilding program. Four Tippecanoe contracts went to builders "west of the Alleghenies," in Pittsburgh and Cincinnati, far from the shipbuilding centers of the East Coast. This industrial mobilization had three roots. First, the administration was under pressure to spread the wealth of government contracting. Second, many officials questioned the loyalty of the areas along the Ohio and Mississippi River valleys and believed that loyalty would increase with prosperity. Third, the shipyards and engine builders of the East Coast were already chockablock with new construction and repairs; to increase ironclad production, the navy would have to involve more producers.[47]

Although the navy did not recognize it, the program was in trouble from the first. Urgency drove the decision to award the contracts before the design was completed, but because the navy required the contractors to build strictly from navy plans, which were barely begun, the navy reaped no benefit from its haste. Worse, in their search for technical perfection,

Fox and Stimers kept changing and adding to the design; Ericsson, nominally the designer, was building eight other monitors and could not give the Tippecanoes adequate attention.

"Better is the enemy of good enough," and "better" was a formidable foe indeed. For the Tippecanoes, "better" first appeared in October 1862, when the navy sent specifications to the contractors. Compared with the specifications upon which the shipbuilders had bid in August, the contract specifications doubled the thickness of the deck armor, changed the original pine armor backing to heavier oak, enlarged the main boilers, and added auxiliary boilers. Besides increasing weight and cost, the changes further delayed production of the drawings for which the contractors were waiting.

Yet the already-ambitious Federal ironclad program became poised to grow even larger when Fox began badgering Ericsson for a light draft monitor to operate in shallow Southern rivers. Ericsson developed a sketch design for a vessel with a six-foot draft that would be simple and quick to build, but when Ericsson's plans arrived in early October 1862, Stimers promptly set to work to modify them. The light draft program thus competed for engineers and draftsmen with the Tippecanoe class ships, and both competed for attention with the ardently desired Passaics. In March 1862, Ericsson had called a dozen monitors "a mere trifle" for the "enormous engineering capabilities of the United States."[48] Nine months later, with more than two dozen coastal ironclads being built, the limits of those capabilities were becoming clearer.

At about the same time, one of the contractors noticed a problem. The advertisement for the Tippecanoes envisioned a slightly modified Passaic class ship. The navy (that is, Fox and Stimers) had made far-reaching changes but had never reviewed the design as a whole. When the changes were totaled, the increased weights overwhelmed the buoyancy. As contractor Charles A. Secor observed, "The vessels would sink the moment they got in the water."[49] The stop-work order and the massive redesign effort that followed it delayed the Tippecanoe program several months. In trying to accelerate the design process by cutting corners, Stimers and Fox had in fact retarded the ships they wanted so badly.

Stimers's involvement in monitor design had expanded his role as general inspector far beyond its official character, but he had never given up his first responsibility: supervising the construction of ironclads. In the autumn of 1862 that had meant the "improved" monitors of the Passaic class, scheduled to be completed from August through October 1862. Delays mounted in this first widespread application of a new technology, and despite intense pressure from Welles and Fox, the first of the Passaics was not delivered until November.[50] As each ship was completed, Welles sent her to Du Pont.

Du Pont's attack on Charleston marked a Union turn for the worse, technically as well as strategically, as the Navy Department reacted to the damage the Confederates inflicted on the monitors. The reason for having ironclads, Stimers said, "was to enable people to go into fights that otherwise they would not be able to approach and remain in them and come out whole." Combat effectiveness thus demanded technical improvements, but those improvements came with costs. Stimers discussed the issue with Fox, and "it was well shown that it would cost a great deal of money to make the changes, and would make great delay." Fox opined, "If we went on in this way and made changes, every time a monitor was in a fight it would cost a million of dollars," but he still considered it "the best plan to pursue."[51]

For the Tippecanoe class and the light draft monitors, Fox's decision brought programmatic disaster. On their original schedule, the Tippecanoes should have been completed in March and April 1863, but the discovery of their lack of buoyancy in late 1862 had already delayed them several months. Still in shipyard hands when Du Pont attacked Charleston, their incompleteness made altering them seem easier. Their turrets and pilot houses provide an example of the process.

To speed construction of all his monitors, Ericsson specified thin one-inch armor plates, laminating them with bolts and rivets to achieve the required thickness. When Confederate gunfire hit the outside, the bolts broke and the flying fragments inside injured or killed crew members. The Passaics, already in service, received a cheap and inelegant but effective fix: fabric or sheet iron fragment screens hung inboard of the armor. The Tippecanoes received a complete armor redesign, and several nearly completed turrets and pilot houses were completely dismantled, modified, and rebuilt, with great cost and delay.[52] The constant changes delayed construction, and the navy's inadequate system for paying for them left the shipbuilders holding the financial bag. Charles A. Secor, with three Tippecanoes under construction and $800,000 owing from the navy, complained to Fox that he would soon run out of capital and have to stop work. Fox replied that if the firm stopped work, he would send marines to take over their shipyard.[53]

The light draft monitors suffered from a similar flood of changes. Ericsson had sent sketches of a simple, cheap ship that could be built quickly, but Stimers and Fox "improved" the design with addition after addition.

The discovery that the Tippecanoe design was overloaded probably impelled Stimers to reexamine the light drafts, and in late November or December 1862 he discovered that they, too, were overloaded. He responded by having his assistant, Theodore Allen, redesign the vessels, making them larger and still more complex.[54]

The light draft design thus followed the same evolutionary path as the Tippecanoes. The original designs for both classes were relatively simple. Both classes received many improvements, added without any quantitative analysis of their impact. And when belated calculations showed that the ships would be too heavy, Fox and Stimers chose to enlarge them rather than to give up any of the "improvements." Technical perfection trumped even Fox's urgently expressed desire for a light draft ironclad.

The light draft design was finally advertised for bids in February 1863. Fox did not communicate with Ericsson about the design until three days before the bids were to be opened. When he did, asking the inventor to confirm that the ships were "all right," he received a reply that must have been an unpleasant surprise. Ericsson wrote that he had not seen the plans until February 24, the day the bids were opened, and Stimers had "frittered away" Ericsson's principles by changes.[55] For reasons explored elsewhere, Fox began to award contracts anyway.

Negotiations with shipbuilders took more time than usual because of the navy's twin desires to mobilize more of the shipbuilding industry and to "spread the wealth" of contracts. With the light drafts, however, Ericsson became the first of the Fox-Stimers-Ericsson troika to realize that nontechnical factors were overtaking technical ones. To minimize demands on the Union's overstretched shipyards and ironworks, his original light draft design emphasized woodworking and mechanical simplicity. To speed construction and ease the burden on the navy's design teams, he planned to return to the prewar practice of decentralization: the navy would provide a general plan and specifications, and each builder would fill in the details. The theory was sound, but the implementation was faulty.

Besides elaborating on Ericsson's original design, Stimers invoked a myriad of minutely detailed specifications. The specifications, which occupied ninety-two pages of small type in what one builder called "the monitor prayer book," made the contractors unwilling to risk having their plans disapproved.[56] In practice, they waited for Stimers's drawings, costing the navy the potential benefits of decentralization. Further delay ensued after Stimers returned from Charleston in April 1863, because the light drafts received the same sort of post-Charleston design changes as the Tippecanoes.[57] Fox could not decide whether technical elegance or speedy construction was more important. He very forcefully pressed the shipbuilders for haste, but had he opted for simpler ships in the first place, he could have had them much sooner. The ships that Fox wanted for early 1863 were still under construction six months later.

Bulloch's ironclads were also experiencing delays, although not from the same causes. The ships were to have been ready in the spring of 1863, but by that time, conditions had changed significantly for the Confederates. In April 1863 the British government seized the steamer *Alexandra*, supposed (correctly) by the U.S. consul in Liverpool to be intended for the Confederate service. The ship's builders and owners were charged with violating the Foreign Enlistment Act, based in part upon the contention that the ship's structure was that of a warship. At the trial in June 1863, the jury found for the defendants, agreeing unknowingly with Bulloch's solicitor that building alone was not an offense under the law.[58] Although this seemed to be a victory for the Confederates, Bulloch reported later that the *Alexandra* decision "has not made our operations in Europe less difficult."[59] Modern scholarship has shown that the case provoked the British to reexamine their policy in a way that proved detrimental to the Confederacy.[60]

Charles Francis Adams, the U.S. ambassador to Great Britain, had an efficient intelligence network. Despite Bulloch's precautions, Adams learned of the "Laird rams" soon after their laying-down and began to bombard the British Foreign Ministry with notes offering evidence of their warlike character and Confederate destination. Among Adams's star witnesses was Acting Assistant Paymaster Clarence R. Yonge, CSN, who had served in early 1862 as Bulloch's clerk. Yonge joined the *Alabama* when she began her cruise, then deserted that vessel and eventually resurfaced in England as an informant for the United States. The Confederates immediately attacked Yonge's credibility, but the intensity of Bulloch's vituperation is a good indication of Yonge's value to Adams.[61]

Adams's campaign against the Laird ironclads did not bear immediate fruit, but Bulloch sensed the changing climate. Although Britain and France had coordinated their response to "the American question," Napoleon III had generally been more willing to recognize the Confederacy and to intervene on its behalf than had the British, and the Confederates placed their hopes upon the French emperor's "most friendly feeling and spirit."[62] The French declaration of neutrality, more strictly worded than the British, was in Imperial practice likely to be considerably more elastic. In France, Bulloch wrote, "Everything might and probably would depend upon the secret purposes of the Chief of the State," and in 1862, the Confederates received assurances from persons "in positions of close relationship with the Emperor" that they could build ships without interference. By 1863 the Confederacy perceived that the environment in France was more supportive than that in Great Britain, and Bulloch accordingly turned to France.[63]

In April 1863, Bulloch contracted with shipbuilder Lucien Arman for four 1,500-ton wooden corvettes. Napoleon III personally knew that the ships were intended for the Confederacy but insisted that their destination be concealed.[64] The French government was not so monolithic as the Confederates supposed, however, and the minister of foreign affairs, Edouard Drouyn de Lhuys, would tell the Confederates only that it was better if he knew nothing about the vessels.[65] The four ships were begun in mid-April, two in Arman's own yard in Bordeaux and two in the shipyard of M. J. Voruz in Nantes. In June 1863 the French minister of marine officially approved arming the ships for "service in the China Seas," and the Confederates' hopes rose.[66]

Construction in the French yards was much more conspicuous than in Britain. Arman's cover story of building ships to trade with China and Japan, armed to protect themselves against pirates, was not implausible, but the true destination of the vessels was widely known. As Bulloch well understood, the attitude of the French government was all-important. As long as the emperor approved, the government would turn a blind eye and French officials would not interfere.

France also seemed likely to solve the problem of increasingly strict British attention to the Laird ironclads. In March 1863, Mallory directed Bulloch to arrange to transfer the ships to a French "owner" and to equip them in a French port, orders which Bulloch received in May.[67] The Confederates chose Messrs. François Bravay and Company of Paris as their "front," since Bravay had recently received inquiries from the Egyptian government regarding the construction of two ironclads in Europe. John Slidell, the Confederate commissioner to France, had even received hints that if the British government objected, the French government would officially voice its support for Bravay. Bulloch consummated the transaction in June, managing it so well that Laird, Sons, which was building the two ironclads, was convinced that the sale was bona fide.[68]

The Confederate ironclad program expanded again when, in late June 1863, Bulloch received instructions to buy armored ships in France.[69] Excessive optimism can charitably explain Mallory's reiteration of his desire to buy an existing ironclad, but it is more difficult to explain why he thought that a deep draft European-style ironclad would be able to enter the Mississippi River. Bulloch, conversant with both European naval construction and European attitudes, knew that the only way to obtain shallow draft ironclads was to build them. He arranged for this with his usual promptness, contracting with Arman in mid-July for two ironclads similar to the Laird vessels.[70]

As the summer of 1863 advanced, however, the odds against actually obtaining a European-built ironclad for the Confederacy continued to lengthen. News of Union victories at Gettysburg and Vicksburg influenced European policies, especially in France, as did the relationship between that country and Great Britain. The Confederacy focused optimistically on the two powers' reasonably coordinated response to "the American question," discounting or ignoring the areas in which other British and French interests clashed. Although Mallory had earlier commented on the "rivalry in naval construction" between France and Great Britain, the Confederates do not seem to have given enough weight to the long history of enmity and suspicion between the two nations.[71] Frightened by the French ironclad program of 1858–60, the British had responded vigorously, and by 1863 the Royal Navy had commenced twenty-four oceanic ironclads. As one author has pointed out, it is difficult to believe that the British government would ever have permitted Laird to deliver ironclads to a French subject.[72]

By August, as the Laird ships neared completion, Federal agents stepped up their pressure on the British government. Adams's campaign eventually culminated in his well-known "this is war" note on September 5, 1863, but by that time Britain had already decided to detain the vessels for further investigation. The British government, recognizing the deficiencies of the Foreign Enlistment Act but unwilling to change it under American pressure, had determined to fulfill its neutral obligations through policy rather than law.[73] The two Laird ships were "detained" in September 1863 and formally seized in October. Bulloch, confident of the legal correctness of his position, hoped for a speedy resolution of the case that would return the ships to Bravay.

The climate in France was also becoming more difficult for the Confederates. The American ambassador, William L. Dayton, pursued the same sort of tactics that Adams used in England and likewise benefited from an informant, who gave him confidential and highly detailed documents from the Voruz shipbuilding firm. Even so, the French situation was more complex than the English; concerned about his Mexican adventure, Napoleon III kept a weather eye on the military situation in North America. The Union victories of 1863 probably influenced the emperor more than they did the British, with results that will be explored below.

By the end of 1863, then, both navies were making progress slowly. The Confederates, handicapped in building ironclads at home by materials and labor shortages, had failed to take advantage of loose European regulations when they had the opportunity. The Federals, with a larger resource base, had wasted much of their advantage by chasing the chimera of technical perfection. The next year would show whether either combatant could get its ironclad program back on track.

CHAPTER SIX

Runners and Blockaders

The one constant feature of the Civil War at sea was the blockade. Offensives waxed and waned, amphibious operations came and went, commerce raiders appeared and were captured, but the blockade continued unabated. Secretary Welles had written in 1861 that blockading was "unattractive and devoid of adventure."[1] Although there were certainly moments of high adventure, by and large blockading was indeed unattractive. It was a tedious job: a constant battle against the sea, boredom, and blockade-runners, enlivened only by the faint chance of prize money.

Most Northerners did not appreciate the difficulties that the blockading fleets faced, and Welles repeatedly received howls of protest from Northern politicians and editors when vessels passed through the blockade. Yet the sea itself, the hydrography of the Southern coastline, and the technological limitations of the age combined to make an "airtight" blockade a daunting goal. Like many seemingly simple military tasks, blockading was much easier to do than it was to do well (see figure 6).

For one thing, human senses imposed strict limits on detection. The primary search sensor was the human eye, aided by optical devices such as telescopes, but at close range the ear contributed as well. All of the things that reduce visibility and audibility at sea—night, fog, mist, spray—helped the runner and hindered the blockader.

Safe navigation was a continuing problem. The U.S. Coast Survey made excellent charts, but they covered only a portion of the Southern coast, and even with good charts it took time for Federal officers to gain detailed knowledge of their operational areas. Inshore operations, at night and in all weathers, required both a very high standard of seamanship and a keen judgment of the boundary between boldness and rashness.

A captain who was rash could lose his ship, but a captain who was too timid would be ineffective. The blockade-runners had the advantage of carrying local Southern pilots, and the pay of Ł700 or Ł800 per round trip ensured that, despite the risks, there were always candidates for those piloting jobs.

Beyond the physical factors, as Carl von Clausewitz noted, "In war, the will is directed at an animate object that *reacts*." The contest between blockade-runners and blockaders quickly became a high-stakes game of move and countermove that involved both tactics and technology.

The underlying motive for private blockade-running was clear: profit. One English participant, Thomas E. Taylor, wrote, "Firm after firm, with an entirely clear conscience, set about endeavouring to recoup itself for the loss of legitimate trade by the high profits to be made out of successful evasions of the Federal cruisers," and he characterized the feeling as one of "adventurous commerce." The trade later came to be "seasoned with the pleasure of doing a good turn to the South," and the Confederate government eventually became directly involved in both regulating and conducting blockade-running, but investors flocked to blockade-running ventures because of the tremendous profit to be made.[2] One blockade-running captain observed, "Unromantic as it may seem, much of [blockade-running's] charm consisted in money-making."[3]

Although many blockade-runners made money, only a few firms returned as much as 40 percent on their capital over the course of the war. Similarly, while some individual runs paid huge returns, fewer than 10 percent of the runners made more than a single trip through the blockade. Despite the oft-repeated tales of fantastic profits, over 100 percent in a single round-trip, a lucky blockade-runner would be more likely to make about 67 percent per voyage, whereas the unlucky runners were captured.[4]

Profit entered the other side of the equation as well. At the tactical and operational level, decisions about the blockade could not help but be colored by financial considerations. The prize money system was the cause.

Sailors received prize money for capturing an enemy's seagoing property, usually a merchant vessel or warship. Dating back to the less professional days before national navies, the system was still very much alive during the Civil War. While prize money appeared to reward gallantry, earning it was in fact influenced far more heavily by chance. Some ships, because of their mission or location, would never have a real chance to take a prize. For officers and men who were stationed ashore, doing the absolutely necessary jobs that kept the fleet at sea, prize money meant nothing.[5]

The Union navy ballyhooed prize money on its recruiting posters, but few sailors gained much of it. For one thing, unless the prize had been more powerful than the capturing vessel, half the prize's value went to the navy's central pension fund. For another, every ship within visual signaling distance of a capture shared equally in the prize money—in a busy area like Charleston, fifteen crews might claim a portion. Finally, the system tilted heavily toward senior officers. A commanding officer received one-twentieth of the amount awarded to his ship; the lieutenants shared another tenth; and so on down through the ranks until it reached the far more numerous seamen and marines, who split 35 percent of the money.

Officers and sailors alike hoped for a prize captured with no other ship in sight, and captains vied for single-ship assignments to rich areas. The uss *Magnolia*'s capture of the outbound blockade-runner *Memphis* in July 1862 was every captain's dream: no other ship was in sight, and *Memphis* and her cargo were worth over half a million dollars. A more representative example would be the sloop *Secesh*, captured off Charleston in the spring of 1863. *Secesh* earned $17,685.69 for her captors, but twelve ships participated in the distribution. A lieutenant's share was probably less than $30—better than nothing, but no bonanza. The only certain way to make prize money was to command a squadron; the admiral commanding received one-twentieth of every prize taken by any of his ships, in his sight or out. Samuel P. Lee gained the most, receiving nearly $110,000 for his tenure as commander of the North Atlantic Blockading Squadron, but Porter received $91,000, Du Pont $57,000, and Farragut $56,000.[6]

Progressing from "Sail ho!" to cash in hand was rarely straightforward or quick. The actual chase and capture were only the first steps in a long legal process that began when an officer from the chasing ship arrived at the suspected vessel to inspect her cargo, examine her records, and question her officers, crew, and passengers. If the evidence indicated that the vessel was a blockade-runner, she would be seized. At this point, legal technicalities notwithstanding, her captors would call her a prize and do a bit of celebrating.

There was still much to do before the captors received any money. Because prizes were shared equally among the ships within visual signaling distance, each ship had to provide an up-to-date listing of her crew so that prize money could be properly distributed. Next, the captured vessel had to be navigated safely to a place where a court could determine whether she was indeed a lawful prize. The capturing vessel or other nearby warships normally provided a small prize crew, but the coming of steam complicated this activity as it had complicated many others. Sailing vessels were enough alike that a trained seaman could literally "learn the ropes" of a prize in very short order, and merchant sailing vessels were built for small crews. Besides the need to master the idiosyncrasies of each engineering plant, though, steamships needed firemen and coal heavers constantly on duty, and U.S. Navy ships rarely had enough of them to be able to provide an adequate engineroom force to a prize.

As Civil War blockade-running evolved, its unique circumstances provided a solution. By 1863 most runner crewmen were Britons or other foreign nationals, shipped for wages rather than for shares in the venture. They had little dedication to the Southern cause and knew that if captured they faced at worst a few weeks detention, closely monitored by the British government.[7] Many were willing to accept temporary employment with their captors, and since few would dare to mutiny to recapture their ship, the United States ran little risk.

Once crewed, the captured ship would be sent to a seaboard city where a federal court would determine whether she had been lawfully seized. Legal precedent, reinforced by Lincoln's original blockade proclamation, stated that captured ships would be sent to "the nearest convenient port," but in practice, prizes were sent to ports all up and down the Atlantic seaboard. The reason was patronage: prize cases meant employment for lawyers and officers of the courts, as well as profits for merchants.[8]

When the prize crew delivered their capture to the court, appointed commissioners would receive the ship's papers and take testimony in each case. After that, the sailors would go their separate ways—the prize crew back to their ships, the merchant mariners generally back to find another blockade-running berth. The court proceedings might take over a year, but eventually the court would either release the prize to the original owners or condemn her and fix an amount for distribution by the treasury. Prize vessels occasionally found their way circuitously back into blockade-running, but the U.S. government bought a number for use as transports or storeships. Some prize vessels, commissioned in the navy, were set to catch other blockade-runners in their turn.

At first, blockade-runners used the same ships upon which the Southern trade had depended before the war. Small sailing vessels carried the

1. A prewar steam frigate, the USS Wabash, photographed in 1863. (U.S. Naval Historical Center photograph, NH44510)

Davis.
Nov 22nd/62.

2. One of the "ninety-day gunboats," the USS Katahdin, on the Mississippi River. (U.S. Naval Historical Center photograph, NH52241)

3. The CSS Atlanta, shown here under U.S. colors after her capture in 1863, was outwardly typical of the Confederacy's casemated ironclads. (U.S. Naval Historical Center photograph, NH61902; courtesy of the National Archives)

4. The USS Passaic, one of the monitors that fought at Charleston, in a drawing by R. G. Skerrett. (U.S. Naval Historical Center photograph, NH42803)

5. The Confederacy had hoped that the "Laird rams" would break the Union blockade. Instead, they were forcibly purchased by the British government and served the Royal Navy as HMS Wivern (shown here) and HMS Scorpion. (U.S. Naval Historical Center photograph, NH52526)

6. The USS Conemaugh, a typical blockader, served in the South Atlantic, North Atlantic, and Western Gulf Blockading Squadrons. (U.S. Naval Historical Center photograph, NH49989)

7. The Advance ran the blockade into Wilmington seven times before she was captured in September 1864. The Union Navy later commissioned her as the USS Frolic. (U.S. Naval Historical Center photograph, NH53958)

8. "The Supply Steamer." (Courtesy Massachusetts Commandery Military Order of the Loyal Legion and the U.S. Army Military History Institute)

9. *The raider* CSS *Florida, photographed at Brest, France, c. 1863–64. (U.S. Naval Historical Center photograph, NH49994)*

coasting trade, while the long-haul trade moved in larger sailing ships and slow steamers traveling directly from Europe to Southern ports. Such ventures became riskier as both the total number of blockaders and the percentage that were steam-propelled grew. By 1863 sailing vessels had become rare because sailing ships large enough to carry any significant amount of cargo could not realistically hope to evade the blockading fleet.[9]

Tactical and legal considerations combined against the long-haul steamers. At first, the runners tried to minimize risk by sending out "old unseaworthy slugs which we could well afford to lose," but the Federals became more aggressive in patrolling and capturing vessels far out to sea.[10] Then the blockade-runners realized that they could eliminate the period of legal open-ocean vulnerability by consigning their goods to neutral ports near the Southern states. The rise of St. George, Bermuda, Nassau in the Bahamas, and Havana as centers of blockade-running commerce stemmed from this realization.

The nearness of these ports to the Confederacy conferred a significant geographic advantage. The direct route from Southampton in the United Kingdom to Charleston is 4,836 nautical miles, and a blockade-runner would be exposed to capture effectively for the entire distance. From Nassau to Charleston, however, is only 507 nautical miles, about two days travel at 10 knots, and Nassau to Wilmington is 561 nautical miles. Even the longer Bermuda to Wilmington run is only 746 nautical miles, or just over three days at 10 knots (chart 7). The Western Hemisphere ports dramatically reduced the "exposed" portion of the voyage.

Nowhere was the charm of money-making more evident than in the Bahamas, where British lieutenant governor Charles John Bayley was strongly pro-Confederate, and in Bermuda. As the United States argued in the postwar "Alabama Claims" case, the neutrality proclamation that "inhibited Her Majesty's subjects from 'breaking, or endeavoring to break, any blockade lawfully or actually established by or on behalf of either of the said contending parties,'" was blatantly ignored, and nowhere more blatantly than in the islands.[11] In March 1864 the British foreign secretary, Lord Russell, asserted that British subjects were "entitled by International Law to carry on the operations of commerce equally with both belligerents, subject to the capture of their vessels and to no other penalty."[12] Lord Palmerston had reportedly phrased it more succinctly: "Catch 'em if you can."[13] The colonial authorities, with a great deal of business at stake, frequently went out of their way to make the catching difficult.

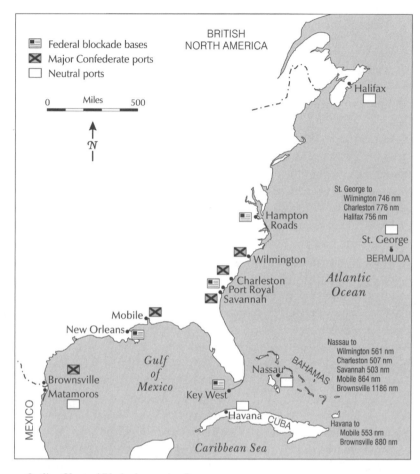

7. *Outline Chart of Blockade-running Ports.*

Besides offering a safe haven, the Western Hemisphere ports also made possible the use of specialized vessels. The first such ships were adaptations of the "Clyde" steamers used around the United Kingdom, but by 1863, the Clyde type had given way to more extreme designs, faster and larger. All were characterized by shallow draft, low silhouette, and side-wheel propulsion (see figure 7). Shallow draft allowed the runners to use channels that deeper draft blockaders dared not enter. Low silhouette reduced their chances of being sighted, while paddlewheels gave both shallow draft and fast acceleration.

These advantages, of course, came with a price. Shallow draft, light construction, and low silhouette made the ships marginally seaworthy in the open ocean, and some were severely damaged by weather during their passages from Great Britain.[14] Paddles were less efficient than propellers, and the combination of small coal bunkers and inefficient propulsion reduced steaming range; a stormy passage or a long chase could force a runner to burn the cabin furniture to reach port. The drawbacks of these extreme designs came to light in service, and by 1864 British builders had generally turned back to slightly broader, sturdier ships.

The steam technology that had so changed blockading strategy and logistics also affected blockading tactics. Although the same technology constrained both blockaders and runners, the effects of the constraints differed because the runner always held the tremendous advantage of initiative: the runner could choose the time, place, and manner of his attempt to penetrate the blockade, and the blockader could only react.[15]

Some of technology's differential effects, for example, turned upon a key characteristic of coal-fired power plants: they require significant time to adjust to large changes in steam demand. As those who have tried to keep a wood fire going in a fireplace will recognize, it takes considerable attention to keep solid fuel burning evenly. Cruising slowly to patrol a blockade station required low but steady production of steam, and the coal fires in the blockaders' boilers would be adjusted to maintain the balance between the steam generated and the steam used. The difficulty came if a runner were sighted. The blockader would start off in chase as rapidly as she could, while her engineers worked feverishly to increase steam using tricks such as burning rosin-filled pine wood or oil-soaked rags. Yet if the blockader built up her boiler fires in anticipation of a chase while still moving slowly, excess steam would be generated. It had to go somewhere, usually up the stack through a blow-off valve. Besides wasting fuel, the noise of blowing off was loud and distinctive, an audible announcement of the blockader's position.

The blockade-runner, able to choose his own time and place rather than having to spend weeks on station, had far less concern for wasting fuel. For him, carrying "high steam" for quick acceleration might mean the difference between success and capture. Yet although "running the blockade" connotes speed, stealth and cunning were even more important, and quietness was frequently a runner's best defense. To carry high steam without making noise, runners rerouted their blow-off pipes to terminate underwater. A letter found in the blockade-runner *Kate* stressed the importance of stealth, speaking of passing through "18 of the Blockading Squadron" without receiving a shot, although other ships that tried to run out of Charleston on the same night were captured or forced back.[16]

Another quirk of coal-fired boilers, the smoke that they produced, generally favored the blockaders. Normal steaming produced smoke, but the amount depended upon the skill of the engineers and firemen and the quality of the coal: soft coal made more smoke than harder coal. Recognizing this, the U.S. government placed strict controls on the export of clean-burning anthracite to keep it out of the bunkers of blockade-runners, and it did its best to provide high-quality coal to the blockaders.[17] Similarly, coal fires had to be kept free of ash and clinkers for best performance, but cleaning fires produced sparks, flames, and smoke that could reveal a ship's position. To meet the twin goals of avoiding detection and being ready to escape if they encountered a blockader, a runner's engineers had to plan carefully when to clean their fires. The importance of engineering shows clearly in the pay of blockade-running crews: chief engineers received $2,500 per run, twice as much as first mates. Only captains and pilots earned more.[18]

Runner captains learned as quickly as did their engineers, and successful tactics spread rapidly as captains and pilots shared their stories in Nassau, Havana, or St. George. Running in and out during the dark of the moon was a natural first step, and each Confederate port sooner or later developed a system of signal lights to help inbound runners find the channels. Other changes showed the effort by runners to reduce the chances of visual detection by trimming the size of their upperworks, reducing the size of their masts, removing their rigging, and painting their ships a neutral gray or dull white to reduce their visibility at night.[19]

Blockade tactics were at first quite basic: the blockaders would anchor near the entrance to the blockaded harbor, out of range of any Confederate batteries, and get under way to chase blockade-runners when they were detected. These tactics sufficed at first, but aided by the shallow draft introduced in the Clyde-style steamers, the runners quickly learned to avoid the normal peacetime channels. Heading inbound, some captains would aim to strike the coast well away from their intended destination, then run along inshore of the blockaders. Besides using every quirk of hydrography, runners turned the blockaders themselves into navigational marks. As late as 1863, sailing blockaders frequently anchored for the night, and when they did, the Confederates ashore would measure their positions and provide them to any blockade-runners who were waiting to run out.[20] In reaction the blockaders stationed small ships or guard boats to give the alarm of a runner's approach and changed their practices by shifting anchorage or getting under way after dark.[21] The Federals also painted their ships to match the runners and removed as much of their own rigging as they could.[22] The effect of the interaction shows in the capture rates of steam blockade-runners, which dropped from 24.4 percent in 1862 to 13.4 percent in 1863, and increased to 15.4 percent in 1864.[23]

As the war continued, the Federals developed a "layered" blockade, seen in its most highly evolved form in the approaches to Wilmington. In this scheme, three lines of ships were used. The inner line placed at least three ships off each entrance (New Inlet and Old Inlet). An intermediate line of two or three steamers was stationed five miles further offshore, with outliers near Masonboro Inlet to the north and Folly Inlet to the south to intercept the runners that tried to run along the coast. Weather permitting, all these inshore blockaders were to "keep underway at night." The farthest line, composed of "steamers of superior speed," was stationed far enough out to intercept an outbound blockade-runner at dawn, according to a formula that assumed that the runner would cross the bar at half flood tide and run outward at 12 or 13 knots.[24]

As an example, October 30, 1864, was the night of a new moon. The Federals always expected blockade-runners during the dark of the moon, and in fact the *Annie, Lucy, Little Hattie,* and *Beatrice* were then preparing to run out of Wilmington. Darkness fell at New Inlet at about 6:30, and half flood tide was about 7 PM Dawn would be about 6 AM, giving roughly eleven hours' run at 12 or 13 knots, or from 132 to 143 miles. The Federals would concentrate near the direct course from New Inlet to Bermuda, so the center of the Federal screen would probably be located around 135 miles bearing 098 degrees true from New Inlet (chart 8). By December 3, with the moon a waxing crescent, half flood tide was about 10 PM and morning civil twilight on December 4 was about 6:30 AM With only eight and a half hours of darkness after half flood tide, the runner would make from 93 to 110 miles and the Federal cruisers would accordingly move closer to shore.[25] The system was the best the Federals could do to try to overcome the unchangeable fact that the runner always held the initiative.

Beyond initiative, the runner had another advantage in that he operated strictly on his own. For the blockade-runner, every ship he sighted was an enemy. In daylight, successful runners kept a sharp lookout and promptly turned away from any vessel they saw.[26] At night, the runner's advantage was even more pronounced. For the blockader, the danger

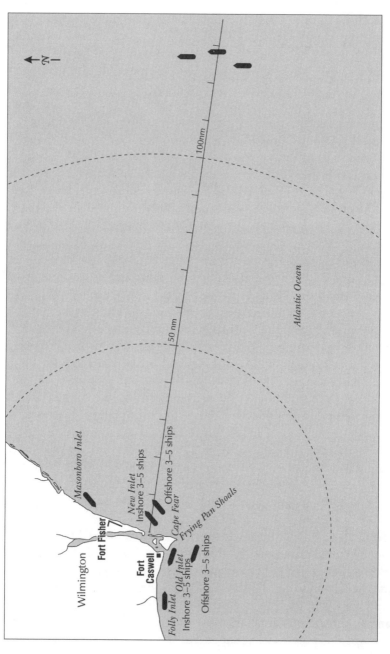

Masomboro Inlet

New Inlet
Inshore 3–5 ships

Offshore 3–5 ships

Cape Fear

Frying Pan Shoals

Fort Fisher

Wilmington

Fort Caswell

Folly Inlet Old Inlet
Inshore 3–5 ships

Offshore 3–5 ships

Atlantic Ocean

50 nm

100nm

N

8. The blockade of Wilmington, North Carolina. Two layers of ships were stationed close to land, with outliers north and south where blockade-runners might make landfall. The location of the offshore ships varied, but they were positioned to catch vessels at dawn that had run out during the night.

of firing into a friendly vessel in the dark was acute, and as the size of the blockading forces grew, so did the problems of coordination. The blockading squadrons evolved a system of daily-changing recognition signals, combining colored lights and prescribed ways to display them. The blockaders normally operated without running lights, but the Charleston squadron's instructions directed vessels "in danger from fire of another" to show running lights as a last resort signal.[27] Near-misses made Federal captains cautious, but given the state of the gunners' art, any hesitation could easily allow a blockade-runner to escape.

Once a runner had been sighted, the blockader had to warn nearby ships as well as give chase. Colored rockets were widely used as warning signals at night, but detected blockade-runners soon took to firing rockets of their own to confuse the blockaders. The actual physical risk to blockade-running crews was small. Blockade runners were frequently fired upon but not as frequently hit, in part because gunnery was an inexact science and in part because a succession of close rounds would often cause a runner to heave to. Inbound runners learned to beach themselves when in extremis; the crews usually escaped, and Confederate authorities could salvage much of the cargo if they could force the Federals to keep their distance. At Fort Fisher, for example, Col. William Lamb organized a "flying battery" of Whitworth rifled guns to cover grounded runners.[28]

In chase, speed became important, but "a stern chase is a long chase," and many factors made it more than a simple race. Both pursued and pursuer depended upon their engineers to squeeze every fraction of a knot from their machinery, but a hard-driven engine could break down and end the chase for either participant. Some sea conditions would affect a shallow draft runner more than they would a deeper draft pursuer, but the natural tendency of crewmen to crowd forward to see what was happening could change a pursuer's trim and reduce her speed. Outbound runners, almost invariably burdened well beyond safe limits, carried much of their load of cotton as deck cargo and could jettison it to lighten themselves and increase their speed.[29] If the chase occurred in darkness, or if the runner could prolong it until darkness fell, he stood a good chance of escaping. One tactic was to run until the blockader was out of sight, turn at a right angle, run for a few minutes more, and stop. The "usual result" left the gunboat "labouring furiously past us and firing wildly into black space."[30]

A number of the Union blockaders had once been runners themselves, but blockading vessels were rarely as fast as the fastest runners. In some cases this might have been because the fastest runners weren't caught, but in general the fastest runners would not make good blockaders. Low and lightly constructed, they sacrificed accommodations, coal capacity, and durability for speed—the Civil War equivalent of a modern drug runner's "cigarette boat." Their "short run" designs made them unsuitable for the extended sea duty that blockading demanded.

A representative example of a runner conversion was the USS *Stettin*, an iron-hulled screw steamer 171 feet long built in Sunderland, England, in 1861. The brig-rigged *Stettin* was captured by the USS *Bienville* while trying to run the blockade into Charleston on May 24, 1862. The navy bought her from the New York prize court in September 1862 and commissioned her on November 12, 1862.[31] Armed with one 30-pounder Parrott rifle and four 24-pounder howitzers, the ship drew twelve feet. Less extreme than many runners, *Stettin* still had to carry coal in her holds as well as in her bunkers to remain on station for a useful length of time. Although her 6 knot speed was unimpressive, especially by late war standards, she captured at least three blockade-runners during her twenty-nine months of commissioned service.

Like most blockade-runners, *Stettin* had been private property, an ordinary merchant ship in law if not in operation. Some runners, however, were operated or owned by the Confederate government. The Confederacy entered the blockade-running business in late 1862, when Confederate army chief of ordnance Josiah Gorgas recognized the danger of allowing profit alone to drive the selection of inbound cargoes. The first Ordnance Department runner, the *Cornubia*, made her maiden run from Bermuda to Wilmington in December 1862, and other government-owned vessels followed. Initially under British registry and manned by Britons, in mid-1863 the government-owned ships were reregistered as Confederate merchantmen, and Confederate naval officers were assigned to operate them. The Confederates, however, tried to conceal the ships' nature. Gorgas instructed his captains to "leave the impression that your steamer does not belong to the Government."[32]

By mid-1863, the Confederacy's blockade-running efforts had begun to overlap and even to conflict. The Ordnance Bureau, other War Department bureaus, the Treasury, the Navy Department, and even state governments all operated runners, competing for cotton, coal supplies, and railroad shipping space in the South and for military supplies in Europe. Recognizing the disarray, the Confederate government made fundamental changes.

One change was centralizing the Confederacy's European purchasing and financial operations. Colin J. McRae had been sent to Europe as the chief agent for the Erlanger loan, and Davis appointed him chief purchasing agent in the autumn of 1863. McRae reorganized Confederate finances, sharply cutting expenses, renegotiating unfavorable contracts, and shifting money among purchasing agents to meet the most pressing needs. Another change was driven by the need to ensure that McRae received enough cotton to fulfill the Confederacy's obligations and that the Confederacy received his purchases promptly: in August 1863 the government ordered the impressment of half of the cargo space on every outbound runner.[33]

The reorganization was timely, because late 1863 brought ill fortune to the Confederacy's blockade-running efforts. All of the Ordnance Bureau vessels and many private ships were lost, some fifteen runners in all. The loss of so much capacity exacerbated the Confederacy's supply shortages and impelled action by the Confederate Congress. In February 1864 that body placed control of imports and exports firmly in government hands. A comprehensive program to regulate blockade-running resulted, and by April 1864 the C.S. Army's Bureau of Foreign Supplies had agents assigned to the major East Coast and Gulf ports. Although strongly opposed to the new controls, British shippers and their Confederate partners reluctantly acquiesced, and by mid-1864 the flow of supplies had been regularized.[34] The action gave the Confederates a double benefit: besides increasing imports, the new plan strengthened Confederate credit in Europe.[35]

To the Union blockading crews, it mattered little who controlled the runners—their lives changed not at all. Those lives were organized around ship's routine, which helped to implement the adage that idle hands are the devil's playground. During the day, crewmen worked, drilled, and cleaned the ship, with a shipwide inspection and divine services on Sunday in place of work and drills. During the night half the men would be on duty at a time, in four-hour watches. Boredom was a constant companion. As one officer observed, "One gets tired of seeing the same faces all the time, hearing the same 'yarns' & laughing at a repetition of old jokes until they become worn out & stale."[36]

The navy supply steamers that visited the fleets every two or three weeks provided an eagerly awaited break (see figure 8). One element was fresh food. The supply ships carried "iced beef," fruit, and vegetables in their refrigerated storage rooms, providing a respite from the salted meat and hard bread that formed the usual at-sea ration. The supply ships also brought mail and provided an opportunity to purchase personal items.[37] The sutlers' schooners that visited the major blockading anchorages also let sailors break the monotony by trying to smuggle liquor aboard. *New Ironsides*'s sailors bought cans of liquor ingeniously disguised as hams and a five-gallon keg of whiskey packed in a barrel of potatoes, but at Port Royal the crews of the colliers provided most of the smuggled liquor. Even with this attraction, the colliers were far less welcome than the supply vessels. The blockaders had to refuel once or twice a month, and the intensely laborious process of coaling left a ship filthy, with coal dust in everything on board.

The mail service was important for reading material as well as for letters. Compared to their army counterparts, sailors left a relatively small literary record. One reason was that sailors were not as well equipped to write. Recent scholarship indicates that most Union sailors came from working-class backgrounds and were less educated than their soldier counterparts. They were also less ideological and had fewer family ties, which may have generated less motivation to write, and the relative sameness of days aboard ship probably meant less to write about.[38]

Despite their drawbacks, the ordinary blockaders were the most habitable ships of the fleet. Most had ample room for their crews, they were well ventilated, and even at their worst they were familiar to sailors. Additionally, these ships had more freedom of action than the ironclads and made more frequent port visits. The wooden cruiser USS *Powhatan*, for example, spent thirteen months on blockade duty, of which fifty-seven days were spent in port. The ironclad *New Ironsides*, in contrast, spent sixteen straight months on the blockade without entering any port at all. The ships of the South Atlantic Blockading Squadron had perhaps the least chance of visiting a "real" port, and ships from that squadron considered themselves lucky to visit Port Royal.

Port Royal was no place a sailor would choose to go, but *New Ironsides*'s executive officer stated the case exactly when he wrote, "Barren and tiresome as Port Royal seems now, it was something of a paradise then to the blockader to go there, and feel sure of not being blown up by a torpedo before morning."[39] A monitor crewman described Port Royal's amenities almost lyrically, and "long nights of refreshing sleep" were near the top of his list.[40] "Refreshing sleep," equally attractive to other crews, was a reaction to the grueling blockade routine. Since blockade-running was almost always carried on at night, so was blockading.

The week or so that bracketed the new moon was always the busiest time on the blockade. Alarms were frequent and exhausting. Paymaster William F. Keeler described a night during which the *Florida* "poked around in the darkness for some time without hearing or seeing anything" before anchoring. Keeler went to bed at 1 AM, but soon "the deafening report of the 9 in. gun directly over my head, followed in a moment or two by the rush of a rocket, slightly disturbed my quiet slumbers."[41]

Dealing with runners at night was bad enough, but the same dark nights that brought the runners brought other challenges. By mid-1863 the threat of Confederate torpedo boats had become all too real, and as the fear of torpedo boats grew, so did the level of anxiety aboard the blockaders. Each night alarm exacted a price in reduced alertness and increased anxiety, and the alarms were not confined to major ports.

On August 9, 1864, as the *Stettin* lay in St. Simon's Sound, her log recorded, "At 2 AM saw a black object floating on the water towards us. Discharged a musket at it and immediately beat to quarters. On examination it proved to be an empty canoe. At 2.30 piped down." Half of the crew had been on watch until midnight, and those men would have less than three hours of sleep when it was again time for them to assume the watch at 4:00 AM. Fishing boats and other Union ships also alarmed the *Stettin*.[42] Aboard *New Ironsides* off Charleston, half the crew would be awake at their stations and half sleeping near their guns. The sailors had to sleep on deck because slinging the hammocks cluttered the gun deck so badly that the ship could not fight.[43] Aboard the monitors off Charleston, turrets were turned at night "every 1/4 and 1/2 hour, guns ready to fire at a second's notice."[44] No one wanted to be the next victim of a torpedo boat.

Similarly, no one wanted to be the victim of a Confederate raid. Ships operating close inshore and in the rivers were in constant danger of ambush. The Confederates succeeded in capturing several vessels, frequently in the sort of fierce night boarding actions that gave them the *Harriet Lane* and *Westfield* off Galveston, the *Water Witch* in Ossabaw Sound, Georgia, the *Morning Light* and *Velocity* off Sabine Pass, and the *Isaac Smith* in the Stono River. The larger ships were not as vulnerable to such methods, but the Confederate navy made enough attempts on them to keep the Federals nervous. The action of the *Manassas* at the Head of the Passes showed the potent psychological effect of an ironclad attack on unarmored ships, and Hampton Roads was in a continual uproar during the autumn of 1862 for fear of Confederate ironclads. The January 1863 raid by the *Chicora* and *Palmetto State* off Charleston intensified Federal concerns about ironclads, and the completion of the CSS *North Carolina* later that spring spread the concern to the blockaders off Wilmington. Even without ironclads, the Confederates were active; wooden gunboats attacked the blockaders off Mobile in early April 1862, and the *Alabama* sank the *Hatteras* off Galveston in January 1863.

Paymaster Keeler, blockading off Cape Fear, described the symptoms of "ram fever . . . brought on by occasional sights at a rebel ironclad": close observation of the channel, "the frequent mistaking of little river steamers & tugs for rebel ironclads & rams," and an inclination on the part of the commanding officer to keep his vessel well out to seaward.[45] The ram fever did not lessen much even when the Federals learned in October 1863 from Confederate deserters that the *North Carolina* was "too shaky and weak to go to sea," because the CSS *Raleigh* had also been completed at Wilmington in early 1863.[46]

The *Raleigh* brought a relapse of ram fever on May 6, 1864, when she and two gunboats sortied from Wilmington on the evening tide. She traded shots with several blockaders during the night, crossing back over the bar at high tide on the morning of May 7. The runner got out safely, but the *Raleigh* ran aground in the Cape Fear River. She became a total loss, and although she was reported late in May to be "badly injured," the Federals could not confirm her destruction until the end of June. Late autumn finally brought an end to ram fever off Wilmington, when an informant reported that the *North Carolina* had sunk at her moorings; a third ironclad under construction at Wilmington was never completed.[47]

Most navy officers believed that the best answer to an ironclad was another ironclad, and from 1863 on, the monitors put iron in the spine of the blockade. Handicapped by slow speed, a monitor would be unlikely to capture a prize herself, but a monitor's crew might share in one that another ship captured. There were no monitors around, however, when the USS *Stettin* encountered the blockade-runner *Diamond*, in an episode that may represent many such interactions. In September 1863, *Stettin* was anchored in St. Simon's Sound, Georgia, where she had been stationed since early July. Her captain was Acting Master Cornelius J. Van Alstine. Although he was a volunteer, Van Alstine knew his business; warranted midshipman in 1833, he had attained the rank of lieutenant before resigning from the navy in May 1859. Van Alstine had ordered that each watch section practice starting the engine and getting under way, and his insistence on practice paid off.

September 23, 1863, began as a routine day on the blockade. *Stettin*'s executive officer, John M. Butler, kept a diary, and that morning he observed, "My soul aches for something to do." The crew had exercised at quarters, and the afternoon had become rainy and breezy when Butler got his wish. *Stettin*'s lookouts sighted a steamer headed southward. That wasn't unusual, but as Butler noted, "She seems too near in for a naval vessel. Now she heads in. We discover black smoke & I think it must be a prize for us."

Stettin's log recorded, "At 3.45 PM saw a one masted St[eame]r outside standing to the Southward. Engine started in 30 seconds." The steamer turned in towards St. Simons, and Van Alstine immediately moved to intercept her. Firing a gun to leeward of the steamer caught her attention; she hoisted the British ensign but did not stop until *Stettin* fired again. Once the steamer had anchored, Butler went aboard to inspect her.

He found that the vessel, the British steamer *Diamond*, had no clearance or manifest, but the papers Butler did find and the conversation of the passengers and crew convinced Van Alstine that the *Diamond* intended to run the blockade. (Butler did not speculate about why her captain would try to do so in daylight.) Van Alstine took the crew and passengers aboard *Stettin* and placed a prize crew under Butler's command aboard the *Diamond*. After three days of preparation, including hiring eleven of the *Diamond*'s own engineers to operate her engines on the way north, Van Alstine sent the ship, with a cargo of "liquors, boots and shoes, cigars, medicine, dry goods, and cutlery," to Port Royal for further disposition. Her crew and passengers, including two men whom *Stettin* had captured once before, were sent to Port Royal aboard the supply steamer *Massachusetts*.[48]

Butler and his prize crew left Port Royal on October 2 and arrived in Washington DC on October 7, "after a hard week's sleepless hours." Butler turned the *Diamond* over to the prize commissioners on October 9 and took leave before attending the prize commission's hearing on October 19 and 20. After a few more days of leave, on October 31 he left Philadelphia for Port Royal. He and his fellow officers of the prize crew returned to the *Stettin* on November 10, having been away almost six weeks.[49] When condemned in January 1864, *Diamond* brought $27,725.02 for her captors. Butler would have received a few hundred dollars as his share—no small amount when a skilled workman's wages were $3 per day.

The success of the Union blockade has been a matter of serious debate. Contemporaries North and South agreed that the blockade crippled the

Confederacy, but second thoughts began in the 1920s. Early studies compared the number of attempts to run the blockade with the number of
arrivals in Southern ports to argue that the blockade was ineffective because it was porous and that the Southerners' own informal embargo
affected the cotton trade far more than did the blockade.[50] Other analysts assert that "defeat did not come from the lack of material" or that
"no Confederate army lost a major engagement because of the lack of
essential supplies and arms." By these lights the blockade was useless or
even counterproductive; it absorbed ships and men that could have been
used elsewhere with more effect on the war's outcome.[51]

More recent scholarship challenges this view. While the percentage
of successful penetrations is certainly important, it does not account for
the deterrent effect of the blockade—the blockade's effectiveness should
be evaluated not only by counting the cargoes that made it through but
also by comparing the prewar volume of trade of the Confederacy's ports
with the sharply reduced wartime trade of the same ports. Just as important, the blockade crippled the South's internal economy by cutting off
coastwise trade, especially in foodstuffs. By forcing the Confederacy back
upon an inadequate railroad network and preventing the importation of
the heavy, bulky materials needed to maintain that network, the blockade
hastened the deterioration of the Confederate transportation system and
the collapse of the Confederate economy. As an additional benefit, the
blockade helped to maintain itself by depriving the Confederate navy of
the imported armor plate and machinery that it needed to compete with
the Union navy's industrial base.[52]

Most important, the blockade dramatically reduced the revenue available to the Confederate government by curtailing the export of cotton.
Southerners and Northerners alike recognized its value; Du Pont called
cotton "almost literally a munition of war—for all the money raised in
Europe, every arm bought, has this cotton pledged for its payment."[53]
When the Civil War began, the South imposed an informal embargo on
cotton exports, hoping to pressure European governments to intervene
in the conflict, and some have argued that a glut of cotton in 1861 and
a downturn in world demand hurt the South's diplomatic position.[54] In
fact, European stocks of raw cotton were not excessively large in 1861, and
the demand for cotton textiles remained strong throughout the war. By
April 1862 the embargo had lost much of its appeal, and had it not been
for the blockade, the embargo would have postponed but not destroyed
the South's cotton revenue.[55]

The spectacular rise in the price of cotton was due almost entirely to the transportation costs imposed by the blockade—the specie price at Southern ports changed little, while the price in England tripled or quadrupled. William Watson, himself a successful blockade-running captain, recorded that runners felt "they could afford to give the Yankees a prize now and then to encourage them to maintain the blockade and keep up the price of cotton." The runners received most of the benefit, and the blockade cost the South at least $500 million in cotton revenue, roughly equal to everything the Union spent on its navy during the war.[56]

By 1864, as the blockade tightened and more Southern ports were sealed, the economic isolation of the South was becoming increasingly effective. The closing of Mobile Bay in August 1864 shifted blockade-running in the Gulf of Mexico to Texan ports—a very long way from the main theaters of war, and the monthly total of inbound and outbound runners combined never exceeded fifteen for all Texas ports combined. A few runners continued to use Charleston, but after mid-1863 Charleston's monthly total of inbound and outbound voyages combined averaged only five, and it exceeded ten in only three calendar months. In 1862 humorist Orpheus C. Kerr had opined that the Federal anaconda had "gathered itself in a circle around the doomed rabbit of rebellion, and if the rabbit swells he's a goner."[57] By the end of 1864 the snake was firmly in control and the much diminished rabbit was in serious trouble.

CHAPTER SEVEN

Privateers, "Pirates," and Raiders

Attacks on seaborne commerce have a long history, but any such campaign has the same basic objectives: to cause so much financial and economic harm that commercial interests force the enemy government to yield, and to affect enemy war-making by cutting off trade in vital materials. The Confederacy had a third objective: to weaken the Federal blockade by forcing the Union to divert ships to chase the commerce raiders. Despite some legendary exploits, the Confederate war on commerce failed on all three counts.

Like the rest of the naval war, the war on commerce was shaped by asymmetry: the North had a flourishing merchant marine while the South had practically none, and the South's overseas commerce had been carried predominantly in Northern and European ships. After war began in 1861, Southern imports moved almost exclusively in European ships. These vessels were neutrals and could be seized only if their cargoes were contraband, destined for the blockaded ports of the Confederacy, or if they actually tried to penetrate the blockaded area. Welles pointed out the asymmetry in 1861, writing, "Those who have engaged in this rebellion have neither commerce nor a navy to reward or stimulate to exertion."[1]

The Union had some early success with intercepting vessels carrying contraband near their European ports of departure, in a rough practical equivalent of commerce raiding. By 1862, however, Europeans had learned the tricks of falsifying bills of lading and of consigning their westbound cargoes to neutral ports in the Western Hemisphere, prominently Nassau, Bahamas, and St. George, Bermuda. Once there, cargoes were transshipped to specialized blockade-running vessels for the final leg of their journeys to the Confederacy. These dodges provided a veneer of neutrality that protected Confederate commerce during the trip across the Atlantic, the longest portion of the voyage from Europe, and eliminated any chance of a Northern analog to the Confederate *guerre de course.* The South could implement Du Pont's strategy of seaborne attacks to "sweep away" enemy commerce without fear of retaliation in kind.

Unfortunately for the Confederates, the sine qua non for sweeping away commerce was a force of seagoing warships, and this the Confederacy lacked. To encourage private citizens to supply the need, the new Confederacy moved quickly to issue letters of marque and reprisal, and the Confederate war against Union commerce began with privateering. One of the earliest privateers helped to impel the Union's de facto recognition of the Confederacy as a belligerent nation rather than a group of outlaws.

In the theory to which the Lincoln administration subscribed, the Confederacy had no legal existence; it was an illegal product of rebellion. Its armed forces were therefore rebels in arms, subject not to the usages of war between belligerent nations but to the civil statutes of the United States. By this logic, a Confederate letter of marque had no legal standing, and a privateersman who took a Northern prize was in fact guilty of piracy. The issue was tested in the case of the privateer *Savannah*.

In May 1861, T. Harrison Baker and seven other businessmen received a letter of marque from the Confederate government, and their schooner, the *Savannah*, sailed from Charleston on June 2, 1861. The privateer's cruise began auspiciously when on June 3 she captured the brig *Joseph*, but it turned sharply downward later the same day when the USS *Perry* captured the *Savannah* in turn. Baker and his crew of twelve were sent to New York City to be tried for piracy—a capital crime.[2]

The Confederacy protested that the men were privateersmen, not pirates, operating lawfully and thus entitled to the status of prisoners of war. The Union pressed on with the prosecution, ignoring the protests, and in August, the Confederate Congress authorized retaliation. By the time their trial began in October 1861, the case of the "Baker's dozen" had attracted much attention. In early November the Confederates chose fourteen Union prisoners of war and vowed to hang them if Baker's crew and another privateersman condemned in a separate case were executed. Clearly the Confederates were playing hardball, and an uneasy standoff ensued.

Paralleling the evolution of de facto belligerency ashore, the practical overcame the theoretical. Although the Union continued to assert the same legal stance throughout the war, it adjusted its policies to acknowledge that the Confederacy was in fact a belligerent nation. In February 1862 the *Savannah*'s crew were deemed to be privateersmen, and later that year they were exchanged. There would be no more criminal trials for piracy, but constant Northern use of the term probably gave pause to would-be privateers. The threat of a piracy trial remained in the background.[3]

Legal issues were more influential than the threat of hanging in suppressing both the number and the impact of the privateers. To give good title and avoid committing piracy, a privateer had to have his prize condemned by a competent court, following the process described in chapter 6. Reaching a Confederate States court in person, however, meant that a Confederate privateer had to bring his prize back through the Union blockade. Getting through the cordon was not a sure thing even in custom-built blockade-running steamers; in a sailing vessel like those upon which the privateers generally preyed, it would be extremely difficult.

Condemnation at a distance was legally possible, but such a "mail order" proceeding took a long time even if the case for condemnation were airtight and the mail service reliable. Since mail to and from the Confederacy had to run the blockade, each iteration of the case or request for additional documents could take months. While the condemnation case was going on, the captor needed a safe harbor for the captured ship— that is, a neutral port with regular mails. When most neutrals followed Great Britain's lead and refused to allow uncondemned prizes to enter their ports, privateering became economically unattractive.

Du Pont had written in July 1861 that the privateers would be short-lived, and his forecast was correct. The last of the Confederate privateers, the *Retribution,* was sold in Nassau in early 1863.[4] Civilians who wanted adventure and riches at sea turned from privateering to blockade-running, which by 1862 had become significantly more rewarding and less risky.

The other means by which the Confederates might attack Union commerce was the commissioned raider. Originally intended to complement the privateers, the Confederate navy's cruisers wound up carrying on the bulk of the Confederacy's anticommerce campaign. The refusal of neutral powers to allow prize vessels into their ports did not seriously hamper commissioned commerce raiders. Warships could legally destroy their captures without reference to prize courts.[5]

The first of the commissioned commerce raiders was the homegrown css *Sumter*, converted from the merchantman *Habana* in New Orleans in late spring 1861. Under Cdr. Raphael Semmes, csn, *Sumter* slipped out of the Mississippi on June 30, 1861, and began her cruise in the Gulf of Mexico. Her first prize, burned on July 3, was followed by six more in two days. One prize's crew recaptured their ship, but Semmes took the other five vessels into Cienfuegos, Cuba, to "test the waters" with regard to Spanish neutrality. Of the two other prizes that Semmes took in late July, one was recaptured as she tried to run the blockade into New Orleans and one was sent to Cuba, whence she, like the other five, was eventually returned to her owners by the Spanish government. Several weeks of cruising in the Caribbean and off Brazil yielded only two more prizes, and in mid-November Semmes entered St. Pierre, Martinique, to coal.[6]

The uss *Iroquois* found him at St. Pierre on November 14, 1861, and blockaded the anchorage from beyond the three-mile limit. The Federals arranged with a Union merchant ship to signal the *Sumter*'s course if she departed at night, and lights from the schooner duly notified the *Iroquois* when Semmes headed south at 8 PM on November 23. Semmes also saw the lights and, his suspicions confirmed, doubled back to the north. Evading the *Iroquois*, he set off for more lucrative cruising in the northern Atlantic. Three prizes and six weeks later, *Sumter* entered Cadiz, Spain, to refuel.[7]

Semmes found that the coal merchants of Cadiz required cash, of which he had little, although the local Spanish navy commandant allowed him to dock the *Sumter* on credit. On January 17, 1862, the Spanish government peremptorily ordered him to depart, still without coal, and he took two more prizes before arriving at Gibraltar on the 18th. Federal influence again kept him from buying coal commercially, and the British government would not sell him any from the Royal Navy's stock. Basing his decision on the difficulty of refueling, the three Federal cruisers watching the port, and the *Sumter*'s "burned out" boilers, Semmes determined to lay up the ship. He left her in mid-April to return to the Confederacy by way of England.[8]

css *Nashville* was active for roughly the same span of time as the *Sumter*. The converted passenger steamer ran out of Charleston in October 1861. The first Confederate warship to visit England took two prizes before returning to Beaufort, North Carolina. Her career as a raider ended in March 1862 when she was sold out of the service to become the blockade-runner *Thomas L. Wragg*.[9] By April 1862, then, the Confederates had no active commerce raiders. The situation would soon change, thanks to the redoubtable James D. Bulloch.

Only two active Confederate cruisers were purpose-built as warships, and both were constructed in England under Bulloch's supervision. Both benefited from the thought Bulloch had given to the characteristics that would suit a ship for commerce raiding. Habitability, speed, and the capacity to carry ordnance played a part, but Bulloch's number one criterion was performance under sail. Recognizing that a Confederate vessel could not depend upon frequent refueling, he insisted upon full rigging and a hoisting screw to reduce drag when not under power.[10]

Bulloch ordered the first of his ships in June 1861 from the Liverpool firm of William C. Miller & Sons. The design of the wooden-hulled *Oreto*, as she was then called, was based on a British gunboat, modified to increase speed, carrying capacity, and sail power. Since the Confederate government had no money available in Europe, Bulloch obtained an advance from the commercial firm of Fraser, Trenholm & Co. to begin her construction.[11]

As noted in chapter 5, British neutrality was governed by the Foreign Enlistment Act of 1819. Bulloch's counsel asserted in 1861 (and the British courts unknowingly concurred with him in 1863) that an unarmed ship was a legitimate article of commerce under the Act. Bulloch determined to follow the letter of the law by maintaining rigid separation between the "building" and the "equipping" of his ships.

In practice, this meant building the *Oreto* as an unarmed vessel and treating the contract as an ordinary commercial transaction between the shipbuilders and a private individual. Although the builders "may both have had a tolerably clear notion" that the vessel would pass to the Confederate government, "they never mentioned their suspicions" and thus technically complied with the Act.[12] Bulloch separately ordered all of the warship equipment needed for the ship, from main battery guns and carriages to sidearms, planning to send it in another vessel to meet the *Oreto* later. He left England to consult with Mallory in October 1862, anticipating that the *Oreto* would be completed about the time he returned and that he would be ordered to command her.

Bulloch's return trip was delayed for nearly two months by the need to run out through the Federal blockade, and while he was away from England, as he had anticipated, the *Oreto* was completed. Following Bulloch's instructions, on February 5, 1862, Fraser, Trenholm & Co. notified James North that the vessel was ready for delivery.[13] North displayed his characteristic lack of energy and perception. First, North wanted to load the ship with arms, which would have undermined Bulloch's carefully devised strategy for obtaining ships and getting them out of England. Then, when Charles Prioleau of Fraser, Trenholm objected to his loading plan, North immediately dumped his problem onto higher authority, writing that he did not want to "take charge of an empty ship" and that he was "very much at a loss to know how to act."[14] When Bulloch returned to England on March 10, he found the ship still not ready to depart, and nearly two weeks of intense labor were needed before she sailed on March 22, 1862.[15]

Mallory had originally intended that Bulloch should command the *Oreto*, but his need for an energetic agent caused him to approve Bulloch's request to command the second ship instead. Neither officers nor crew were available to take the *Oreto* to the Confederacy, but she had excited the suspicion of the U.S. ambassador, who had begun pressing the British government to seize her. Bulloch placed the vessel in the care of one of his junior officers and sent her, as a merchant ship with a merchant captain and crew, to the Bahamas. There he hoped to place her in the hands of Lt. J. N. Maffitt, CSN. Her outfit would follow as freight in the steamer *Bahama*.[16]

Oreto arrived in Nassau on April 28, 1862, and the U.S. consul there promptly began agitating for her detention. The British authorities seized, released, and reseized the ship, and after a trial, on August 2, the verdict was "insufficient evidence" to prove a violation of the Foreign Enlistment Act. Maffitt left the harbor immediately, and on August 9 the newly commissioned CSS *Florida* (figure 9) rendezvoused with the merchant ship *Prince Albert*, which carried her armament.[17]

Unfortunately for Maffitt, essentials such as sponges and rammers had been overlooked in transshipping the armament from the *Bahama* to the *Prince Albert* to the *Florida*, and without them, the crew could not fire the guns. Worse, he had only thirteen men and four other officers for his crew, and worse yet, yellow fever broke out on board. Maffitt evaded several U.S. cruisers and made his way to Cardenas, Cuba, where he himself caught the *vomito*. His executive officer managed to engage another dozen men, and with them *Florida* sailed for Havana on August 31, 1862.

The recovering Maffitt found that the Spaniards' strict interpretation of neutrality prevented him from refitting or recruiting, so he decided to run the blockade into Mobile. On September 4, he hoisted British colors and boldly approached three U.S. blockaders off the Mobile bar.

Here, the derivation of the *Florida*'s design from a British gunboat stood Maffitt in good stead. Cdr. George H. Preble, concerned about insulting the Royal Navy, held his fire until it was too late to stop the *Florida*, and the Confederate vessel steamed past his force in a hail of fire and gained the shelter of Fort Morgan.[18] The Confederates reported that the ship was seriously damaged, but Welles's unhappiness was manifest. Telling his diary that Preble had exhibited "sheer pusillanimous neglect, feebleness and indecision," he wrote that the case should be investigated "and an example made." Preble was promptly dismissed from the service, and *Florida* spent several months repairing and refitting.[19]

Meanwhile, the second of Bulloch's cruisers also neared completion. He had contracted for her with John Laird, Sons & Co. of Liverpool on August 1, 1861, and she was laid down as Laird's hull number 290. Bulloch noted his disappointment with her slow progress when he returned to England in March 1862, but after her launching in May, Laird was able to make up the time by quickly installing her engines and equipment. The *Enrica*, as the *290* had been christened, ran her trials in mid-June 1862, and Bulloch made ready to take her to sea as her commanding officer. Her armament and "warlike stores," long since ordered, were placed aboard the purchased barque *Agrippina*, and plans were made for her rendezvous with the *Enrica* outside British jurisdiction.[20]

At this point, Bulloch's status as the Confederate navy's "indispensable man" in Europe interfered with his earnest desire for command at sea. Cdr. Raphael Semmes, it will be recalled, had laid up the CSS *Sumter* in Gibraltar in April 1862 and taken passage for the Confederacy via England and the Bahamas. When he called in England, Bulloch offered him command of the *Enrica*, but Semmes refused to override Mallory's orders. When he reached Nassau, however, Semmes received orders directing him back to England—to command the *Enrica*. Bulloch received orders of similar date to turn the ship over to Semmes and to take charge of the Confederacy's ironclad construction program in Europe. Semmes and his officers had not yet arrived in England when events forced Bulloch's hand.[21]

Bulloch had been reluctant to dispatch the *Enrica* and her tender *Agrippina* until Semmes arrived, but the pressure applied by the U.S. consul in Liverpool and the U.S. ambassador had steadily increased. Bulloch noted that the Foreign Enlistment Act was a "domestic enemy" upon which he had to keep a watchful eye, and on July 26, he received word from a "most reliable" source that the *Enrica* would not be safe in Liverpool for another forty-eight hours.[22] On Tuesday, July 29, a "trial trip" was begun with guests on board, but the guests were offloaded to a tug that afternoon and the *Enrica* sailed for a remote anchorage. Bulloch rejoined her on July 30, the crew was shipped for the voyage, and just after midnight on July 31, the ship got under way to round Ireland north-about. Bulloch left the ship later that day, and the *Enrica* pressed on for her rendezvous with the *Agrippina* at Praya Bay, Terceira, in the Azores.

Semmes, his officers, and Bulloch set out by chartered steamer on August 13, arriving at Terceira on August 20. On August 24, Semmes commissioned the *Enrica* as the css *Alabama* and Bulloch returned to Liverpool, where he turned his attention to the additional duties that had caused Mallory to keep him in England.[23] Semmes and his crew began to shake down the *Alabama* and commenced a cruise that would last almost two years.

In August 1862, then, the Federals knew that the *Oreto*, commissioned as the *Florida*, was in Cuba. They also knew that the *290/Enrica* had escaped from Liverpool, but they could not know what had transpired since then. On September 4, Welles told his diary, "Something energetic must be done" about the *Oreto*, then in Cuba, and "Steamer *290*, both piratical, British wolves."[24] The "something energetic" Welles did was to organize a "flying squadron" to pursue raiders in the West Indies and, under pressure from Lincoln and Seward, to appoint Charles Wilkes of *Trent* affair notoriety as its commander. Meanwhile, the *Alabama* took and burned her first prize on September 5, 1862, in the vicinity of the Azores.

Within two weeks Semmes's score was up to ten, and by the end of October, he had captured and destroyed or ransomed twenty-one vessels. In early November 1862, Fox wrote Du Pont, "The '290' is giving us a sick turn," and advised him that the Navy Department had sent out several fast ships to catch her.[25] November 19 brought Semmes an encounter with the uss *San Jacinto* in Martinique, but, as Semmes noted, the *Alabama* was faster than the "old wagon" and escaped in a squall that same evening.[26] November also brought Semmes three more victims and December another two, including the outbound California steamer *Ariel*, released under bond.[27]

In early January 1863 Semmes decided to attack the transports that were carrying Maj. Gen. Nathaniel Banks's troops to Galveston, but found instead several Union warships. He succeeded in luring uss

Hatteras away from her fellows, and on January 11, 1863, he sank her in a brief engagement.[28] Semmes rescued the crew of the *Hatteras* and set sail for the West Indies.

Florida, meanwhile, had completed her refit at Mobile, and she spent several weeks waiting for an opportunity to run the blockade. Her crew was eager to commence their work; as Maffitt wrote, "all hands are very restive," chief among them Lt. Charles W. Read, who "suffers particularly in this and has become somewhat bilious."[29] On January 16, 1863, Maffitt escaped from Mobile and on January 19 took his first prize near Cuba. After a short visit to Havana, Maffitt took two more prizes near Cuba on January 22 and added another on February 12 before heading for Brazil.

In early May, the *Florida* captured the brig *Clarence*, and Read, apparently still restive, proposed to use the vessel to raid Hampton Roads. Maffitt agreed, equipping the vessel with twenty men and a single gun, and sent her off under Read's command.[30] The *Clarence* took six prizes, including the bark *Tacony*, which she captured on June 12. Transferring his force to the *Tacony*, Read burned the *Clarence* and continued his cruise along the U.S. coast. Word of Read's exploits reached Welles late on June 13, and the secretary reacted by ordering "every vessel to proceed to sea without delay in search of this wolf that is prowling so near us."[31]

The wolf continued to prowl, and Read's northbound trip along the coast yielded fourteen prizes before he captured the fishing boat *Archer* on June 24. On June 25 he transferred his command to the *Archer*, burned the *Tacony*, and headed for Portland.[32] On June 27, he and his men cut out the U.S. revenue cutter *Caleb Cushing* but could not evade the pursuit organized by the collector of customs using chartered steamers. Setting fire to the *Cushing*, Read and his crew took to their boats and were captured, and the *Archer* was retaken later that day.[33] The *Florida* continued her cruise in the West Indies and North Atlantic, arriving in Brest for extended repairs in August 1863.

Wilkes meanwhile was making much commotion without achieving any notable results. The Danish, Mexican, Spanish, and British governments had all lodged formal complaints about him, and in addition Wilkes had commandeered every U.S. Navy ship that passed through his area. An example was the USS *Vanderbilt*, sent by the Navy Department to pursue the *Alabama*: Wilkes overrode Welles's orders and made her his flagship. Wilkes also diverted the *Chippewa*, en route to Du Pont's South Atlantic Blockading Squadron; the *Oneida*, sent by Farragut to chase the *Florida;* and the *R. R. Cuyler*, en route to Farragut's West Gulf Blockading

Squadron from the North. Farragut complained to Welles in June 1863, but by the time Farragut penned this protest, Wilkes was already on his way home.[34]

Wilkes's antics in the West Indies and his inability to adjust to the new paradigm of centralized command finally eroded his support within the administration, and Welles decided in May to replace him. Wilkes's disregard of orders clearly affected Welles's decision, but the other primary determinant was the commodore's effect on Anglo-American relations. Incidents such as the controversial seizures of the British steamers *Peterhof* in February and *Dolphin* in March 1863 combined with British memories of Wilkes's role in the *Trent* affair to impel his departure "unless we are ready for a war with England."[35] In the end, neither his popular acclaim for twisting the British lion's tail nor his wife's intercession with Welles could save Wilkes's command.

Replacing Wilkes was a positive step, but Welles clearly had his own difficulties with the British. Although Welles confided to his diary the need to avert war by removing Wilkes, he added that he sometimes thought that war was "not the worst alternative, [England] behaves so badly."[36] It must have seemed to Welles that no sooner was one raider eliminated or neutralized than another British-built vessel replaced her, and his frustration at the British government's unwillingness or inability to restrain its subjects grew apace. The year 1863 in fact marked the high point for Confederate raiders, with seven vessels at least nominally active at one time or another.

Two of those seven vessels were the work of Matthew Fontaine Maury. Maury, whose failed gunboat scheme had apparently not endeared him to Mallory, was sent overseas on "special service" in late 1862. His primary objective was to investigate "submarine defences," but his orders also allowed him to buy and dispatch commerce raiders.[37] Operating circumspectly through a Dutch friend and a cousin, he bought the iron-hulled screw steamer *Japan* in March 1863 and the wooden-hulled dispatch boat *Victor* in November 1863. Outfitted in the usual way, the *Japan* became the css *Georgia* in April 1863. The *Victor*, hastily removed from British jurisdiction, was commissioned as the css *Rappahannock* on her way across the English Channel but was never outfitted.[38]

Unfortunately for the Confederates, Maury's operational acumen did not match his scientific success, and neither of the ships he purchased was a successful raider. The *Georgia* had too little sail power to cruise without using her engines, and after a six-month cruise and a few prizes, she spent most of the rest of her career in French ports. She was sold out of the Confederate service in Liverpool in June 1864. The *Rappahannock*, her engines defective from the start, could carry only six weeks worth of provisions. She never cruised, and spent her entire commissioned life in Calais as a sort of depot ship for the Confederate navy.[39]

Other British-built vessels never served the South. The *Texas*, built under the cover names *Pampero* and *Canton* for Lt. George T. Sinclair, CSN, was to be an "improved *Alabama*." James and George Thompson launched her at Clydebank in early November 1863, but Federal agitation kept her from the Confederacy until the war's end.[40] Several ships were intended for conversion to cruisers after running the blockade, but the *Georgiana* was wrecked off Charleston in March 1863 and the *Olustee*, *Vicksburg*, *Waccamaw*, and *Black Warrior* were not completed in time to be delivered to the Confederacy.[41]

The best publicized raider was, of course, the *Alabama*, commanded by the dashing and egotistical Raphael Semmes. After sinking the *Hatteras* in January 1863, Semmes took several prizes in the West Indies before heading for Brazilian waters. Three months in and out of Brazilian ports netted more prizes, including the bark *Conrad*. Semmes armed the *Conrad*, commissioned her as CSS *Tuscaloosa*, and sent her off under Lt. John Low. She captured two prizes in her short career, which was terminated by British authorities in Cape Town who seized her in December 1863 when they determined that she had not been legally commissioned.[42] Semmes operated between Africa and Brazil until September 1863, when he departed for the Indian Ocean and China Sea. He returned to Cape Town six months later, having taken seven prizes, and in late March 1864 he set out for European waters with the intent of overhauling the well-worn *Alabama*. He entered Cherbourg, France, on June 11, 1864.

Word spread quickly, and on June 14, the USS *Kearsarge*, under Capt. John A. Winslow, arrived to blockade the *Alabama*. The *Kearsarge* was of roughly equal size and armament, and Semmes told Flag Officer Samuel Barron, "The *Kearsarge* is off the port, which I understand, of course, as a challenge."[43] He decided to leave port and offer battle. On Sunday, June 19, the *Alabama* steamed out at midmorning to meet her adversary. Semmes opened the firing just before noon at a range of about a mile and a half, intending to close the range and, if possible, to board.

The battle, one of the very few such ship-to-ship actions of the Civil War, did not go as Semmes had hoped. By maintaining his distance instead of permitting the *Alabama* to close, Winslow maximized the advantage of his somewhat heavier guns. Winslow also benefited from luck, since a number of *Alabama*'s shells failed to explode. One of the duds lodged in the *Kearsarge*'s sternpost—had it exploded, it would have ended the battle on the spot with a Confederate victory—but after an hour and a half of fighting, the *Alabama* struck her colors and quickly sank. Semmes and many of his crew were rescued by an English yacht and transported to neutral England.

After the battle, Semmes discovered that Winslow had covered *Kearsarge*'s sides with anchor chains. In a typically arrogant assumption of his own nautical superiority and gentlemanly nobility, the beaten Confederate sought solace in asserting that his opponent had not fought fairly; Winslow had played a "Yankee trick" and had "cheat[ed]" by being "ironclad" and not telling Semmes about it beforehand. [44] It is difficult, however, to reconcile Semmes's decision to fight the *Kearsarge* with his mission of commerce destruction. He had slipped out of port past a vigilant Federal cruiser before. Why not try it again? One suspects that the desire for a glorious ship-to-ship action caused Semmes to forget his purpose. His uncritical admirers lionized him as much in defeat as they could possibly have done in victory, but Semmes's desire for glory robbed the Confederacy of its most effective raider and boosted the Union's morale when a boost was seriously needed. [45]

Destroying commerce raiders was certainly the most satisfying and the most publicly appreciated way of protecting the North's shipping, but other methods existed. Passive methods such as detours and camouflage do not seem to have been much used. Most of the vulnerable vessels were sailing ships for which evasive routing would have been difficult, and in the absence of governmental control, merchant captains did as they pleased, trusting to the "little ship, big ocean" theory to avoid raiders.

Confederate authorities expressed surprise that the Union did not "keep guard" at "those well-known points towards which the trade of the world converges," but in fact the Union did its best to cover the critical areas. [46] In this game of hide-and-seek, the raider held all the advantages. Successful interception required timing so precise as to be extremely improbable: if the hunter intersected the raider's course two hours too early or too late, or at night, or in heavy weather, the ships would never sight each other. [47] If the raider unknowingly missed a merchant ship in this way, it made no difference. There were plenty of merchant ships, and each was as good prey as any other. For the hunter, only one ship mattered. Unlike his critics, Welles had arrived empirically at the conclusion that World War II operational analysts proved mathematically. A raider has far more opportunities to sight and attack merchantmen sailing independently than a hunter has to sight and attack the raider.

Open-ocean convoys were not a significant feature of the Civil War, although the California mail ships and other high-value units were escorted. Direct defense was also insignificant; the navy offered to provide guns and navy gun crews to arm some high-value merchant ships on the California and West Indies routes, but shipping lines preferred that their ships be escorted.[48] Commerce defense was thus mostly indirect. The indirect methods included chasing the raiders and blockading or conquering their bases, but the effort was not entirely military; the State Department also worked to suppress commerce raiding. The vigilance and energetic protests of U.S. ambassadors and consuls in Britain and France delayed or prevented the delivery of several potential raiders.

Welles was constantly the object of abuse from citizens who felt that the navy should do more against the raiders. One anonymous correspondent indignantly wrote the secretary to demand the capture of "that pirate *Alabama* . . . catch the dam [*sic*] thing if it takes the whole navy."[49] Others proposed various schemes to "decoy and destroy" or capture the *Alabama*, all of which had the common denominator of wanting the navy to pay for them.[50] Welles reacted to such pressure on occasion during the early months of the war, but as the conflict continued, he became less inclined to divert ships from the blockade to the needle-in-a-haystack search for raiders. In December 1863 the secretary told his diary that it would be folly to detach vessels from the blockade: "When I sometimes ask the fault-finders to tell me where the Alabama is or can be found, assuring them I will send a force of several vessels at once to take her on being satisfactorily informed, they are silenced."[51] By his staunch defense of the blockade as the Union navy's top priority, Welles negated one of Mallory's major hopes for the Confederate cruisers.

Welles also had to defend the blockade against public demands for naval protection. Confederate cruisers produced a climate of fear on the Northern seaboard, and the North experienced much of the same public concern for coastal defense as did the South, although with much less reason. Parochial requests for naval protection assaulted Welles from every side. Boards of trade and chambers of commerce passed resolutions, governors sent frantic telegrams, state legislatures sent delegations and memorials, and politicians at all levels applied all the pressure they could.[52] Their concerns ranged from the possibility of a Confederate cruiser raiding the coast to the potential activities of nonexistent vessels like the "four iron clad rebel vessels similar to the Merrimac [*sic*] at Norfolk" and the "war steamer" fitting out in France "to capture N. York."[53]

As Du Pont had foreseen, trying to defend each locality with a naval force would cause "endless vexation, dissatisfaction, and dispute," and Northern states and cities raised precisely the sort of clamor that Du Pont had feared would keep the navy at home.[54] New York, the most populous and influential city in the nation, contained the "most easily terrified and panic-stricken" men in the country, but Boston seems to have been a close second.[55] Each seaboard city and town urgently pressed its case through its congressional delegation, state governor, and influential citizens, painting the direst possible picture of the results of a sudden Confederate "descent" upon it and demanding that substantial naval forces be assigned to permanent guard duty.

While the threat of a Confederate raid might frighten the North, such raids were unlikely. As Fox pointed out during a New England panic about the raider css *Alabama*, "She is doing a better business with less risk than attacking Boston."[56] Both he and Welles saw that the navy could not provide ships to every potentially threatened locale without crippling the blockade and gutting the raider-pursuing cruiser squadrons.[57] In addition, defending the major seaports was the responsibility of the army, a responsibility Welles did not intend to assume. As Fox wrote, the Army Corps of Engineers had been working on the defenses of New York harbor for sixty years, and they "ought to be able to keep one steamer out."[58]

With Lincoln's apparent backing, Welles remained focused upon larger issues. He stated his philosophy in a letter to Massachusetts governor John Andrew, writing that with so many undefended points, "If the armed vessels of the United States were to be distributed to each one for the purposes of defence, there would be no vessels left for the blockade or for the purpose of pursuing the pirates on the high seas."[59] He passed many of the plaints to the secretary of war, responsible for coastal defenses, or the secretary of the treasury, whose Revenue Service was the predecessor of the modern Coast Guard.[60]

Welles did yield to the heaviest political pressure, but even then he yielded pragmatically. When he absolutely had to assign a guard ship, he would try to designate a ship already under repair in the "threatened" port. This usually gave the governor or mayor a (perhaps mistaken) sense of security without taking ships away from more important operations. The concerns of Northern constituencies about coastal defense were predominantly what one businessman called "spasmodic attacks of the Shakes," and the most the Confederates ever managed were pinpricks compared with the operations the Union mounted against the Southern coasts.[61]

Confederate privateers and raiders also sowed panic in Northern commercial circles, a panic reflected in dramatically rising insurance rates, accelerated transfer of ships to neutral flags, and anguished wails for protection. Yet commerce was not "swept away." Exports of wheat jumped from four million bushels in 1860 to thirty-one million in 1861, then averaged over twenty-seven million bushels per year during the war years. Meat exports rose in value from $14 million in 1860 to $35 million in 1865. Exports of finished manufactures averaged $30.2 million per year for the war years, compared with $32.4 million per year for the five years before the war.[62] The Union's overseas commerce simply moved to neutral flags, and American ships were sold to neutral owners. U.S. merchant ships carried 66.5 percent of all U.S. foreign trade in 1860 but only 27.7 percent in 1865, though total imports and exports increased during the war.[63]

The increasingly evident failure of commerce raiding led the Confederacy to consider alternative ways to affect the Union's commerce. One such method, for which planning began in late 1864, involved clandestine operations to destroy neutral merchant ships that were carrying goods to the North.[64]

The plan was based upon the Confederates' growing technological mastery of torpedo warfare. A major element would be the Courtney torpedo, made of cast iron in the shape of a lump of coal. It was designed to be placed surreptitiously on a coal pile, whence it would eventually be shoveled into a ship's boiler. The ensuing explosion would likely be blamed on a boiler failure.[65] "Horological torpedoes" with clockwork time fuzes were also available. In August 1864, Confederates planted such a time bomb at the Union army's City Point supply depot, causing an explosion that killed and wounded over 160 men and destroyed $4 million worth of supplies.[66]

The torpedo operators would be organized under a Confederate law passed February 17, 1864, that provided for "bodies for the capture and destruction of the enemy's property by land or sea."[67] The cover for the "destructionists" apparently remained in the Confederate army's engineer bureau.[68] Although the act was secret, it soon became known to the Federals. Admiral Porter, enclosing a captured operator's commission, observed that the Confederates had "just appointed a torpedo corps . . . for the purpose of blowing up property of all kinds."[69] The attack on merchant shipping did not mature in time to affect the war, but the "destructionists" achieved some notable successes, including the City Point explosion and the sinking of Benjamin Butler's headquarters ship *Greyhound* on the James River.[70]

In another "unconventional" effort, in May 1864 Mallory ordered Acting Master Thomas E. Hogg to lead a group of men to capture one of the Pacific mail steamers that ran between Panama and California. The party would pose as passengers and take control of the chosen ship at sea, a method already proven feasible by the Confederate capture of the steamer *Chesapeake* off Cape Cod in December 1863. Hogg and his men were detected and captured, and this attempt to "strike a blow at the California trade and whalemen in the Pacific" failed.[71]

The Confederates did not rely only on covert means to attack commerce in the Pacific. After the *Alabama* was sunk, Bulloch had begun to look for another ship, and when funds came to hand, he bought the merchant steamer *Sea King* and dispatched her in his usual way. In late October 1864 the newly commissioned *Shenandoah* left Madeira, headed south to round Africa and attack the U.S. whaling fleet in the Indian and Pacific Oceans.[72]

In the aggregate, commerce destruction was a good bargain for the Confederacy. The dozen or so commissioned raiders and their slightly more numerous privateer cousins captured or destroyed about 110,000 tons of United States shipping and caused over 800,000 tons more to be transferred to neutral flags. At the peak, over fifty U.S. Navy ships were searching for at most four or five active raiders. Once the war was over, the U.S. merchant marine never recovered its former dominance.[73]

Yet although commerce raiding was a good bargain, and romantic to boot, it did not seriously hamper the Northern war effort. Union shipowners' and merchants' cries of pain did not force the United States to give up the war. Except on a temporary basis, the raiders did not force the Union to reallocate naval assets away from the blockade; while fifty ships were searching for raiders, over six hundred were not. Even the spectacular decline of the U.S. merchant marine is attributable less to the Confederates than to changing economic conditions and national priorities.[74] The raiders provided a number of exciting tales and a legacy of anti-British feeling in the North, but in terms of their impact on the war, they were what one pro-Southern naval historian objectively characterized as a "minor counterstroke."[75]

CHAPTER EIGHT

The Naval War, 1864–65

As 1864 opened, Federal arms seemed to be making little progress. Ulysses S. Grant had been appointed general in chief, but the eastern armies awaited good weather in much the same positions they had occupied a year earlier. At sea, Confederate raiders still operated against Yankee shipping, blockade-runners still eluded Yankee pursuers to make huge profits, and Charleston still defied Dahlgren's ironclad fleet.

The first real naval news of the year was bad for the Union: on February 10, 1864, the commerce raider CSS *Florida* escaped from the port of Brest, France. This news reached the Navy Department at about the same time as word of the sinking of the steamer USS *Housatonic* by the submersible CSS *Hunley* on February 17. Neither piece of information was encouraging, and the *Housatonic* episode raised fears that the "whole line of blockade will be infested with these cheap, convenient, and formidable devices."[1]

Capt. Francis D. Lee of the Confederate army had been working for over a year to give the Confederates the benefit of such an infestation. His torpedoes had seen action on the *Torch* and the *David* in 1863, but despite Beauregard's unwavering advocacy, Lee had limited success in obtaining support from the army establishment. Even after convincing the War Department that torpedo boats should be funded by the army engineers as harbor defenses, he still encountered official hostility. His request through channels for the services of a machine shop was returned by the commander of the Charleston Arsenal with an endorsement that the mere request, "if not an assumption of authority, is at least highly prejudicial to military discipline."[2]

By late January 1864, however, Lee had found a sponsor. One of his letters attracted the attention of the Confederate army's Torpedo Bureau.

In addition to orders from the War Department placing him in charge of constructing "torpedo-bearing steam-boats," Lee received the Torpedo Bureau's financial backing, including the authority to purchase items abroad using the Bureau's "sterling money."[3] The support apparently reinvigorated Beauregard's torpedo program, which eventually planted over 175 torpedoes. At least eight torpedo boats based on the *David* design were commenced at Charleston in 1864.[4]

Other torpedo boat projects were also under way. On the James River, the Confederates built four vessels to a design that was more conventional than the semisubmersible *David*. As with other types of ships, the Confederates tried to supplement local construction with European building. In July 1864, Mallory told Bulloch to have six torpedo boats and a number of additional engines built in England. Mistakes in the plans supplied from Richmond delayed the work, and these six vessels and six more ordered in November 1864 were not completed in time to serve in the war.[5]

Mallory's increased interest in torpedo warfare probably stemmed from the sense that its effectiveness was increasing. In March 1864 the *David* attacked the USS *Memphis* near Charleston, but the torpedo failed to explode. In April and May 1864 the fuzes worked better, and the Confederates sank three Federal transports on the St. John's River with moored torpedoes.[6] Also in April, *Squib*, commanded by Lt. Hunter Davidson of the Confederate Naval Submarine Battery Service, torpedoed and slightly damaged the USS *Minnesota* in Hampton Roads.[7]

These successes heartened the Confederates, but straws in the European wind foreboded ill news. Bulloch had once been confident that his sham sale of the Laird rams to the French Bravay firm would allow the ships to reach the Confederacy. By January 1864, though, he was convinced that the only way to get the ships out of England would be to have the French government ask officially for their release. Napoleon III's refusal to do so caused Bulloch to characterize the emperor's "personal sympathy" as "sheer mockery, when we had been buoyed up with the expectation of something more."[8] Bulloch and the Confederacy's European diplomats would continue their efforts to free the rams throughout the spring and summer.

As March began, Grant was preparing for the coming campaigning season. He planned to force action with the Confederacy's armies by aiming at strategic targets for which the Confederates would have to fight; as he instructed Maj. Gen. George G. Meade, commander of the Army of the Potomac, "Lee's army will be your objective point."[9] The plan would turn the Union's exterior lines to advantage by pressing the Confederacy all around its frontiers.

In the east, Meade's army would try to slide past Lee's right flank to strike at Richmond. In the West, Maj. Gen. William T. Sherman's main army would set out for Atlanta and a smaller force under Nathaniel P. Banks would join Farragut to take Mobile. Unfortunately, Banks's troops were already committed to take Shreveport, Louisiana, supported by Rear Adm. David Porter's fleet on the Red River. Grant could not cancel this presidentially inspired expedition, but he limited its objectives and ordered Banks to be ready to move against Mobile by mid-April 1864.[10]

Although Welles and Fox were undoubtedly gratified by the proposed attack on Mobile, Grant's plan of all-around pressure naturally stressed the Confederacy's land frontiers. The Navy Department, intent on tightening the blockade, wanted more help from the army, and Wilmington was its primary focus.

In early 1863, Wilmington's blockade-running traffic had begun to grow, a trend that received impetus from the near-closure of Charleston in the summer and autumn of 1863. Although Wilmington was farther from the primary blockade-runner haven of the Bahamas than was Charleston, it was closer to the Virginia theater of war, and it was a much more difficult port to blockade. Statistics reflect this difficulty—Wilmington saw more blockade-running in 1863 and 1864 than Charleston saw during the entire war, with a peak of nearly twice that of Charleston in its prime.[11] Although by 1864 the danger of European intervention was receding, Welles still received much abuse over the porosity of the blockade at Wilmington.

Material and tactical improvements in the blockading fleet barely kept up with similar improvements among the runners, and Wilmington remained an almost intractable problem. In January 1864, Welles asked Stanton for army cooperation to shut off Wilmington by taking Fort Caswell, the earthwork that guarded the mouth of the Cape Fear River at Old Inlet.[12] Despite Grant's close association with Porter and his undoubted appreciation for water transport and gunboat support, at that point the general in chief would not detach troops to cooperate with the navy against the Confederate coast. The navy would have to maintain and tighten the blockade without help.

Besides tightening the blockade, Welles hoped to renew the assault on Charleston, but both that effort and the Red River campaign stalled almost before they began. Dahlgren had earlier opined that he would not make another major attempt on Charleston unless he received the ironclads earmarked for Admiral Farragut.[13] When the ships went to Farragut, the Charleston effort succumbed to a combination of Dahlgren's caution and his preoccupation with the death of his son, Ulric, killed in action near Richmond in early March. Meanwhile, on the Red River, the expected spring flood did not materialize. By early April Porter's gunboats were in an uncomfortable position, unable to move either upriver or down.

April brought another rude shock for Welles and Fox, thanks to the much-delayed Confederate ironclad program. The loss of the Confederacy's major shipbuilding ports in 1862 had forced Mallory to regroup, and late in that year the Confederacy laid down eighteen casemated ironclads at "interior" sites such as Richmond, Columbus, Georgia, and Selma, Alabama.[14] Gilbert Elliott and William P. Martin had duly received contracts to build two ironclads in North Carolina, and they began work on one of them in the autumn of 1862 at Edwards Ferry, on the Roanoke River. The work made halting progress, slowed by the common Confederate handicaps of scarcity—insufficient skilled labor, inadequate tools, underdeveloped metalworking industries, and inadequate transportation— but by early 1864 the *Albemarle* was nearing completion.

Slow, mechanically unreliable, and poorly armed and armored, the *Albemarle* was no prize even for a Confederate ironclad. Her combat life against a monitor would probably have been even briefer than the *Atlanta*'s. *Albemarle*'s hole card, however, was her draft. Since she needed only six feet of water in which to float, while the smallest monitors needed more than ten, she was highly unlikely to encounter a Federal ironclad.

Fox had foreseen the need for such shallow water work, and the twenty light draft monitors ordered in the spring of 1863 were intended to fulfill it. John Ericsson had developed a minimalist design with a simple iron hull moved by the simplest possible machinery, with the avowed intent of producing light draft armored ships as quickly as possible. He told Fox that his design could be built in ninety days.[15] Unfortunately for the Union, minimalism did not suit Fox and Stimers. They added so many features and so much delay that by the spring of 1864 none of the light drafts was ready; in fact, in February 1864, none had even been launched. Like their Tippecanoe class counterparts, the light drafts had been delayed by abundance—the abundant industrial resources that encouraged Fox and Stimers's quest for technical perfection.

The Union had controlled North Carolina's sounds since early 1862, but as *Albemarle* neared completion she clearly threatened that control. Fox was seriously concerned, and he poured out his feelings in a letter to Stimers in which he wrote that the "additions, alterations, and improvements" he had approved would be "fatal" to the monitor program. "The first monitor did more than all the others put together," he wrote, "because she was in time."[16] Stimers, who had just had a professional and personal falling out with Ericsson, replied that he was "so very blue that your letter could depress me no further."[17] In early March 1864, Stimers and his assistant Theodore Allen went to Boston to hurry the light draft monitor *Chimo* to completion. There was much left to do, and *Chimo* had not yet been launched when the Confederates commissioned the *Albemarle* on April 16, 1864.

Albemarle promptly made her mark. At 3:30 AM on April 19, the ram engaged two wooden gunboats, the USS *Southfield* and the USS *Miami*, off Plymouth, North Carolina. After a fierce action in which she sank the *Southfield*, the *Albemarle* drove off the *Miami* and two lighter ships. That night and the next morning, she shelled the defending Federal troops, reversing the usual state of affairs that had Confederate troops receiving fire from Union gunboats, and the Confederates captured the town on April 20. Almost simultaneously, the Confederates completed a second North Carolina ironclad, CSS *Neuse*, on the Neuse River at Kinston, North Carolina.

The uproar over the loss of Plymouth shook the Navy Department. Since the light drafts were still not ready, Fox entreated Ericsson to develop a system of pontoons to lift a Passaic class monitor enough to enter the sounds and engage the Confederate ironclad.[18] This scheme came to nothing, and two weeks later the *Albemarle* started for New Bern, North Carolina, to support another Confederate advance. On May 5, four wooden gunboats drove her back to Plymouth after a desperate fight. The Confederate troops were then redeployed to Virginia to meet Grant's 1864 offensive, but the Union could not immediately know this. *Albemarle* continued to threaten Federal control of the sounds, and Fox and Stimers continued to force the completion of a light draft to meet the threat and help retake Plymouth.

By coincidence, May 5 also marked the launching of the *Chimo*, the first of the light draft monitors. Stimers and Allen continued to press the work on her, but by the end of May, it was clear that they had wasted their effort: when equipped for combat, the light draft monitors would be too heavy to float. For Stimers, this was exceptionally bad news. The light drafts had been built to his design, under his supervision, and he was the engineer responsible for a multimillion-dollar mistake.

The mistake combined with the changing circumstances of the war to end Stimers's reign as head of monitor construction. In 1862, Welles and Fox had seen the monitor program as a matter of national survival, and ironclad construction was the U.S. Navy's top priority. Ericsson understood the urgency, and his Passaic class ships balanced technical refinement with quick production. The delays caused by Fox and Stimers's unbalanced stress on technical improvements undermined the urgency of the program. The unfinished ships seemed much less vital in 1864, since even without them the nation was gaining the upper hand over the Confederacy. As the perception of urgency declined, so did Stimers's leverage. Eventually, the delays, cost overruns, and technical failures destroyed confidence in his ability to manage the program at all, and in June 1864 he was removed as general inspector of ironclads and assigned to sea duty as the chief engineer of one of the light draft monitors he had designed. [19]

Stimers's departure left the navy with two problems: the technical matter of ships that would not float, and the political matter of a multimillion-dollar mistake. Stimers's professional demise and an embarrassing congressional investigation covered the political side, but it took an expensive and time-consuming redesign and reconstruction effort to address the technical side. Under Ericsson's direction, the navy altered the light drafts so that they would float and turned several into questionably effective torpedo boats. Only three were completed in time to serve in the war.

May thus brought little relief to the Union in North Carolina. *Neuse* had run aground just below Kinston, and although the Confederates eventually gave up trying to salvage her, the Union had to consider her a threat until the Confederates burned her almost a year later. On May 6, the css *Raleigh* sortied from Wilmington to attack the blockading fleet and enable a blockade-runner to escape. Returning upriver, the ironclad grounded and broke her back, but as with the *Neuse*, it would be some time before the Union could confirm that she was no longer a threat. About the only real encouragement for the Union was the escape of Porter's Mississippi Squadron, floated across the Red River rapids by an ingenious system of dams built by the army. Even that was overshadowed by the total failure of the Red River expedition and the cancellation of the joint operations against Mobile.

As spring turned to summer, the Confederacy seemed to be regaining strength. The Army of the Potomac had begun its campaign on May 4, and Grant's persistent attempts to turn Lee's right flank had resulted in costly battles such as the Wilderness and Cold Harbor. By the end of June the Army of the Potomac again appeared to have been stalemated in front of Richmond, no closer to capturing that city than it had been in 1862, while the Confederates were once again on the march in the Shenandoah Valley. Some historians consider the early summer of 1864, marked as it was by growing war weariness in the North, to be the true "high point of the Confederacy."

The Union navy certainly showed the strain. Operationally, the chronic manpower shortages of 1863 had become acute, and in March 1864 between thirty and forty vessels were tied up awaiting crews. At the same time, shortages of skilled labor delayed the navy's shipbuilding and repair.[20] Poor national planning and ill-conceived legislation had placed the navy in a serious bind.

The ironclad *New Ironsides* illuminates the problem. In June 1864 the ship was preparing to return to the North after sixteen months on blockade duty, and Dahlgren ordered Capt. Stephen C. Rowan to transfer all sailors with more than six months remaining service to other ships of Dahlgren's South Atlantic Blockading Squadron. Rowan protested, but Dahlgren's answer showed the extent of the manpower problem: the squadron was 1,300 men short, and the shortage was getting worse.

The law allowed commanders to hold men thirty days beyond the end of their enlistments, but Dahlgren had already stretched that law: Although it was intended for limited peacetime circumstances, he applied it to every sailor in the squadron whose enlistment had expired. He had also offered a month's furlough to those who would reenlist for one year.[21] Writing that it would be unfair to keep some men over and send back those who still had months to serve, Dahlgren of course prevailed. *New Ironsides* transferred 135 sailors and 33 marines (over 40 percent of the crew) and in return received 121 time-expired men for passage north.[22]

The manpower shortage was not unique to Dahlgren's squadron, and it stemmed from the lack of a balanced national manpower policy.[23] Union conscription was army-oriented—so army-oriented, in fact, that it permitted the army to draft men who were already serving in the navy.[24] Under the law, each town's draft quotas were offset by the number of men who had enlisted, but navy enlistments did not count, and the volunteer bounties paid to soldiers were not matched by bounties for sailors. Between the carrot of bounties and the stick of conscription, mariners joined the army rather than the navy.[25]

The navy worked to solve its problems in several ways. One was to increase recruitment of African Americans. At first the navy limited "contrabands," or former slaves, to the lowest ratings aboard ship. By December 1862, competition from the army for recruits brought a policy change that allowed contrabands to advance and to be paid the same as white sailors. By war's end some 15 percent of Union navy enlistments were African American. Aboard *New Ironsides* herself, black crew members rose from 6.9 percent in April 1863 to over 12 percent in January 1865. [26]

Another way was to recruit Southerners. In 1862, *New Ironsides*'s crew of 545 men included seven white Southerners, about 1.3 percent, and twenty border state men. In 1864 she carried forty-nine white Southerners and three border state men, over 13 percent of her reduced crew of 390. Fifty of the fifty-two appear to have been "white-washed rebs" or "galvanized Yankees"—former prisoners of war who enlisted in exchange for release from prison. [27]

The most important thrust, however, was to change the conscription law. In February 1864 Congress took a first step by approving the transfer of seaman volunteers from the army to the navy. [28] Little appears to have come of this in practice. The regulations effectively gave army commanders control of the process, and they were not likely to give up good men without a struggle. Welles's lobbying finally paid off in mid-1864, when Congress changed the law to give bounties for navy enlistments and to credit navy enlistments to the towns. [29] The change started a stampede for navy recruiting offices.

As Welles recorded, "A desire to enter the Navy to avoid the draft is extensive," and by October 1864, so many landsmen applied for enlistment that the Bureau of Equipment and Recruiting had to turn them away. In those days before centralized recruit training, Welles noted, "There are no means by which to teach landsmen to become sailors except on shipboard," and many of the seamen the navy needed were already in the army. [30] Still, untrained bodies were better than no bodies at all. After reaching their peak in the summer of 1864, by the end of the year the navy's operational manpower difficulties were on the wane.

Conscription also affected the navy's construction program. Shipbuilders had begun lobbying for draft exemption for their workers in 1862, when Ericsson asked Fox to obtain it. "If you cannot, the Country must then look to its soldiers alone for protection for a long time to come." [31] A blanket exemption was not forthcoming, but Welles worked with the War Department to obtain discharges for individuals who had been drafted.

In 1862 this system seemed to balance the army's need for men with the navy's need for skilled workers to build and repair its ships.

The climate quickly changed, as Secretary of War Stanton insisted that the army-oriented conscription act be strictly enforced. By July 1863, Welles told shipbuilders that Stanton "declines to grant exemptions from draft, or to suspend its operations, in any case."[32] Even the revised draft legislation of 1864 never satisfactorily allocated the Union's manpower among army, navy, and war production.

The Confederacy had the same problem of allocation, and similarly never solved it, although the Confederate navy's difficulties quantitatively matched the smaller scale of its operations. Confederate law stated that soldiers who applied for transfer to the navy and whose applications were approved by the secretary of the navy would be transferred.[33] The army naturally dragged its feet, and instead of transferring men to the navy, army commanders preferred to detail them, as soldiers, to support the naval vessels operating in their areas.[34] Similarly, while the Confederate army was not entirely unwilling to detail skilled workmen from the army to industries that supported the army, it generally turned a deaf ear to requests for details to navy-oriented industry.[35]

Mallory had begun to complain as early as 1862, when in August he told his diary, "The President refuses to permit a man to leave the army to work on gunboats or for the navy."[36] In mid-1864, Mallory queried the commanders of his industrial facilities about their manpower shortages, and the major facilities at Charlotte, Atlanta, and Selma asked for 124 skilled metal workers.[37] The equivalent of slightly more than one infantry company, detailed piecemeal from the Confederate army, could have dramatically increased the Confederacy's production of ordnance.

As the Union army's 1864 campaigns seemed stalemated in early summer, the only real signs of hope for the North were at sea, and some of them were not immediately evident. Perhaps most important in the long run, Bulloch's hopes for the Laird ironclads were finally dashed. After several months of negotiation, the British government, "with the law-suit in one hand and the valuation in the other," offered to buy the two ships from Messrs. Bravay. The sale was consummated in May 1864, and the Laird rams no longer threatened to form the nucleus of a Confederate European Squadron that would break the blockade of the Confederacy.[38] Under similar duress, James North's "Scottish Sea Monster" was sold to Denmark in June 1864.[39]

June also marked the elimination of a major irritant, although Welles did not hear the news until early July. As described in chapter 7, the cruiser *Kearsarge* sank the raider *Alabama* off Cherbourg. Semmes escaped, but it was still an important material and psychological victory for the Union. The unsuccessful pursuit of the *Alabama* had long been a favorite target for Welles's critics, and as the secretary told his diary, the victory was "universally and justly conceded a triumph over England as well as over the Rebels."[40]

The loss of the *Alabama* was particularly painful for Bulloch, but he received even more bad news when Napoleon III personally commanded Arman to sell the ironclads and the corvettes he was building to European governments.[41] Arman sold the two ironclads, then known as *Cheops* and *Sphinx* in keeping with their supposed Egyptian destination, to Prussia and Denmark, respectively, but neither could be delivered immediately because Prussia and Denmark were at war. With this setback, Bulloch reluctantly gave up his hopes of breaking the blockade and turned with his usual energy to running it. By mid-September 1864, Bulloch had contracted for fourteen new runners.[42]

July and August brought continued Union discouragement ashore and pinpricks at sea. Gen. Jubal Early's Confederates briefly occupied Silver Spring, Maryland, on the outskirts of Washington itself. The cruiser css *Florida* captured several vessels off the Maryland and Virginia coasts before disappearing again. Sherman seemed to be getting no closer to Atlanta, and Grant's Eastern campaign was mired in the siege of Petersburg. The war seemed to many to be a failure, and in August Lincoln enunciated his own discouragement, writing that it seemed likely that he would not be reelected.

Even before Lincoln expressed his depression, however, the navy was beginning to relieve it. Farragut had planned to attack Mobile after New Orleans, but the Navy Department had instead ordered him to Vicksburg. The admiral's focus from mid-1862 to mid-1863 had thus been on the Mississippi River offensive, with the blockade as second priority and other coastal operations a distant third. On August 1, 1863, Farragut transferred his responsibility for the lower Mississippi to Porter's Mississippi Squadron and went north to consult with Welles and to restore his health. For the remainder of the year, Farragut's absence and Dahlgren's efforts at Charleston meant that offensive operations in the Gulf would have to wait.

Part of the difficulty was that Dahlgren's fruitless siege had kept most of the navy's seagoing ironclads at Charleston, and the Navy Department could not withdraw them without giving the public impression of failure. In 1863, Farragut's lack of ironclads had not been critical. By late January 1864, though, the Confederates at Mobile had completed the css *Tennessee*. Commissioned in mid-February, this ironclad would provide a solid nucleus for pugnacious Adm. Franklin Buchanan's small Confederate naval force. The *Tennessee* shared the propulsion drawbacks of most Confederate ironclads, with the added one of poorly protected steering gear. She also drew too much water to cross the shallows outside Mobile itself, and it took Buchanan until May to get her down Mobile Bay to a position near the forts that protected its entrance. Still, as Farragut again looked to attack Mobile, it was clear that he would need ironclads.

With the loss of New Orleans, Mobile was the Confederacy's primary port on the Gulf Coast, but its distance from Nassau and from the Virginia theater kept its blockade-running traffic low. Most of its traffic passed through Havana, 553 miles away. Mobile counted only seventeen inbound and twenty-seven outbound blockade-runners during 1863, predominantly between April and July 1863 when the Federals depleted their blockading squadron for the Mississippi River campaign. In the first six months of 1864, Mobile accounted for sixteen inbound and fifteen outbound runners; twenty-two of the thirty-one runs occurred from April through June when Farragut was preparing his ships to attack Mobile. [43]

Mobile did not depend solely on Buchanan's squadron for its protection. Forts Morgan and Gaines guarded the main entrance to Mobile Bay, and Fort Powell covered the shallower west entrance. The ship channel passed close under Fort Morgan before making its shallow, winding way some thirty nautical miles up the bay to the city of Mobile itself (chart 9). The hydrographic conditions in Mobile Bay favored torpedo warfare, and the Confederate underwater defenses were correspondingly elaborate. The Confederates sent a torpedo expert, Brig. Gen. Gabriel J. Rains, to the area in August 1863, and he returned in February 1864 for a three-month stay to further bolster its defenses. [44]

Farragut returned to the Western Gulf Blockading Squadron in mid-January 1864 after a five-month absence and promptly wrote to Porter asking for river monitors to "hold the gunboats and rams in check" at Mobile. [45] Counting on the joint expedition that Grant had directed, Farragut began to prepare for an attack in April. Banks's and Porter's difficulties up the Red River delayed the return of Banks's troops, and delay followed

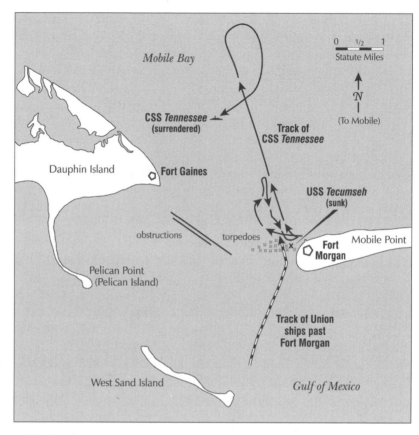

9. *The Battle of Mobile Bay (Redrawn from "Chart showing the entrance of Rear Admiral Farragut into Mobile Bay, 5th of August 1864. Drawn & compiled by Robt. Weir, for Rear Admiral D. G. Farragut, Novr. 1st 1864." Library of Congress Geography and Map Division, Washington* DC, *at http://hdl.loc.gov/loc.gmd/g3972m.cw0110000; and "Approaches to Mobile, Ala. 1864," U.S. Coast Survey, Library of Congress Geography and Map Division, Washington* DC, *at http://hdl.loc.gov/loc.gmd/g3972m.cw0109000.)*

delay until the joint attack on the city of Mobile was finally cancelled. By July 18, Farragut and Maj. Gen. Edward R. S. Canby had decided to forego taking Mobile itself and settle for closing the port. Farragut would take his squadron into the bay and attack the Confederate naval forces, while the army landed on the beaches and invested the forts.[46]

In preparation for the attack, Farragut began to assemble his ships. The admiral received his first ironclad, the new Tippecanoe class monitor

Manhattan, in July, and by August 2 the river monitors *Winnebago* and *Chickasaw* had joined her in a sheltered anchorage off Mobile. *Manhattan*'s sister *Tecumseh* should also have been there, but she was delayed in Pensacola. Farragut grew increasingly irritated, until on August 3 his flag captain wrote that if the *Tecumseh* weren't ready on August 4, the admiral would not wait for her.[47] *Tecumseh* reached Mobile on the evening of August 4 and joined the rest of the fleet in making ready for battle on the 5th.

Farragut had coordinated his attack with the army, and as he later wrote, Brig. Gen. Gordon Granger's landing on Dauphin Island was "up to time."[48] For his own attack, Farragut planned to form his ships into line, lashed together in pairs so that if one were disabled, the other could still propel them both. The four monitors would form a separate line between the wooden ships and Fort Morgan, the closest Confederate fortification. Once inside the bay, the ships would separate to engage the Confederate squadron. Farragut specifically detailed the *Tecumseh* and *Manhattan*, carrying 15-inch guns, to attack the ironclad *Tennessee*.[49]

Farragut knew that the Confederates had blocked most of the channel with obstructions and torpedoes. He received intelligence reports from the army and obtained his own from Confederate deserters and civilians, but he also reconnoitered the bay. A raiding party from the uss *Oneida* captured six Confederates on July 22, and on July 25, Farragut's flag lieutenant, J. C. Watson, led one of several boat expeditions to investigate the harbor entrance. Over the next week, Watson and his men buoyed the outer channel and marked the outer limits of the Confederate mine-field.[50] On August 3, they returned at night to clear as many torpedoes as possible.[51] Despite all this activity, rough weather hindered Federal reconnaissance, and flag captain Percival Drayton wrote on August 1 that it "would not be a bad thing to get also an idea of the obstructions."[52]

Farragut's fleet entered Mobile Bay shortly after 6 AM on August 5. His fourteen wooden ships, lashed together in pairs, formed one column, and the four monitors formed the other. *Tecumseh*, leading the line of armored ships, commenced the action shortly before 7 AM by firing on Fort Morgan. Confederate admiral Franklin Buchanan, in the ironclad ram *Tennessee*, led his squadron out to meet the Federals, and the *Tecumseh* turned to engage the ram. Almost immediately the monitor struck a mine and sank within seconds. This unmistakable evidence of torpedoes caused the commanding officer of the *Brooklyn*, leading the line of wooden ships, to hesitate. In planning the attack, Farragut's captains had dissuaded him from leading the line due to the perceived risk of torpedoes, but in this extremity he took simple, forthright action. Directing his flagship *Hartford* to haul out to starboard and pass the *Brooklyn*, his "Damn the torpedoes!" assumption of leadership restored the momentum of the Federal attack. In the general action that followed, the monitors *Manhattan* and *Chickasaw* pounded the *Tennessee* until the ram, unable to steer, surrendered, and two of the other three Confederate vessels were captured or sunk.[53]

Although the victory would not be complete until the Confederate forts were taken, by August 8 only Fort Morgan remained in Southern hands. Farragut's ships assisted the army by bombarding Morgan for two weeks before the Confederate garrison surrendered on August 23. The Union's uncontested mastery of Mobile Bay closed the South's last major port on the Gulf Coast, and the city of Mobile, left to wither, eventually fell in the last weeks of the war. The blockade-running trade shifted west to Texas, but the inefficiencies of trying to move cargo to and from the Texas ports rendered this route much less desirable for the Confederates.[54]

By the time the good news of Mobile reached the Navy Department, so had reports of another Confederate cruiser. css *Tallahassee* ran the blockade out of Wilmington on August 6 and captured her first prize off New England on August 11. Six more followed that day. By August 12 the hunt was up, but *Tallahassee* had already taken thirteen vessels.[55] Sixteen U.S. ships had joined the chase by August 15. Welles anticipated that the raider would try to refuel in Halifax, Nova Scotia, and on August 14 he directed the uss *San Jacinto* to guard that port. On August 18 he discovered that the *San Jacinto* had not sailed, and on the same day the *Tallahassee* entered Halifax without opposition, with thirty prizes to her credit.[56] Peremptory orders sent uss *Pontoosuc* after her, but *Tallahassee* departed just in time, so hastily and opportunely that Welles suspected collusion with the British authorities.[57]

By the time *Tallahassee* returned to Wilmington on August 25, she had taken thirty-one prizes and demonstrated once again that finding a raider at sea, even with many pursuers in a very limited area, required tremendous luck. She had also invited unwanted attention to Wilmington, which manifested itself in the increased size of the blockading fleet. Clerk John B. Jones wrote that the raider's presence had "caused the loss of one of our blockade-runners, worth more than all the vessels destroyed by the *Tallahassee*, and the port is now guarded by such an additional number of blockaders that it is with difficulty our steamers can get in with supplies."[58] Both General Lee and Maj. Gen. W. C. Whiting, the commander of Wilmington's defenses, suggested that Wilmington would be more valuable to the Confederacy as a supply port than as a base for commerce raiders, but to no avail.[59] Mallory persisted in his policy, and *Tallahassee* and another raider, css *Chickamauga*, both cruised from Wilmington later that autumn.[60]

By mid-September, Lincoln had become more optimistic than he had been in August. Farragut's victory at Mobile was good for the administration, and Sherman's September 3 announcement that "Atlanta is ours, and fairly won" was even better. The Confederates had withdrawn from the vicinity of Washington DC, and after an initially ineffectual pursuit, Grant put Maj. Gen. Philip Sheridan in command and told him to follow the Confederates to the death. Sheridan put paid to Jubal Early's Confederate force in the battles of Winchester, in mid-September, and Cedar Creek, in mid-October. By November, Union successes in battle had derailed the Confederacy's political strategy of ending the war by promoting Lincoln's electoral defeat.

For the navy, the capture of Mobile Bay left Wilmington as the only major port still in Confederate hands. Welles's January 1864 proposal to take Fort Caswell was but one of a series; closing Wilmington had been a navy objective since early 1862, but a joint expedition was necessary, and Welles and Fox could not persuade the army to participate.[61] This situation changed in 1864 when, at the end of August, Grant agreed to provide troops for a combined expedition. *Tallahassee*'s depredations probably gave more force to Welles's arguments, but Grant also guessed what the closure of Wilmington would mean to Lee's supply situation.[62] Although Grant could not know it, Lee agreed with his assessment of Wilmington's importance to the Army of Northern Virginia.[63]

On September 5, 1864, Welles put the expedition in motion when he ordered Farragut to command the North Atlantic Blockading Squadron. His letter crossed one from Farragut, however, in which the admiral requested leave because his health was giving way. When he learned of Farragut's request, Welles chose David D. Porter to lead the fleet in its attack on Wilmington.

While Porter was traveling from the Mississippi to take up his new command, Cdr. Napoleon Collins of the uss *Wachusett* relieved Welles of another burden. The css *Florida* had escaped from Brest, France, in February 1864 and had been operating with modest success in the North Atlantic. She took several prizes off the Delaware Capes in early July, coaled in Tenerife in the Canary Islands in early August, and made her way to Bahia, Brazil. When she arrived on October 4, 1864, she found the *Wachusett* already at anchor.

Collins, *Wachusett*'s captain, had served under and admired the impetuous Wilkes, and he remembered Wilkes's instructions to take the *Alabama* wherever he found her "unless under the guns of a fort strong enough to protect her." Moreover, the U.S. ambassador to Brazil told Collins's officers that he had directed other commanding officers to attack Confederate cruisers in any Brazilian port and that he would "make it all right with Brazil."[64] With this background, Collins decided to capture the *Florida* "for the public good." At 3:00 AM on October 7, *Wachusett* rammed the *Florida*, captured her, and towed her to sea in what the Confederates denounced as an "assassination." This flagrant violation of Brazilian neutrality, of course, caused a major international incident. Secretary of State Seward disavowed Collins's action and ordered that the *Florida* be returned to Brazil, but before that could happen, she sank at her moorings at Newport News. A postwar twenty-one gun salute satisfied Brazilian honor, and Welles undoubtedly considered the *Florida* cheap at the price.[65]

The eventful month of October continued with the similarly cheap destruction of the *Albemarle*. Her appearance in the North Carolina sounds had precipitated a matching crisis in the U.S. Navy's shipbuilding program, and for the reasons noted above, there would be no light draft ironclads available to oppose her in the foreseeable future. Into this atmosphere came Lt. William B. Cushing, a young Naval Academy graduate who had already earned a reputation as a daredevil for his reconnaissances into Confederate territory. In July he persuaded Admiral Lee and Secretary Welles to approve an expedition against the *Albemarle*.[66] Cushing went to New York, where he bought two small steam-driven boats and converted them to carry spar torpedoes. On the way back South, one of the boats ran aground in Virginia and was burned to prevent its capture by the Confederates, but Cushing reached North Carolina safely with the second boat on October 24, 1864.

Cushing and his volunteer crew started up the Roanoke River on October 26, but the launch grounded and Cushing postponed the expedition. The next evening, the expedition slipped past the Confederate pickets and made it almost to the *Albemarle* before being sighted. As the Confederates responded to the alarm with small arms fire, Cushing discovered that they had placed a boom of logs around the ironclad to protect her from torpedo boats. Coolly circling to gain speed, he hit the log barrier and crossed it. Once inside, he dropped the torpedo into the water and detonated it just as *Albemarle* fired her first heavy gun. The combination of the blast and the gunfire sank the launch, but the torpedo sank the *Albemarle*. Of the fifteen men in the attacking party, only Cushing and one other escaped death or capture. [67] With the *Albemarle* gone, the Union immediately attacked Plymouth, recapturing it on October 31, 1864. Federal control over the North Carolina sounds had been emphatically reasserted, but to Fox's chagrin, no monitors, light draft or otherwise, had been involved.

As Collins was bringing the captured *Florida* to the United States in mid-October, her place was being taken by the ship that would be the last Confederate cruiser. For some time, Bulloch's shortage of funds had prevented him from augmenting the raiding force, but the forced sale of the Laird ironclads in mid-1864 yielded enough to allow Bulloch to replace the *Alabama*. Money, however, was not the only obstacle. As Bulloch wrote, the British government's increasingly stringent enforcement of the Foreign Enlistment Act had made it very difficult to get a British subject "fit for the trust" to agree to serve as the ship's "ostensible owner," but ship and subject both came to Bulloch's hand in mid-September 1864. [68]

Bulloch lost no time in embarking again on the familiar process of covert dispatch, rendezvous, and arming, and the merchant steamer *Sea King*, commissioned as the css *Shenandoah* under Lt. James I. Waddell, left European waters in late October. Psychology played a major role in dispatching the *Shenandoah*—with a raider operating, no one could say that the Confederate flag had been driven from the sea. Psychology also appears to have played a major role in Bulloch's and Waddell's choice of targets. Destroying the Pacific whaling fleet would have little effect on the Union war effort, but the losses would disproportionately punish New England shipowners. [69]

As the *Shenandoah* headed for the Pacific, Porter began to assemble in Hampton Roads the ships he would need for the Wilmington expedition. His objective was Fort Fisher, an earthwork fortification located near the tip of the peninsula that formed the eastern bank of the Cape Fear River. In 1862, when the navy had begun its planning, Fort Caswell on the mainland had been the objective and Fort Fisher was an afterthought. Col.

William Lamb, CSA, had changed that in two busy years as commander of Fort Fisher.

In 1864, Fort Fisher's "sea face" stretched three-quarters of a mile north from the Mound Battery to the northeast bastion, where the "land face" turned west to cross the spit. A detached work, Battery Buchanan, covered the fort's rear and the Cape Fear River. In December 1864 the fort mounted twenty-four guns on the sea face and twenty on the land face.[70]

Divided command bedeviled the Fort Fisher expedition as it had so many others. Porter commanded the navy component and Grant assigned Maj. Gen. Godfrey Weitzel to command the army component. The military department in which Fort Fisher lay, however, belonged to Maj. Gen. Benjamin F. Butler, who saw a chance for glory and insisted upon taking personal charge.

Butler formed the idea that he could flatten the fort by exploding a ship filled with gunpowder near it. Porter detailed the USS *Louisiana*, and preparing the ship and loading her with over two hundred tons of powder further delayed the expedition. Butler finally had his force of transports and supply ships ready to sail on December 9, but storms delayed it until December 14. Meanwhile, the navy ships gathered off Beaufort, North Carolina.[71] The Confederates knew the Federals were coming and prepared as best they could; although Porter blamed "too many leaky people" for the lack of surprise, Wilmington was the only conceivable Confederate target for so large an armada.[72]

The fleet arrived twenty miles off New Inlet on December 19, but Butler's troops were again delayed, this time because they had run out of food, water, and coal. The fleet weathered a violent gale without loss, and fleet and transports finally rendezvoused off New Inlet on December 24.

A volunteer crew ran the powder boat ashore the night of December 23 and exploded it, but the effect was so small that the Confederates thought a blockader's boiler had blown up.[73] On December 24, Porter's ships began to bombard the fort. Four monitors and *New Ironsides* formed the inmost line, and they opened fire early in the afternoon. Five hours of shelling bore little fruit, and only a few transports had arrived. The landing was rescheduled for Christmas Day.

The bombardment resumed on Christmas morning, with the ships firing slowly, "only sufficient to amuse the enemy while the army landed." Butler put his troops ashore some four miles up the spit and advanced south toward the fort, but soon decided that his force was too weak to capture it. He took most of the men and departed for Hampton Roads, leaving some seven hundred soldiers to be rescued by the navy on December 27. The fleet arrived back at Beaufort on December 29.

It soon became clear that the naval bombardment, which had seemed so impressive, had been ineffectual. In fact, the garrison had suffered only sixty-four casualties, compared with eighty-three for the navy, and half of those eighty-three navy casualties came from the bursting of the fleet's own Parrott guns. Lamb and his men quickly remounted three of the four guns dismounted by the Federal bombardment and repaired the fort's earthworks.

Porter was highly displeased at the failure, and Grant was hardly less so, in part because the headstrong Butler had ignored Grant's explicit instructions not to withdraw if he obtained a foothold. Grant relieved Butler, placed Maj. Gen. Alfred H. Terry in command, and sent the same troops back to try again.[74] Porter, meanwhile, refined his bombardment plans to improve their effectiveness. For the second try, he would station his ships closer to the fort and prohibit the sort of shooting at symbolic targets, such as flagstaffs, that had diverted the fleet's gunnery during the first attack. Porter also formed a landing force of seamen and marines to assist the soldiers.

The troops started out on January 6, 1865, but another heavy gale delayed the operation. The troops again landed several miles up the spit and moved south, while the naval bombardment that opened on the morning of January 13 concentrated on the landward defenses. Thanks to Porter's recalibration of his captains, the fort suffered much more heavily than it had in December. The wooden ships withdrew at dusk, but the ironclads kept up an effective harassing fire all night. By 2:00 AM on January 14, Terry's troops were only two miles from the fort.

The bombardment resumed at dawn. The primary target was the fort, but the ships also engaged a Confederate gunboat in the Cape Fear River and forced it to withdraw. After landing its artillery, the army moved down the river side of the peninsula to within a mile of the fort. Every attempt to stop the Federals with artillery "[drew] upon the gunners the fury of the fleet," and by dusk only three or four guns remained intact on the land face.[75] Gen. Braxton Bragg, in charge of Wilmington's defense, refused to counterattack despite Lamb's pleas.

Late the next morning, Porter landed 1,600 sailors and 400 marines to attack the seaward side of the fort while the army attacked the land side. The sailors and marines charged the fort at 3:00 PM, but the Confederates drove them back in less than half an hour. Although the navy assault failed, it allowed the army to gain a foothold on the northwest corner of the fort's land face. In that area only one heavy gun had survived the three days of bombardment.[76]

Once the troops were inside, naval gunfire supported them as they advanced against stubborn Confederate resistance. Besides destroying the fort's artillery and driving off a transport carrying Confederate reinforcements, the ironclads supported the army directly, firing on individual traverses with "deadly precision." Lamb wrote, "Just as the tide of battle seemed to have turned in our favor the remorseless fleet came to the rescue."[77] In the evening the remaining defenders withdrew toward Battery Buchanan, only to find that the battery's Confederate navy garrison had spiked the guns, taken the boats, and departed. The surrender of Battery Buchanan at about 10:00 PM on January 15 meant the end of large-scale blockade-running east of the Mississippi.

Events in Georgia had not waited. After capturing Atlanta on September 2, Sherman decided to strike for Savannah. After much persuasion, Grant approved Sherman's plan, and on November 16, the army left Atlanta. By early December Sherman's columns were paralleling the Ogeechee River, and they reached Savannah's defenses on December 9. As he approached Savannah, Sherman arranged for resupply by sea, arrangements that were especially critical in view of the shortage of forage for his animals. On December 13 Sherman's troops bypassed Savannah to capture *Montauk*'s old adversary, Fort McAllister on the Ogeechee, and open communications with Dahlgren's South Atlantic Blockading Squadron.

Savannah boasted the ironclad *Savannah*, the ironclad floating battery *Georgia*, and two smaller vessels among its naval defenses. Since the ships could do little against Sherman's army, on December 14, Secretary Mallory told Flag Officer W. W. Hunter to fight his way to Charleston if Savannah fell. Three days later, the chief of the Office of Orders and Detail reiterated Mallory's orders, saying it would be better "for the vessels, for the navy, for our cause and country," to fight and lose than to have the ships "tamely surrendered to the enemy or destroyed by their own officers."[78] Hunter tried to clear the Confederates' own torpedoes from the harbor, but when he could not, he elected to destroy his ships instead of trying to fight or sweep his way out. Self-destruction was an all-too-common story for the Confederacy; as one author noted, "There is good reason to believe that the Confederate navy would have served the nation better had it been less professional in its outlook and continued each fight until the last ship had been sunk."[79] Sherman took Savannah on December 21, 1864, and began refitting his army there for the spring campaign.

As the Union's hopes rose, the Confederacy's fell, but Butler's initial failure at Fort Fisher helped to counterbalance Sherman's success at Savannah. December 1864 provided another glimmer of hope for the Confederacy, this time concerning ironclads. The Confederates, under duress, had sold the French-built *Cheops* and *Sphinx* to Prussia and Denmark in July 1864. The conclusion of the Prusso-Danish War left the Danes with no particular need for an ironclad, and when the *Sphinx* arrived in Copenhagen in November 1864, she was very much a white elephant. Bulloch had maintained his contacts with the French shipbuilder Lucien Arman for just such an eventuality. When the Danes manifested a willingness to sell the ship back to Arman, Bulloch jumped at the chance to retrieve the Confederacy's fortunes with a ship that was beyond the reach of either the British or French governments.

By mid-December 1864 the financial arrangements were completed, and Bulloch turned his attention to gathering a crew and essential stores. Capt. Thomas Jefferson Page, CSN, joined the ship in Copenhagen, and the ironclad, carrying a temporary crew and the equally temporary name *Olinde*, left Copenhagen on January 7, 1865. Bulloch's windfall ironclad received her Confederate crew from the blockade-runner *City of Richmond* off Quiberon Bay on January 24 and was commissioned as CSS *Stonewall*.[80]

Only Bulloch's usual superb timing had allowed him to repurchase the vessel. Had she become available much sooner or any later, he would not have had the funds to buy her. The military and political defeats of 1864 had eroded the Confederacy's ability to sell its bonds, and the money raised by the Erlanger Loan was exhausted. The Confederates had earlier "sold" ships under construction as a ploy to evade British and French scrutiny, but by mid-1864, the impact of tighter European neutrality policies led the Confederates to sell ships bona fide. Although the proceeds gave Bulloch's finances a boost, much of the money had to be used in autumn 1864 to pay the interest on the Erlanger bonds and to cover outstanding purchases made for the Confederate army.[81] Besides the *Sphinx*, the ironclad money allowed Bulloch to contract in September 1864 for two iron-hulled twin-screw vessels, intended for conversion into gunboats to defend Wilmington. *Ajax* left the William Denny yard at

Dumbarton on January 12, 1865, headed for Wilmington via Ireland, the Bahamas, and Bermuda, but the fall of Fort Fisher apparently caused her merchant captain to turn back.[82] Her sister *Hercules* was not completed during the war.[83]

The Confederacy's financial straits were evident at home, too, and the flow of cotton could not yield enough foreign exchange to meet the Confederacy's obligations. Clerk Jones recorded in early January 1865 that the 1865 budget for the War Department alone was $670 million, with "a deficiency of $400 million," and a month later he noted that the Confederacy's debt was actually $400 million more than had been estimated.[84] In December 1864, Mallory told Bulloch to "aid the Treasury" whenever he could.[85] In late January 1865 the Confederate Congress officially and secretly directed the navy to transfer £250,000 to the Treasury Department, but Bulloch had already bought back his ironclad.[86] By spring 1865, Bulloch had suspended all Confederate navy purchasing to devote the money to the "general and pressing claims upon the Treasury."[87]

At about the same time, in late January, the Confederate James River Squadron made its only significant attempt to attack the Federals. The James River had been obstructed by one side or both since 1862, but on January 23, 1865, a freshet washed away some of the obstructions while the monitor *Onondaga* was the only Union ironclad in the James. The Confederates sent three ironclads downriver that evening, and Cdr. William A. Parker, USN, disobeyed orders and withdrew the *Onondaga* downstream. One Confederate ironclad passed the obstructions, but the other two grounded above them and the third ship rejoined them instead of continuing the attack.

About 11:00 AM the next day, the *Onondaga* returned and opened fire at long range with her 15-inch guns. She caused some damage before the Confederates refloated their ships on the rising tide and retired. Although the raid fizzled out, the threat to Grant's supply base at City Point had thoroughly alarmed the Union army high command.[88] Grant demanded action from Parker, telling him that it would be "better to obstruct the channel with sunken gunboats" than to let the Confederates reach City Point, but fast response was not Parker's strong suit, and Grant immediately went over Parker's head.[89] When the general in chief told Fox and Welles that Parker "seem[ed] helpless," they reacted much more rapidly.[90] By the evening of January 24, Welles had fired Parker and directed the commandant of the Norfolk Naval Station to "send all the ironclads within your reach immediately up James River."[91] Four Union ironclads, including *New Ironsides*, were on station at City Point by the 26th, and the Confederates did not renew their challenge. It was the Richmond ironclads' last sortie.

During the spring, the Confederacy's situation became more fragile by the day. For 1865, Grant planned to continue the same sort of all-around pressure that he had envisioned in 1864. He himself would remain with Meade's Army of the Potomac to maintain the pressure on Richmond and Petersburg. Sherman would march north through the Carolinas, and Maj. Gen. John M. Schofield's corps, detached from the army in the west, would join the drive through North Carolina to meet Sherman. Canby would move from New Orleans to take the city of Mobile, but would then strike for Selma and Montgomery, Alabama, seat of much of the Confederacy's remaining heavy industry, and move on to Columbus and Macon, Georgia.

Sherman left Savannah on January 19, 1865. Opening his march with feints toward Augusta, Georgia, and Charleston, he actually moved to take Columbia, South Carolina, supported by the navy's control of the rivers.[92] Sherman's troops cut Charleston's communications, and the Confederate defenders evacuated the city on February 18. Dahlgren's force entered the harbor that day, moving carefully for fear of the torpedoes that had sunk the monitor *Patapsco* in January. The Union navy's long campaign against the "Cradle of the Rebellion" was over.

Charleston had long since been overshadowed as a cotton shipping port, but with Wilmington gone, every bale counted, and five ships had run out of Charleston in January and seven in February. The loss of Charleston changed the Confederate outlook from bleak to hopeless. The nearly complete cessation of cotton exports definitively ruined the South's credit and rapidly placed its agents in Europe in "great financial straits."[93]

Thomas J. Page, the commanding officer of the ram *Stonewall*, was thus operating on a shoestring. Setting out for North America after her commissioning, the ram entered Ferrol, Spain, on February 2, 1865. Repairs to leaky rudder fittings took some time, and the U.S. steamers *Niagara* and *Sacramento* soon arrived to watch the port. Captain Page consulted with Confederate authorities in Paris, who determined that "no possible effort that could be made from Europe should be abandoned," and the *Stonewall* left Ferrol on March 24.[94] Page was convinced that the U.S. ships would attack him, but they were as worried about the ironclad as

Page was worried about them, and the Confederate vessel proceeded to Lisbon unmolested by the U.S. Navy.[95] Leaving Lisbon on March 27, Page set course to attack the Union base at Port Royal.[96]

The Confederates' increasing financial difficulties in Europe paralleled their increasing military difficulties at home. Gen. Joseph E. Johnston had taken command in the Carolinas in late February, but he could conjure no defensive miracle against Sherman's determined pressure. Under the circumstances, Mallory directed Catesby Jones to investigate moving the machinery of the Selma works. In doing so, Jones wrote, "Our machinery is very heavy and there is a great deal of it. Under favorable circumstances it would require weeks to remove it."[97] From the tone of the letter, Jones was also at a loss as to where the machinery should go. The noose had continued to tighten, and by mid-March the remaining strength of the Confederacy lay between Sherman's army in North Carolina and Meade's army in Virginia.

Lee had not given up, and on March 25, he attacked the Union lines around Petersburg. Lee hoped to give himself some breathing room, but the attack failed, and Grant took advantage of the Confederate repulse to begin an offensive move of his own.

In May 1864, the Confederate Congress had secretly given President Davis the authority to move the capital if "the public exigencies shall require."[98] Those "exigencies" came suddenly on April 1, 1865, when Sheridan's attack at Five Forks turned the flank of the Confederate defenses around Richmond and Petersburg. Lee began to retreat toward Lynchburg, Virginia, hoping to escape Grant and join Johnston's army, and Davis hastily departed Richmond for Danville, Virginia, on April 2. Escorted by midshipmen from the Confederate Naval Academy, the Confederate archives and treasury left the city on April 3. On the same day, Adm. Raphael Semmes destroyed the ironclads of the Confederate James River Squadron, and Brig. Gen. James H. Wilson's Federal cavalry destroyed the Selma works.[99]

While Grant and Sherman were closing the vise, the navy's war was winding down. The process of retrenchment had begun after the fall of Charleston, when it became evident that Confederate commerce had been extinguished. In late February, Welles directed his commanders to reduce expenses, and he began to decommission the ships that were not needed to support the army.[100] An example was the *Stettin*, then blockading St. Helena Sound. Ordered north, she left station on March 22, 1865, for a passage that brought her to Boston on March 29. After unloading ordnance stores and powder at anchor, the ship moved alongside a pier at the Charlestown Navy Yard and the crew transferred to the receiving ship *Ohio,* where they lived for the few days needed to empty *Stettin* of her stores. On April 6, 1865, John M. Butler made the final entry in *Stettin*'s log, noting, "Hauled down the Ensign and pennant and put the ship out of commission."[101]

Hundreds of other vessels followed a similar course as the Confederacy's dissolution became clear even to the most die-hard Southerner. Succumbing finally to Federal pursuit, Lee surrendered the Army of Northern Virginia at Appomattox on April 9, 1865, and Johnston negotiated an armistice with Sherman on April 18. In the interim Lincoln had been assassinated and Andrew Johnson had become president. Sherman's armistice with Johnston was repudiated, and on April 26 Johnston surrendered on the same terms as Lee. Jefferson Davis himself was captured on May 10, and although it took some time before the last Confederate forces surrendered, Johnson lifted the blockade on June 23, 1865. By July 1865 the blockading forces had dropped from January's 471 ships to about 30. On August 14, 1865, the Mississippi River command was discontinued, and by the end of 1865, the improvised wartime navy was practically gone, with 340 vessels already sold out of the service and many others decommissioned. Most of the wartime volunteers left the service as well.[102]

The collapse of the Confederacy left the *Stonewall* in an anomalous position. The Federals had tracked the vessel's progress across the Atlantic as best they could, receiving information that became more current as the ram approached the Western Hemisphere. Word of the *Stonewall*'s April 1 departure from Tenerife reached the Navy Department on April 28, and Welles immediately ordered the Navy Yard commandants to full defensive readiness.[103] *Stonewall* arrived at Nassau on May 6, and this news reached the Navy Department on May 12.[104] The ram reached Havana on May 11, and Capt. Charles S. Boggs of the uss *Connecticut* found her there on May 15. On the 17th, Boggs recommended to Captain Page, an old acquaintance, that Page surrender the *Stonewall*.[105] Page politely refused, but at the same time, he knew that he could not meet the odds against him, "even if I believed that I had a Government and a country to fight for." Page pledged the ship to the Spanish governor general in return for enough money to pay his crew's wages, and *Stonewall* was decommissioned on May 19, 1865.[106]

The Confederacy's collapse also left the blockade-running firms high and dry. Their ships were of little value for peacetime commerce, and demand for the military goods and luxury imports that were their stock in trade had dropped precipitously.[107] Since the high wartime price of cotton had been primarily due to the cost of transportation through the blockade, any cotton they had on hand declined sharply in value as well— the average specie price per bale in Liverpool fell from about $215 in 1864 to $153 in 1865.[108] Although several firms returned a considerable aggregate profit to their shareholders, all lost money at the end of the war.[109] Hardest hit was Fraser, Trenholm, which had wagered its future upon Confederate success. Had the Confederacy maintained its independence, the firm would have dominated postwar Southern trade. But with Confederate failure, Fraser, Trenholm's holdings in Confederate obligations, securities, cotton certificates, and goodwill became worthless. After a two-year struggle, the firm finally declared bankruptcy in May 1867.[110]

The last organized Confederate unit was the raider *Shenandoah*, which had been engaged in destroying the U.S. whaling fleet in the North Pacific Ocean. On August 2, 1865, Waddell learned authoritatively from a British vessel that the war was over. Fearing the consequences of capture by the United States, he determined to disarm his vessel and return to England. A masterful feat of seamanship brought him nonstop to Liverpool on November 6, where he hauled down the last Confederate ensign and turned his ship over to British authorities. The war at sea had ended.

CHAPTER NINE

Winners and Losers

The American Civil War ended in the military and naval defeat of the Confederacy and its dissolution as a nation, but underneath that bald statement there is ample room for nuance. Assessing the operations, strategies, technologies, and organizations of the combatants helps to illuminate the paradoxes of America's bloodiest war, in which the Napoleonic art of war coexisted with the industrialized version. The navies similarly juxtaposed new and old elements, with similarly mixed results—the new began to push out the old, only to find that the old sometimes pushed back with just as much vigor.

Operationally, the Civil War at sea looked much like the American Revolution and the War of 1812. In each case the dominant naval power enjoyed great freedom of action and hampered its enemy's war-making by blockade. In each case the dominant power could strike the other's seacoast almost at will. In each case, if the dominant power's armies maintained contact with the coast, they could be supplied, supported, or evacuated, as required. In each case the weaker naval power attempted to hamstring the stronger by commerce raiding and to protect its own coastline passively. In each case the weaker power failed.

In 1861, Welles had enunciated three major concepts for Federal naval strategy: blockading Southern ports, attacking the Southern coast, and suppressing Southern attacks on Union commerce. With the addition of opening the Mississippi River, transferred from army to navy responsibility in 1862, the Federals maintained their focus on these concepts throughout the war. Although hindsight shows many areas that could have been improved, the Union balanced its naval resources to embody all four strategic concepts in successful campaigns.

First, despite its undoubted porosity, the blockade worked, and its success was the single most salient feature of the naval war. Never airtight, the blockade was constricting enough that the South was constantly gasping for economic breath. It beggared the Confederate government by reducing its foreign exchange and increasing the price of its imports. It disrupted Southern coastwise trade, forcing the Confederates to rely on their inadequate rail net, and then helped to overload and ruin the Southern railroads by forcing the South to transport its cotton to seaports far from the cotton belt. It limited vital imports: the rails and rolling stock the South needed to maintain its railroads, the machinery it needed to be industrially self-sufficient, and the armor plate and steam engines it needed to challenge the blockading fleets.

In starving the South of foreign exchange, the blockade exerted both direct and indirect effects. Directly, lack of foreign exchange hampered the Confederacy's ability to purchase war materials. Indirectly, the Confederacy supported considerably less of its war effort from taxation than did the Union, and in the absence of specie, its paper money inflated at a correspondingly greater rate.[1] Runaway inflation led to hardship for the families of Confederate soldiers, hardship that by 1864 contributed significantly to rising Confederate desertion rates.[2] To indulge in counterfactual speculation, without the blockade, inflation might have been better kept in check and fewer Confederate soldiers might have deserted, leading to a smaller Union preponderance in the land campaigns of 1864–65.

Second, despite the lack of Normandy- or Inchon-style landings, the coastal campaign worked. The Union's amphibious efforts kept the Confederates on edge, and even after Lee reorganized Confederate coastal defense, the threat of Union incursions impelled local authorities to hoard ordnance and men that might have bolstered the Confederacy's field armies. Besides their role in capturing supply points and blockade bases, naval forces allowed the Union to hold coastal areas that would otherwise have required an inordinate number of troops. Raids, such as the Union navy's continuing strikes against coastal salt works, denied critical resources to the Confederates and kept them off balance.

Third, despite the well-publicized exploits and escapes of the Confederate cruisers, the commerce protection campaign worked. Shipping losses did not force the United States to make peace or to weaken the blockading squadrons appreciably in favor of chasing the raiders. Commerce protection encompassed considerably more than pursuit, and convoys, diplomatic pressure, and the blockade itself all combined to ensure that Confederates' commerce raiding neither curtailed the Union's overseas commerce nor hampered its war effort.

Finally, the Mississippi River campaign worked. Again, the impact of Union control was twofold: the Union gained the use of the great river system, both for commerce and for military purposes, and denied it to the Confederacy. Union control of the Mississippi kept the Confederates from fully exploiting the resources and the ports of the trans-Mississippi states when they were most needed.

Mallory never enunciated his strategic objectives as clearly as Welles did, but they encompassed protecting the Confederate coast, breaking the blockade, and destroying Union commerce. To implement his key strategic decisions, Mallory depended heavily upon technology. Although the Confederacy's industrial weakness hampered him at every turn, the Confederacy still commenced some fifty ironclads and completed twenty-four of them. "Industrial determinism" is insufficient to explain Confederate failure.

The defense-in-depth strategy implemented by Robert E. Lee proved reasonably successful in delaying or deterring Union amphibious operations. Yet the Confederate navy's contribution to that defense was overshadowed by that of the army. The defenders relied primarily upon obstructions, torpedoes, and forts, not ironclads, to keep the Union navy out of Charleston, Richmond, Savannah, and Wilmington, and those obstructions and forts were predominantly the army's. Even underwater warfare was a joint army-navy responsibility. Given what the Confederate navy actually accomplished with its ironclads, Beauregard may not have been far off in his low estimate of their value relative to their cost.

The lack of useful ironclads contributed to the failure of Mallory's second strategic objective, that of breaking the blockade. Although several Confederate ironclads sortied at different times to try to raise the blockade or to cover the escape of blockade runners, lack of seaworthiness and slow speed made them ineffective. Foreign-built ironclads might have done more, but the only one to fly the Confederate flag inspired little confidence even in her own commander.

That left commerce raiding, which had the dual objectives of weakening the blockade and of applying pressure to the Union to end the war. The Confederacy's material weaknesses came again into play here, since more raiders might have caused the diversion of more Union cruisers from the blockade. More importantly, however, Welles's counterstrategy was effective. In reply, the Confederates do not appear to have devised anything beyond "more of the same."

Technologies also developed winners and losers. A major winner was steam propulsion, as the Civil War marked the maturity and ubiquity of steam. Marine steam engines, largely experimental only twenty years earlier, had become useful and reliable. Steam swept away operational and tactical constraints that had governed naval operations for centuries, but at the same time steam imposed new restrictions of its own. The new constraints were predominantly those of logistics, of fuel supply and machinery repair, and it took time to adjust to them. Managing the extensive logistics system needed to support a steam-powered fleet demanded everything that the U.S. Navy's shore establishment could give. Although the Union's system had become reasonably effective by 1863, it lacked much in efficiency and required constant effort to overcome the "friction" of war. The Confederates, with a smaller fleet but even fewer resources in proportion, seemed less able to support their operating forces.

Two other infant technologies succeeded in reaching adolescence, although by the end of the war they were still far from being mature. One was armor, which began the leapfrog race it would run with ordnance for the next eight decades. The other technology, that of underwater ordnance, was strategically more significant. The mines and obstructions that the Confederates learned to build kept the Union navy at bay during the last two years of the war.

In this area, the Confederates clearly took better advantage of their resources than the Federals, and the organizational contrast is especially sharp. In general, Welles's Navy Department was better organized to deal with technology than was Mallory's. The Confederacy, however, institutionalized torpedo warfare in several secret organizations, including the Army Torpedo Bureau and the Naval Submarine Battery Service. The Federals never similarly institutionalized their mine countermeasures efforts; instead of providing "lessons learned," centralized guidance, or standardized equipment, the Union navy left its commanders on their own.[3]

Assessing the civilian leadership of the two services, the North comes off as the winner. Mallory made less effective use of the resources available to him than Welles made of the admittedly greater resources available to him. Examples include Mallory's organization of the Confederate Navy Department; his deference to senior officers and his inability to overcome the detrimental effects of the seniority and judicial systems; his erratic ability to impel his officers to fight; and his willingness to divert resources to projects that might benefit the Confederate navy in the very long term but would decrease the Confederacy's chances of winning the war.

Mallory's organizational failures are especially apparent in the areas of shipbuilding and marine engineering. The Confederate Navy Department included four offices, modeled roughly on prewar U.S. Navy bureaus: Orders and Detail, Ordnance and Hydrography, Provisions and Clothing, and Medicine and Surgery. Conspicuously absent was a counterpart to the U.S. Navy's Bureau of Construction, Equipment, and Repairs. Until 1863, the Confederate navy had no formal construction and repair organization, which meant that no one below the secretarial level had the formal responsibility or the authority to coordinate ship design and construction. By the time Mallory appointed a chief constructor in autumn 1862, the Union navy had already split its single construction bureau into two to give adequate emphasis to steam propulsion.

The Confederacy's engineering organization was similarly deficient. Union engineer in chief Benjamin Franklin Isherwood designed simple, durable engines and provided the sort of technically conservative operating instructions that inexperienced wartime engineers needed. By contrast, the Confederate navy did not even have an engineer in chief until after a year of war. When Mallory appointed William P. Williamson as engineer in chief, Williamson busied himself designing ineffective machinery for nonexistent vessels, meanwhile leaving his subordinates to their own devices. Mallory's failures in construction and engineering are the more surprising in light of his early adoption of a "technology strategy" for his service.

Mallory's organization and operation of his department were hampered significantly by the senior uniformed leadership of the Confederate navy. The prewar U.S. Navy promoted its officers by seniority alone, a method clearly not calculated to elevate the best and most vigorous men to important commands, and both Welles and Mallory had to deal with this entrenched system. Welles succeeded early in breaking the grip of seniority, passing over ineffective senior officers in favor of more junior but more capable commanders like Du Pont, Goldsborough, Porter, and Charles H. Davis. Mallory was much less successful; despite his 1863 creation of the provisional navy as a way to bypass the seniority system, it was not until mid-1864 that he actually began to use it. The time and energy that senior Confederate navy officers invested in squabbles over seniority could have been much better used, but Mallory never managed to quell the disputes.

The Confederate navy's emphasis on seniority may also provide insight into the service's frequent operational failures; one author has noted that Confederate officers were more likely to destroy their own ships to prevent capture than to give battle against odds that they, as naval professionals, could calculate as being nearly hopeless. Mallory seems to have been unable to prod his officers into action; although he went so far as to explicitly order them to fight rather than to destroy their ships to prevent capture, the results bore a depressing sameness.[4]

This illuminates another of Mallory's failures: his investment of scarce resources in projects that could benefit only a postwar navy. He seemed at times to be focused upon the long run at the expense of the immediate problem of winning the war; the money and instructor talent lavished on the Naval School is an example. Yet this "long run" emphasis might have been counterproductive even if the Confederacy had maintained its independence. A "long run" C.S. Navy would likely have needed a defining mythos, comparable to the one that the U.S. Navy took from the War of 1812, but the Confederacy's cautious, long-view policies provided little naval glory upon which to build.[5] In fairness to Mallory, this concentration on the future to the detriment of the present was apparent in other areas of the Confederate government and political system. As one Confederate lamented, "In future revolutions, never let a 'permanent government' be established until independence is achieved!"[6]

For his part, Welles presided over a major advance in naval administration and over only one major flop, both of which were connected with the monitor building program. The advance was the development of a flexible, effective system to manage ship matériel; the flop came when that system was carried to extremes.

To build and support its fleet of high-technology monitors, the navy established a "project office" form of management practically independent of the existing navy administrative system. Under de facto head Alban C. Stimers, the project office provided desperately needed drive and direction during the critical months of 1862 and 1863, spearheading the navy's attempt to broaden its industrial base. It supported a fleet of high-technology vessels while incorporating the lessons of combat.

Unfortunately, the exclusive focus on monitors that permitted the project office's early successes led eventually to failure. The turf-conscious Stimers too eagerly accepted the added scope that success brought, and the monitor bureau's workload mushroomed. By late 1862 overwork was forcing Stimers to cut technical corners, but he refused to ask for or permit assistance from the bureau chiefs, Lenthall and Isherwood. Over the next year Stimers's chickens came home to roost. In terms of the engineering shortcuts he had taken, "There's never time to do it right, but there's always time to do it over." The Tippecanoe class monitors that followed the Passaics became mired in change upon change, and the light draft monitors Stimers designed in 1863 were a total fiasco—when launched, they would not float. Stimers's failure discredited "project management" in the navy so badly that it vanished for eighty years, until the success of the Polaris Fleet Ballistic Missile program made the "project office" all the rage.

Welles had depended upon Fox to keep tabs on monitor construction, but Fox as much as Stimers sought technical perfection at almost any cost. At first blinded by his enthusiasm for the monitors, Fox was later trammeled by his public espousal of them, and he did not make it clear to Welles how badly the program was doing until the launch of the first light draft made failure incontrovertible.[7] Welles's failure to "pull the string," however, may be said to have been balanced by Mallory's decision to choose James North as his European agent for ironclads and to maintain him in that position for a year, despite North's lack of appreciation for the urgency of the Confederacy's need.

In some areas, neither Welles nor Mallory made much headway. Army-navy cooperation, for example, was never institutionally resolved on either side. Despite the potential advantages of unified defense for New Orleans or Wilmington, or of unified offense against Charleston, joint command would be for a later era.[8] Similarly, the development of naval and joint strategy remained ad hoc and fragmented.

Each secretary had tried to mobilize his nation's industry, with mixed results, but neither made much long-term impact. Most of the Confederate navy's industrial buildup disappeared in the ruin of defeat. Some facilities were destroyed by retreating Confederates, but the Federals did their share: the Columbia powder works fell to Sherman's troops, while Federal cavalry raiders destroyed the Naval Ordnance Works at Selma and the Naval Iron Works at Columbus. Had they been spared, as the famed Tredegar Iron Works was, the navy's industrial facilities could have served as vital postwar industrial hubs. Instead, the Confederacy's investment went literally up in smoke.[9]

The industries mobilized for the Union navy ended less spectacularly, victims of the loss of their navy markets. The wartime shipyards of Pittsburgh and Cincinnati vanished; combined with the draft restrictions imposed by the Mississippi River system, high costs made construction there unattractive. In the East, the builders whose core competencies were machinery and ironwork returned to their roots, but by the end of the decade the prominent Eastern shipyards were largely out of business or in serious trouble.

Although the North was the victor tactically and strategically, the end of the war caused the U.S. Navy to fall upon hard times, and Harold and Margaret Sprout asserted, "A visitor returning in 1870 after ten years' absence might never have guessed that the navy had passed through any war at all."[10] The most visible parts of the navy—the cruising ships and their ordnance—were indeed little changed. The war's invisible influence on service culture would not become manifest until the junior officers of the 1860s, whose formative professional years had been shaped by steam, reached positions of significant authority.

Even "winning" technologies suffered in the postwar years, as the navy displayed the "conservative reaction" of accumulated sociotechnical momentum. "Once the disruptive force—in this case, war—is removed, the prewar context again prevails."[11] The technologies that flourished in the hothouse atmosphere of the war seemed to wither in the peace that followed, although they took firm root in Europe.

The withering had multiple causes, many of which bore only indirectly upon the technologies themselves. Among the factors that affected technological advance in general were internal preoccupation, lack of a foreign threat, and the accelerating pace of technology.

The years after the end of the Civil War marked a national preoccupation with internal affairs. The Western frontier, made sharply more accessible by the transcontinental railroad, joined with Southern Reconstruction to divert attention from foreign affairs. The inward look was accentuated by the lack of a foreign threat, as the demise of French adventurism in Mexico and the resolution of the *Alabama* claims with Great Britain muted public and legislative support for the navy. Another broadly applicable factor was the accelerating pace of technology. U.S. ironclads completed in 1865 were obsolete ten years later, but Americans persisted in "the false but soothing perception that military goods once appropriated were durable and good for generations."[12] Even as clear-sighted an expert as Ericsson asserted that his monitors would be "good for *fifty* years."[13] Absent an evident threat, many preferred to allow other nations to conduct expensive experiments.

These factors affected some technologies more than others. Submarine mine development, for example, was derailed by interservice priorities. The navy, treating mines as a means of coastal defense, preferred to focus on ships and leave mining to the army. The end of the Civil War, however, returned the army's attention to the American West, where the Indian Wars that began two and a half centuries earlier still continued. Facing the same rigid financial constraints as the navy, the army had little to spend on mines.

In contrast, steam engineering suffered most from intraservice politics. Although the navy's "return to sail" is often used as an example of mindless, moss-backed reaction, it was in fact both an economy move and a way for one power group within the navy to undercut another.

Economical peacetime operations, especially for a navy lacking overseas bases, required maximum reliance on sails for propulsion. In 1867 Daniel Ammen wrote that since the United States was "burdened with a debt of three thousand millions of dollars," rejecting "the aid of the winds" would be wasteful. Ammen was pragmatic, though; he sailed the *Piscataqua* while the trade winds lasted, steamed across the doldrums, and hauled fires again when the trades returned.[14]

More important than the economic aspect was the long-drawn feud between line officers and naval engineers. The wartime emphasis on steam propulsion had increased the relative prestige of the engineers, and feelings ran high on both sides. In their total dependence upon steam power, the ironclads were truly engineers' ships, and as such they became a focus for discontent. When opportunity arose, senior line officers struck hard at the engineer corps and at the steam propulsion that had given it such prominence; the repression of ironclad technology was a side effect.[15] Unlike the other major technologies, however, steam was widely used, and commercial steam engineering picked up the torch that navy engineers were forced to drop.

Among winners and losers, the American merchant marine was clearly a loser, although the extent to which the Confederacy caused its extended decline is debatable. Wartime losses amounted to over half of the prewar

U.S. merchant fleet, but over 85 percent of the losses were not destroyed, merely transferred to foreign ownership. Under existing U.S. law, however, they could not be repatriated. Shipping interests trying to change the law failed in the face of opposition from Western states, which wanted the cheapest possible transportation for grain exports, and shipbuilders, who were beguiled by the mirage of replacing the transferred ships with new ones.

In 1860, American ships had carried 66.5 percent of U.S. foreign trade; in 1865, only 27.7 percent. Yet the immediate postwar years saw a resurgence, and by 1870, U.S. ships carried 35.6 percent of U.S. trade. The sharp decline after 1870, to 25.8 percent in 1875 and 15.5 percent in 1882, clearly cannot be attributed to the Confederacy.[16] In the end the Confederates "accomplish[ed] by catastrophe what might otherwise have come about through a long decrepitude."[17] The issue is still debated, but it seems that the failure of the merchant marine to recover was based as much on technological and economic factors as upon the exploits of Semmes and Maffitt. The British maintained a technical and economic lead in iron shipbuilding that American builders, hampered by high labor costs and a high protective tariff on iron, could not overcome. That British advantage combined with the inability or unwillingness of most U.S. shipbuilders to switch to iron and the diversion of capital to the American West to ensure that there would be no resurgence of American trade.[18]

Overall, the war years brought tremendous change to a service that did not always welcome it. Innovative technologies flourished in the hothouse atmosphere, and a rising generation of naval leaders would carry the memory of combat into the long peace that followed. The death of the Confederacy meant the death of its navy, but a hundred years later, ships bearing the names of Confederate heroes like Tattnall, Buchanan, Waddell, and Semmes would steam beside those named for Union heroes like Farragut, Du Pont, Porter, and Worden. Over time, the U.S. Navy again became truly the navy of the reunited states.

Notes

1. SECESSION AT SEA

1. Richard Franklin Bensel, *Yankee Leviathan: The Origins of Central State Authority in America, 1859–1877* (New York: Cambridge University Press, 1990), 238–39.

2. U.S. Census Office, 8th Census, 1860, *Population of the United States in 1860* (Washington DC: Government Printing Office, 1864).

3. U.S. Census Office, 8th Census, 1860, *Manufactures of the United States in 1860* (Washington DC: Government Printing Office, 1865). Harold Wilson emphasizes those 115 "manufactories" and argues that "in many critical areas the slave states possessed the sinews of war," but despite its expansive title, Wilson's work deals almost exclusively with textiles. Harold S. Wilson, *Southern Industry: Manufacturers and Quartermasters in the Civil War* (Jackson: University of Mississippi Press, 2002), xv–xix.

4. Gideon Welles, *Diary*, 3 vols., ed. Howard K. Beale (New York: W. W. Norton, 1960), 1:23–26; Gideon Welles, "Fort Pickens," in *Selected Essays by Gideon Welles: Lincoln's Administration*, ed. Albert Mordell (New York: Twayne, 1960), 110–12 (originally published in *Galaxy* 11 [January 1871]; Gideon Welles, "Facts in Relation to the Expedition Ordered by the Administration of President Lincoln for the Relief of the Garrison in Fort Sumter," ibid., 57–58 (originally published in *Galaxy* 10 [November 1870]).

5. Beauregard to Leroy P. Walker, April 8, 1861, in *The War of the Rebellion: A Compilation of the Official Records of the Union and Confederate Armies*, 128 vols. (Washington DC: Government Printing Office, 1880–1901; hereafter OR), ser. 1, 1:289, 291; Walker to Beauregard, April 10, 1861, ibid., 298. The OR is also in CD-ROM format as *The Civil War CD-ROM: The War of the Rebellion: A Compilation of the Official Records of the Union and Confederate Armies* (Carmel IN: Guild of Indiana, 1997).

6. Fox's report, April 19, 1861, *OR*, ser. 1, 1:11.

7. Virginia's state convention, for example, decided to secede only by a vote of 88 to 55.

8. The U.S. Navy had 7,600 enlisted men when war broke out. *Report of the Secretary of the Navy, 1864–65*, xiii. In 1860 the Union states reported 56,623 mariners, the border states 4,449, and the Confederate states 4,904. Adding potentially maritime categories of boatmen, steamboatmen, and fishermen, the totals were Union 99,691, border 8,801, Confederate 10,466. *Population of the United States in 1860.*

9. William S. Dudley, *Going South: U.S. Navy Officer Resignations and Dismissals on the Eve of the Civil War* (Washington DC: Naval Historical Foundation, 1981); Welles, "Facts in Relation to . . . Fort Sumter," *Selected Essays*, 90.

10. Edward William Sloan III, *Benjamin Franklin Isherwood, Naval Engineer: The Years as Engineer in Chief, 1861–1869* (Annapolis: Naval Institute Press, 1965), 21–25.

11. From "A Journal Kept by Comdr. Stephen C. Rowan, December 1859–April 1861," file microcopies of records in the National Archives: no. 180, Papers of Stephen C. Rowan; William N. Still Jr., *Iron Afloat: The Story of the Confederate Armorclads* (Columbia: University of South Carolina Press, 1985), 10, 18–23.

12. The loss figures given in the Senate inquest into the loss of the yard are markedly exaggerated. Senate Report 37, 37th Cong., 2d sess.; Samuel R. Bright Jr., "Confederate Coast Defense" (Ph.D. diss., Duke University, 1961), 37–43.

13. Early Union counterintelligence is described in Edwin C. Fishel, *The Secret War for the Union: The Untold Story of Military Intelligence in the Civil War* (Boston: Houghton Mifflin, 1996), 8–28, 53–76.

14. Gideon Welles, "Nomination and Election of Abraham Lincoln," in *Selected Essays*, 40–41 (originally published in *Galaxy* 22 [October 1876]).

15. The secretary may have underestimated the sense of personal honor shared by many officers. The thought of betraying a trust extended to former officers; James D. Bulloch, a former U.S. Navy officer then serving as master of a merchant ship, resisted attempts to seize his vessel in New Orleans, and returned her to her owners in New York before going South. James D. Bulloch, *The Secret Service of the Confederate States in Europe; or, How the Confederate Cruisers Were Equipped* (1884; repr., New York: Modern Library, 2001), 25–27.

16. Welles, "Facts in Relation to . . . Fort Sumter," *Selected Essays*, 58–59; Welles, "Fort Pickens," ibid., 110–11.

17. Dudley, *Going South*, 34–35, 11–13.

18. Scott to McClellan, May 3, 1861, *OR*, ser. 1, 51, part 1: 369–70.

19. Theodore Ropp, "Anacondas Anyone?" *Military Affairs* 27 (Summer 1963): 74.

20. C. Mark Grimsley's *The Hard Hand of War: Union Military Policy toward*

Southern Civilians, 1861–1865 (New York: Cambridge University Press, 1995) discusses Federal policy.

21. *Report of the Secretary of the Navy, 1860–61*, 3.

22. Samuel F. Du Pont, *Report on the National Defences* (Washington DC: Gideon, 1852), 4, 10–11, 19.

23. K. Jack Bauer, *The Mexican War, 1846–1848* (1974; repr., Lincoln: University of Nebraska Press, 1992), 174, 344–45. The defensive context of Du Pont's report appears to offer a logical reason why he does not mention a navy's "sea control" role. However, his explicit characterization of raids as "the kind of warfare we must look to" indicates that his thoughts about "mastery of the seas" did not approach the modern conception of "sea power."

24. Copies of proclamations in Welles to Silas Stringham, May 1, 1861, in *Official Records of the Union and Confederate Navies in the War of the Rebellion*, 28 vols. (Washington DC: Government Printing Office, 1894–1922; hereafter ORN), 5:620–21. The ORN is also found in CD-ROM format as *The Civil War CD-ROM II: Official Records of the Union and Confederate Navies in the War of the Rebellion* (Carmel IN: Guild of Indiana, 1999). All references are to series 1 unless indicated.

25. Welles to Lincoln, ORN, 5:53–56.

26. In July 1861 the British foreign secretary, Lord Russell, notified Lord Lyons, the British ambassador in Washington, that Britain would not observe a "legislative closing" of the southern ports. Regis A. Courtemanche, *No Need of Glory: The British Navy in American Waters, 1860–1864* (Annapolis: Naval Institute Press, 1977), 20.

27. The Navy Department's organization had been established by law in 1842. It comprised five "bureaus," each responsible for a functional area of naval administration. They were the Bureaus of Yards and Docks; of Construction, Equipment, and Repairs; of Provisions and Clothing; of Ordnance and Hydrography; and of Medicine and Surgery. The bureau chiefs (some civilians, some naval officers) reported directly to the secretary of the navy. Their meetings in this context are recorded in National Archives Record Group (hereafter NARG) 45, subject file, OL (Mobilization and Demobilization), box 412, minutes of Board of Bureau Chiefs on subjects of supplying blockading squadrons.

28. See, e.g., Stringham to Enoch G. Parrott, May 18, 1861, ORN, 5:640–41.

29. Samuel Novotny, "The Board of Strategy and Union Military Planning for Sea Operations against the Southern Confederacy" (Master's thesis, Old Dominion University, 1978), 3–4; NARG 45, subject file, ON (Operations), box 453, rough drafts of proceedings and reports of the Blockade Strategy Board.

30. Du Pont to Sophie Du Pont, June 28, 1861, in *Samuel Francis Du Pont: A Selection from His Civil War Letters*, ed. John D. Hayes, vol. 1, *The Mission: 1860–1861*; vol. 2, *The Blockade: 1862–1863*; vol. 3, *The Repulse: 1863–1865* (Ithaca NY: Cornell University Press for the Eleutherian Mills Historical Library, 1969) (hereafter *Du Pont Letters*), 1:85–86. The reports were later published. Three Atlantic Coast

reports are first ORN, 12:195–98; third (labeled second), ibid., 198–201; fourth (labeled third), ibid., 201–6. The actual second report is in OR, ser. 1, 53:67–73. The three Gulf Coast reports are ORN, 16:618–30, 651–55, and 680–81.

31. C. H. Davis to Mrs. Davis, May 22, 1861, quoted in Charles H. Davis, *Life of Charles Henry Davis, Rear Admiral, 1807–1877* (Boston: Houghton Mifflin, 1899), 121.

32. Welles to Du Pont, August 3, 1861 ORN, 12:207; Du Pont to Sophie Du Pont, July 26, 1861, *Du Pont Letters*, 1:113.

33. Joseph L. Harsh, *Confederate Tide Rising: Robert E. Lee and the Making of Southern Strategy, 1861–1862* (Kent OH: Kent State University Press, 1998), 7, 10.

34. Bright, "Confederate Coast Defense," 3.

35. Raimondo Luraghi, *A History of the Confederate Navy* (Annapolis: Naval Institute Press, 1996), 189.

36. Proclamation of April 17, 1861, ORN, 5:796–97. The first privateers were not commissioned until early May 1861. William Morrison Robinson Jr., *The Confederate Privateers* (New Haven: Yale University Press, 1928), 25, 26–28, 17.

37. Du Pont to Henry Winter Davis, July 18, 1861, *Du Pont Letters*, 1:106.

2. IMPROVISED NAVIES

1. See, e.g., the attacks of Senator John P. Hale in *Congressional Globe*, 37th Cong., 2d sess., 219–21, 245–49.

2. Gregory discusses his appointment in *Report of the Joint Committee on the Conduct of the War*, "Light Draught Monitors," 38th Cong., 2d sess., 1865, 73. He was made rear admiral on July 16, 1862.

3. Later "double-enders" were actually identical fore and aft, but the first dozen were built to nine different designs by seven shipyards; their "double-endedness" was only in having a rudder at the bow as well as at the stern.

4. Kurt Henry Hackemer, "From Peace to War: U.S. Naval Procurement, Private Enterprise, and the Integration of New Technology, 1850–1865" (Ph.D. diss., Texas A&M University, 1994), 5–10.

5. J. Thomas Scharf, *History of the Confederate States Navy from Its Organization to the Surrender of Its Last Vessel* (1887; repr., New York: Fairfax, 1977), 24–25.

6. Mallory's July 1861 report listed fourteen more purchased steamers. Mallory to Davis, July 18, 1861, ORN, ser. 2, 2:76–77.

7. Mallory to C. M. Conrad, May 10, 1861, ORN, ser. 2, 2:69.

8. Luraghi, *History of the Confederate Navy*, 69.

9. Mallory to C. M. Conrad, May 10, 1861, ORN, ser. 2, 2:69; Secret Act 117, approved May 10, 1861, in *Laws and Joint Resolutions of the Last Session of the Confederate Congress Together with the Secret Acts of Previous Congresses*, ed. Charles W. Ramsdell (Durham NC: Duke University Press, 1941), 158. A companion law, Secret Act 116, approved $1 million for cruising ships.

10. Mallory to Jefferson Davis, July 18, 1861, ORN, ser. 2, 2:76–79; George M. Brooke Jr., ed., *Ironclads and Big Guns of the Confederacy: The Journal and Letters of John M. Brooke* (Columbia: University of South Carolina Press, 2002), 22, 25 (Brooke journal entries for June 23 and 28, 1861); Still, *Iron Afloat*, 5–17, 19; James Phinney Baxter III, *The Introduction of the Ironclad Warship* (Cambridge: Harvard University Press, 1933; repr., Hamden CT: Archon, 1968), 229.

11. Mallory to Davis, February 27, 1862, ORN, ser. 2, 2:152.

12. Mallory to Bulloch, May 9, 1861, ORN, ser. 2, 2:64–65; Mallory to North, May 17, 1861, ibid., 70–72. Bulloch's mission was allocated $1 million, while North's received $2 million. Ibid., 66–67.

13. In modern parlance, torpedoes are self-propelled to impact with their targets; mines wait for targets to come to them.

14. Milton F. Perry, *Infernal Machines: The Story of Confederate Submarine and Mine Warfare* (Baton Rouge: Louisiana State University Press, 1965), 6–7; William A. Tidwell, *Come Retribution: The Confederate Secret Service and the Assassination of Lincoln* (1988; repr., New York: Barnes & Noble, 1997), 156.

15. Naval History Division, U.S. Navy Department, *Civil War Naval Chronology, 1861–1865* (Washington: Government Printing Office, 1971) (hereafter *Naval Chronology*), I-19.

16. Isaac N. Brown, "Confederate Torpedoes in the Yazoo," in Robert Underwood Johnson and Clarence C. Buel, eds., *Battles and Leaders of the Civil War*, vol. 3, *Retreat from Gettysburg* (1887; repr., New York: Castle, 1956), 580; W. W. Mackall to Leonidas K. Polk, October 17, 1861, OR, ser. 1, 4:456; Tidwell, *Come Retribution*, 160–61.

17. Hunter S. Davidson to Jefferson Davis, December 5, 1881, in "A Chapter of War History Concerning Torpedoes," *Southern Historical Society Papers*, 24:285.

18. Welles to Joseph Smith, May 30, 1861, NARG 45, subject file, OL, box 412, minutes of Board of Bureau Chiefs, minutes of meetings of May 30, May 31 and June 1, 1861.

19. House Executive Document 69, *Report of the Secretary of the Navy in Relation to Armored Vessels*, 38th Cong., 1st sess., 1864, 1–2. The proposals are listed in NARG 19, plan file, BuShips Plan 80–11-3. James Russell Soley castigates the Navy Department for "negligence . . . in postponing the building of iron-clads," but given the nature and complexity of the Union's naval problems, Welles moved quite rapidly. Soley, "The Navy in the Peninsular Campaign," in Robert Underwood Johnson and Clarence C. Buel, eds., *Battles and Leaders of the Civil War*, vol. 2, *North to Antietam*, (1887; repr., New York: Castle, 1956), 267.

20. The board's choices are described in William H. Roberts, "*The Name of Ericsson*: Political Engineering in the Union Ironclad Program, 1861–1863," *Journal of Military History* 63 (October 1999): 823–44, and USS *New Ironsides in the Civil War* (Annapolis: Naval Institute Press, 1999). Recent authors have again

disinterred the myth that Navy skeptics inserted a unique performance guarantee clause in Ericsson's contract. Merrick's contract for *New Ironsides* and Bushnell's for *Galena* contained the same sort of provisions for progress payments and performance guarantees as did Ericsson's contract for *Monitor*.

21. At the time, as a disappointed rival pointed out, Eads "had no timber, no machinery, and no boat yard." Eads's connections with Attorney General Edward Bates, also of St. Louis, and the argument that St. Louis desperately needed the business overcame this minor difficulty and trumped the political pressure applied by other firms. Quoted in James M. Merrill, "Union Shipbuilding on Western Rivers during the Civil War," *Smithsonian Journal of History* 3 (Winter 1968–69): 19–20.

22. By April 1862, when the Passaic class monitors were begun, the Union had already commissioned the seven City (or Cairo) class ironclads and two converted vessels. The riverine ironclad program peaked in late 1862 at fourteen armored vessels under construction or conversion simultaneously, totaling some 14,000 tons. At that time, the coastal program had twice as many ironclads under construction, totaling nearly 70,000 tons. The coastal program peaked in 1863 with nearly 99,000 tons under construction.

23. In August 1861 John Laird's New York agent, John Howard, approached the navy with hopes of building ironclads for the Union. Howard, in the fashion of lobbyists, exaggerated to Laird the encouragement he had received from Fox, but the navy never entered serious negotiations with any foreign shipbuilder. Welles, *Diary*, entries for May 2, 1863, 1:291; August 7 and 10, 1863, 394–96; August 13, 1863, 401; William Joseph Sullivan, "Gustavus Fox and Naval Administration, 1861–1866" (Ph.D. diss., Catholic University of America, 1977), 165–68.

24. Roberts, *"The Name of Ericsson,"* 833–35.

25. Mallory to Buchanan, March 7, 1862, *ORN*, 6:780. On March 14, 1862, Mallory asked Brooke, Porter, and Chief Engineer Williamson about sending *Virginia* to New York; they told the secretary that she "could not be rendered seaworthy without rendering her inefficient as a man of war." Brooke journal, entry for March 14, 1862, in Brooke, *Ironclads and Big Guns*, 81. Buchanan independently pointed out the impracticality of the proposal in Buchanan to Mallory, March 19, 1862, quoted ibid., 236.

26. Attorney General Edward Bates, quoted in Bruce Catton, *Terrible Swift Sword* (Garden City: Doubleday, 1963), 116. All concerned, including the British, agreed that if Wilkes had arrested the *Trent* entire rather than only the passengers, his actions would have been far less objectionable. Howard Jones, *Union in Peril: The Crisis over British Intervention in the Civil War* (Chapel Hill: University of North Carolina Press, 1992), 85–87.

27. Welles to Hale, February 7, 1862, NARG 45, entry 5.

28. George E. Belknap, "Reminiscent of the Siege of Charleston," in *Naval*

Actions and History, 1799–1898 (Boston: Military Historical Society of Massachusetts, 1902; repr., Wilmington NC: Broadfoot, 1990), 188.

29. In the author's naval experience, most people take about a year to become fully productive aboard ship. Neither shore-based training nor nonseagoing navy experience reduces this time significantly. This meshes with the observation of *New Ironsides*'s captain that when landsmen enlisted for one year, "their term of service expires about the time they have learned to be useful." Stephen C. Rowan to John A. Dahlgren, October 3, 1863, *ORN*, 15:26.

30. Oscar W. Farenholt, "The Volunteer Navy in the Civil War," *Proceedings of the United States Naval Institute* 45, no. 10 (October 1919): 1691–94; William G. Saltonstall, "Personal Reminiscences of the War, 1861–1865," in *Naval Actions and History, 1799–1898*, 278; Donald Chisholm, *Waiting for Dead Men's Shoes: Origins and Development of the U.S. Navy's Officer Personnel System, 1793–1941* (Stanford CA: Stanford University Press, 2001), 307–10; Charles Oscar Paullin, *Paullin's History of Naval Administration, 1775–1911* (Annapolis: Naval Institute Press, 1968), 299, 314–15.

31. Fox, however, emphasized to Senator J. W. Grimes that the Naval Academy was essential because "the merchant service does not give us the men professionally, or morally." Fox to Grimes, September 22, 1862, in *Confidential Correspondence of Gustavus Vasa Fox, Assistant Secretary of the Navy, 1861–1865*, 2 vols., ed. Robert Means Thompson and Richard Wainwright (Freeport NY: Books for Libraries, 1918–19) (hereafter Thompson and Wainwright, *Correspondence of Fox*), 2:386.

32. From NARG 15, Bureau of Pensions, pension file, survivor's certificate 30941, s.v. John M. Butler, and other sources.

33. Responding to R. B. Forbes's request for "active employment" for the Massachusetts Coast Guard, Welles wrote, "We must preserve unity in the Navy—must sustain its nationality," and he called state naval organizations "more than questionable." Welles to Forbes, June 27, 1861, NARG 45, entry M209, roll 23, 64:441.

34. The appointment of flag officers from captains and commanders, without regard to seniority, was authorized by law in December 1861. Chisholm, *Waiting for Dead Men's Shoes*, 283.

35. One officer wrote that his commanding officer, a former lieutenant recently returned to the navy as an acting master, was "sore. I know why. He can't get a Lieutenancy." Entry for July 27, 1863, John M. Butler Diary, William Pendleton Palmer Collection of Civil War Manuscripts, Western Reserve Historical Society, Cleveland OH, MSS 3947 (microfilm) (hereafter Butler Diary).

36. Chisholm, *Waiting for Dead Men's Shoes*, 308–10.

37. Butler Diary, entries for January 2, February 13, 1863.

38. Charles A. Post, "A Diary on the Blockade in 1863," *Proceedings of the United States Naval Institute* 44 (October 1918): 2346.

39. Robert M. Oxley, "The Civil War Gulf Blockade: The Unpublished Journal of a U.S. Navy Warrant Officer Aboard the uss *Vincennes*, 1861–1864," *International Journal of Naval History* 1, no. 1, online at http://www.ijnhonline.org/volume1_number1_Apr02/article_oxley_journal_blockade.doc.htm

40. Tom Henderson Wells, *The Confederate Navy: A Study in Organization* (Tuscaloosa: University of Alabama Press, 1971), 14.

41. Brooke to Lizzie Brooke, July 7, 1862, in Brooke, *Ironclads and Big Guns*, 98–99. Raphael Semmes charitably observed that while the "old gentlemen" could have commanded "well-appointed and well-officered" squadrons, they were "entirely unsuited for such service as the Confederacy could offer them." Raphael Semmes, *Memoirs of Service Afloat during the War between the States* (1868; repr., Seacaucus NJ: Blue & Grey, 1987), 368.

42. *The Statutes at Large of the Confederate States of America*, ed. James M. Matthews (electronic edition from University of North Carolina, Chapel Hill digitization project, Documenting the American South, at http://docsouth.unc.edu/imls/confdocs.html; hereafter *Confederate Statutes*), 1st Cong., 3d sess., chapter 85; Wells, *Confederate Navy*, 28–31.

43. Craig L. Symonds, "Rank and Rancor in the Confederate Navy," MHQ: *The Quarterly Journal of Military History* 14, no. 2 (Winter 2002): 14–19. The few regular promotions that were granted, including James D. Bulloch's and John M. Brooke's, caused intense resentment. For example, Catesby ap R. Jones to Brooke, February 5, 1862, and Brooke journal, September 21, 1862, quoted in Brooke, *Ironclads and Big Guns*, 65, 111.

44. Joseph T. Durkin, *Confederate Navy Chief: Stephen R. Mallory* (Columbia: University of South Carolina Press, 1954), 149. This was partly the result of a strong state's rights political philosophy. A contributing factor was the Confederate navy's inability to protect the states, which led frequently to urgent needs to raise local defense forces.

45. Mallory to Davis, July 18, 1861, ORN, ser. 2, 2:78–79; John K. Mitchell to Mallory, April 28, 1864, ibid., 640.

46. Dudley, *Going South*, 18–19.

47. Frank M. Bennett, *The Steam Navy of the United States* (Pittsburgh: W. T. Nicholson, 1896; repr., Westport CT: Greenwood, 1974), 205.

48. For example, two different types of torpedo boat engines for which the drawings contained evident errors and for which the specifications and the drawings did not match. Bulloch to Mallory, October 24, 1864, ORN, ser. 2, 2:739, and January 26, 1865, ibid., 790–91.

49. Wells, *Confederate Navy*, 95, 107–9, 111–13, 117. Ship repairs belonged to the Office of Ordnance and Hydrography until 1863, but the Office of Orders and Detail acted on repair-related correspondence in 1862. Robert M. Browning Jr., "The Confederate States Navy Department," in *The Confederate Navy: The Ships,*

Men, and Organization, 1861–65, ed. William N. Still (London: Conway Maritime, 1997), 25–26, 32–33; Franklin Buchanan to J. R. Tucker, February 8 and 24, 1862, ORN, 6:765 and 776.

50. Mallory asked the Confederate Congress to appoint Porter chief constructor. Mallory to A. G. Brown, September 20, 1862, ORN, ser. 2, 2:271–72.

3. EARLY OPERATIONS

1. Welles to Stringham, May 1, 1861, ORN, 5:619–20; Garrett J. Pendergrast to Stringham, May 13, 1861, ibid., 5:630; Welles to Stringham, May 21, 1861, ibid., 5:660–61.

2. John Fraser MacQueen, *Chief Points in the Laws of War and Neutrality, Search and Blockade* (London and Edinburgh: William and Robert Chambers, 1862), 29–30.

3. Welles to Mervine, May 7, 1861, ORN, 16:519–20, and May 14, 1861, 16:523–24.

4. For example, see Welles to Stringham, May 6, 1861, ORN, 5:624–25.

5. Stringham to Welles, June 29, 1861, ORN, 5:753–54.

6. Courtemanche, *No Need of Glory,* 23–24; Jones, *Union in Peril,* 106. The capture rate for all would-be blockade-runners in 1861 averaged 3.1 percent, but was increasing; in 1862, the capture rate was 40.9 percent. Stanley Lebergott, "Through the Blockade: The Profitability and Extent of Cotton Smuggling, 1861–1865," *Journal of Economic History* 41, no. 4 (December 1981): 873.

7. David G. Surdam, *Northern Naval Superiority and the Economics of the American Civil War* (Columbia: University of South Carolina Press, 2001), 12.

8. Bright, "Confederate Coast Defense," 6.

9. Bright, "Confederate Coast Defense," i.

10. Civil War amphibious operations were called "combined" operations, meaning "army and navy." Modern usage calls operations involving two or more services of the same nation "joint"; "combined" are multinational operations.

11. For example, the army force sent to capture Port Royal could not operate inland because it lacked cavalry and artillery. Robert M. Browning Jr., *Success Is All That Was Expected: The South Atlantic Blockading Squadron during the Civil War* (Dulles VA: Brassey's, 2002), 42.

12. Bauer, *Mexican War,* 239–44; Sean Desmond Griffin, " 'All the Watery Margins': The Limitations of Waterborne Strategy, 1861–1865" (Master's thesis, Ohio State University, 2000), 14–15. Stringham wrote that the Confederates were "an enemy much more intelligent and formidable" than the Mexicans at Vera Cruz. Stringham to Fox, September 15, 1861, ORN, 6:205.

13. The correspondence appears as enclosures to Whiting to James A. Seddon, March 12, 1864, OR, ser. 1, 33:1219–29.

14. Fox to Du Pont, June 3, 1862, *Du Pont Letters*, 2:96.

15. Capt. Louis Goldsborough to Fox, June 16, 1862, Naval History Society Collection, Gustavus Vasa Fox Papers, New-York Historical Society (hereafter Fox Papers), box 3. Courtesy of the New-York Historical Society.

16. Rear Adm. David Dixon Porter to Fox, May 24, 1862, Thompson and Wainwright, *Correspondence of Fox*, 2:107.

17. Donald A. Petrie, *The Prize Game: Lawful Looting on the High Seas in the Days of Fighting Sail* (Annapolis: Naval Institute Press, 1999), 11.

18. William Reynolds to Dahlgren, January 30, 1865, NARG 45, entry 395, subseries E-95, Correspondence of Cdr. William Reynolds, vol. 1.

19. Welles, *Diary*, 1:57.

20. Welles, *Diary*, 1:67–69.

21. Quoted in Benjamin P. Thomas and Harold M. Hyman, *Stanton: The Life and Times of Lincoln's Secretary of War* (New York: Alfred A. Knopf, 1962), 174.

22. Thomas and Hyman, *Stanton*, 151.

23. William E. Doster, *Lincoln and Episodes of the Civil War* (New York: G. P. Putnam's Sons, 1915), 116–17.

24. McClellan to Thomas A. Scott, October 17, 1861, OR, ser. 1, 6:179.

25. Du Pont to Fox, November 11, 1861, Thompson and Wainwright, *Correspondence of Fox*, 2:68.

26. Du Pont to Sophie Du Pont, May 29, 1862, in Journal Letter 60, May 29–June 1, 1862, *Du Pont Letters*, 2:79.

27. Benjamin Butler to John E. Wool, August 30, 1861, OR, ser. 1, 4:584–85; Charles Dana Gibson and E. Kay Gibson, *Assault and Logistics: Union Army Coastal and River Operations, 1861–1866* (Camden ME: Ensign, 1995), 9.

28. E. D. Townsend to John E. Wool, August 21, 1861, OR, ser. 1, 4:579; Stringham to Fox, September 15, 1861, ORN, 6:205.

29. Butler to Wool, August 30, 1861, ORN, ser. 1, 4:581–86; other reports at ORN, 6:119–45.

30. Welles to Du Pont, October 12, 1861, ORN, 12:214–15.

31. Conference report of July 13, 1861, OR, ser. 1, 53:67; NARG 45, subject file, ON, Minutes of Conference Meeting of June 29, 1861; Du Pont to Sophie Du Pont, October 17, 1861, *Du Pont Letters*, 2:170–71. Du Pont had not settled on Port Royal as late as October 24. Du Pont to Sophie Du Pont, October 24, 1861, *Du Pont Letters*, 2:182–83.

32. Sherman to Adjutant General, November 8, 1861, OR, ser. 1, 6:3–4.

33. Browning, *Success Is All That Was Expected*, 32. The expedition left New York with its ammunition "stored at the bottom of [the] ships," and Sherman had to borrow 350,000 rounds from Maj. Gen. John E. Wool at Fort Monroe. Wool had to furnish rations as well, since they were similarly stowed "where they cannot be got at without several days' delay." Wool to Simon Cameron, October 28, 1861, OR, ser. 1, 6:184.

34. Regarding the army's participation, Wool observed, "I will venture to assert that a worse-managed expedition could not well be contrived." *OR*, ser. 1, 6:184.

35. Browning, *Success Is All That Was Expected*, 36–39, 42.

36. Browning, *Success Is All That Was Expected*, 41; Rowena Reed, *Combined Operations in the Civil War* (1978; repr., Lincoln: University of Nebraska Press, 1993), 31.

37. Bright, "Confederate Coast Defense," 57, 92, 97.

38. Fox to Stringham, September 14, 1861, *ORN*, 6:210–11; Stringham to Welles, September 16, 1861, ibid., 216–17. Du Pont thought Stringham had "the sulks." Du Pont to Sophie Du Pont, September 17, 1861, *Du Pont Letters*, 1:149.

39. Welles to Goldsborough, September 18, 1861, *ORN*, 6:233–34.

40. Du Pont to Sophie Du Pont, September 18, 1861, *Du Pont Letters*, 2:150.

41. For a popular discussion, see John Steele Gordon, *A Thread across the Ocean: The Heroic Story of the Transatlantic Cable* (New York: HarperCollins Perennial, 2002).

42. Johnson, *Rear Admiral John Rodgers*, 126.

43. Welles, *Diary*, entries for April 8, 10, 12, 1863, 1:264, 265, 267.

44. By 1863 Union outposts had been wired into a network that extended from Tybee Island near Savannah through Port Royal to Morris Island off Charleston. Fox lobbied for a submarine cable along the coast, but the Senate denied the request.

45. Fox to Du Pont, February 20, 1863, Unofficial, *Du Pont Letters*, 2:450.

46. Du Pont to Fox, March 2, 1863, *Du Pont Letters*, 2:464 (Du Pont's emphasis).

47. George E. Belknap observed, "It was a happy circumstance that our naval captains during the Civil War were unhampered by constant touch with Washington," but his retrospective has a rose-colored tinge. "Naval Administration in Times of War," George E. Belknap Papers, Library of Congress, Speeches and Articles, box 2.

48. Heather Cox Richardson, *The Greatest Nation of the Earth: Republican Economic Policies during the Civil War* (Cambridge: Harvard University Press, 1997), 13–15.

49. Charles R. Wilson, "Cincinnati a Southern Outpost in 1860–1861?" *Mississippi Valley Historical Review* 24, no. 4 (March 1938): 473–82; William G. Carleton, "Civil War Dissidence in the North: The Perspective of a Century," *South Atlantic Quarterly* 65, no. 3 (Summer 1966): 390–402.

50. Steven Z. Starr, "Was There a Northwest Conspiracy?" *Filson Club History Quarterly* 38, no. 4 (October 1964): 323–41. The Committee of Conference correctly noted that the Northwest was "bound to the East" by railroads and water connections. Conference report of August 9, 1861, *ORN*, 16:627.

51. Welles to Mervine, July 31, 1861, *ORN*, 16:596.

52. Mervine to Welles, September 5, 1861, *ORN*, 16:656.

53. Welles to Mervine, August 23, 1861, *ORN*, 16:644–45.

54. Du Pont to Henry Winter Davis, September 4, 1861, *Du Pont Letters*, 2:143.

55. Mervine to Welles, September 29, 1861, *ORN*, 16:693; Welles to Mervine, October 2, 1861, ibid., 694–95.

56. John Pope to McKean, October 14, 1861, *ORN*, 16:782.

57. Welles to Farragut, January 9, 1862, *ORN*, 18:5; January 20, 1862, ibid., 7–8; January 25, 1862, ibid., 9–10.

58. Lovell to Samuel Cooper, May 22, 1862, *OR*, ser. 1, 6:512; Lovell to Judah P. Benjamin, March 6, 1862, ibid., 841.

59. "The Opposing Forces in the Operations at New Orleans LA," in Johnson and Buel, eds., *Battles and Leaders of the Civil War*, 2:75.

60. Lovell to George W. Randolph, April 15, 1862, *OR*, ser. 1, 6:876.

61. Still, *Iron Afloat*, 44–45; *ORN*, ser. 2, 1:754–62; Charles B. Dew, *Ironmaker to the Confederacy: Joseph R. Anderson and the Tredegar Iron Works* (Richmond: Library of Virginia, 1999), 121–22.

62. Lovell to Samuel Cooper, May 22, 1862, *OR*, ser. 1, 6:513; Report of Brigadier General Duncan, April 30, 1862, *ORN*, 18:262.

63. Welles to Farragut, February 10, 1862, *ORN*, 18:14–22.

64. Douglas Buckley Dodds, "Strategic Purpose in the United States Navy during the Civil War, 1861–1862" (Ph.D. diss., Queen's University, Kingston, Ontario, December 1985), 113.

65. Porter thought up the mortar fleet but later declared that running past the forts was his plan all along; David D. Porter, "The Opening of the Lower Mississippi," in Johnson and Buel, eds., *Battles and Leaders of the Civil War*, 2:25–26, 38. For a view in better accord with documentary evidence, see William T. Meredith, "Farragut's Capture of New Orleans," ibid., 70–72.

66. Instructions from Cdr. H. H. Bell, April 20, 1862, *ORN*, 18:138; Farragut to John De Camp, April 23, 1862, ibid., 140; Farragut to Welles, May 6, 1862, ibid., 156.

67. Mitchell to Mallory, August 19, 1862, *ORN*, 18:292–93. Porter even had the Coast Survey chart all the shell craters, but the fighting power of the forts does not seem to have been significantly diminished.

68. C. H. B. Caldwell to Farragut, April 24, 1862, *ORN*, 18:225–26.

69. Kennon's colorful account is in Beverly Kennon, "Fighting Farragut below New Orleans," in Johnson and Buel, eds., *Battles and Leaders of the Civil War*, 2:76–89.

70. Farragut to Welles, May 6, 1862, *ORN*, 18:158.

71. Some equated delay with treachery. When the Confederate Congress investigated the navy in late 1862, the Northern-born Tifts received much hostile scrutiny. *ORN*, ser. 2, 1:431–809.

72. Farragut to Fox, April 25, 1862, *ORN*, 18:155.

73. Farragut to Fox, April 25, 1862, *ORN*, 18:155.

74. Fox to Farragut, May 12, 1862, *ORN*, 18:245; Fox to Farragut, May 16, 1862, *ORN*, 18:498; Fox to Farragut, May 17, 1862, *ORN*, 18:499.

75. Welles to Farragut, August 2, 1862, *ORN*, 19:36.

76. Welles to Farragut, July 21, 1862, *ORN*, 19:81.

77. Dodds, "Strategic Purpose," 284.

78. The tone of McClellan's March 19 letter to Stanton shows that the navy had not agreed to McClellan's plans, which seemed to be in flux as late as that date. McClellan to Stanton, March 19, 1862, *OR*, ser. 1, 5:58.

79. McClellan to Fox, March 14, 1862, Fox Papers, box 4.

80. Rowena Reed asserts that McClellan must have discussed the campaign extensively with the navy and that Fox and Goldsborough lied to Congress when they said he had not. Reed, *Combined Operations*, 126. As Dodds points out, "To base an argument on the evidence of hypothetical documents, and to fabricate a conspiracy to explain their non-existence, seem questionable" (Dodds, "Strategic Purpose," 282n52). Dodds is too charitable: Reed indicted Fox based on the absence of evidence in the notoriously incomplete published version of his correspondence.

81. Fox to Goldsborough, April 23, 1862, Thompson and Wainwright, *Correspondence of Fox*, 1:262; also Fox to Goldsborough, March 17 and 24 and April 19, 1862, ibid., 250, 251, 256, and Goldsborough to Fox, April 21, 1862, ibid., 259–61.

82. Goldsborough to Fox, April 21, 1862, Thompson and Wainwright, *Correspondence of Fox*, 1:261.

83. For McClellan's anxiety, Barnard to Fox, March 12, 1862, Fox Papers, box 3; Dodds, "Strategic Purpose," 282.

84. Goldsborough to Welles, May 23, 1862, *ORN*, 7:419–20; Wool to Goldsborough, May 22, 1862, ibid., 422.

85. McClellan to Stanton, May 11, 1862, *OR*, ser. 1, 14:164.

86. Welles to Goldsborough, May 11, 1862, *OR*, ser. 1, 14:164. Fox had hoped to attack Charleston in June 1862, but he deferred this plan. "Our summer's work must be Charleston by the navy." Fox to Du Pont, April 3, 1862, Thompson and Wainwright, *Correspondence of Fox*, 1:114–15.

87. McClellan to Goldsborough, June 27, 1862, *OR*, ser. 1, vol. 11, part 3: 267.

88. Brooke to Lizzie Brooke, July 5, 1862, in Brooke, *Ironclads and Big Guns*, 97. He added, "I wish our cities were in the interior."

89. McClellan's report, *OR*, ser. 1, vol. 11, part 1: 53.

90. Du Pont to Sophie Du Pont, May 29, 1862, in Journal Letter 60, Mau 29–June 1, 1862, *Du Pont Letters*, 2:79.

91. Fox to H. B. Anthony, August 5, 1862, Thompson and Wainwright, *Correspondence of Fox*, 2:347.

92. Goldsborough to Welles, July 8, 1862, *ORN*, 7:549; July 13, 1862, ibid., 569. Goldsborough earlier described the *Galena* as "entirely beneath Naval criticism."

Goldsborough to Fox, April 24, 1862, Thompson and Wainwright, *Correspondence of Fox*, 1:263.

93. One correspondent wrote Welles that the ship "Should be only commanded by an active, truly Loyal, man of Northern birth, Education and Principles." George A. Sawdell to Welles, September 5, 1862, NARG 45, entry M124, roll 418:149.

94. Fox to Lee, October 2, 1862, Thompson and Wainwright, *Correspondence of Fox*, 2:217, 218; Lee's reply is Lee to Fox, October 13, 1862, ibid., 220. Du Pont later found Turner "very sound" and "very anti-South on the war." Hayes, *Du Pont Letters*, 2:372. "Harpers Ferry" alludes to the impression that Col. Dixon S. Miles, who surrendered Harpers Ferry during the Antietam campaign, had not done his utmost.

95. Welles, *Diary*, entry for August 10, 1862, 1:72; Goldsborough to Welles, August 29, 1862, ORN, 7:688; Welles to Goldsborough, August 29, 1862, ibid., 689; S. P. Lee to Welles, September 12, 1862, ibid., 8:14.

96. Fox to Alban C. Stimers, September 5, 1862, enclosure to Francis H. Gregory to Lenthall, June 18, 1866, NARG 19, entry 64, box 7, "Volume 11" (January–June 1866): 9.

97. Lee to S. Cooper, January 8, 1862, OR, ser. 1, 6:367.

4. MATURING UNDER FIRE

1. W. L. Burt to N. P. Banks, OR, ser. 1, 15:203–4; other reports are at ORN, 19:437–77. *Harriet Lane* was captured; *Westfield* was destroyed to prevent her capture.

2. Semmes, *Memoirs of Service Afloat*, 540–50; ORN, 2:18–23, 683–85.

3. J. B. Magruder to S. Cooper, January 24, 1863, OR, ser. 1, 15:237–38; Farragut to Welles, January 29, 1863, and other reports, ORN, 19:553–73.

4. Du Pont's report of February 3, 1863, is at ORN, 13:577–78; other reports at ibid., 579–623; Still, *Iron Afloat*, 117–25.

5. Beauregard's proclamation is at ORN, 13:617.

6. Butler Diary, entry for January 31, 1863.

7. Butler Diary, entry for February 11, 1863; Fox to Du Pont, June 3, 1862, Thompson and Wainwright, *Correspondence of Fox*, 1:128.

8. Fox to Du Pont, March 11, 1863, *Du Pont Letters*, 2:488.

9. Fox to Du Pont, June 3, 1862, *Du Pont Letters*, 2:96.

10. Du Pont initially told a kinsman that he wished he were forty again, "to go in for ironclads, etc." Du Pont to Lammot Du Pont, July 1, 1862, *Du Pont Letters*, 2:147.

11. Du Pont to Benjamin Gerhard, January 30, 1863, *Du Pont Letters*, 2:394; Du Pont to Welles, January 28, 1863, ORN, 543–44. The *Rattlesnake* had been the raider CSS *Nashville*, and the Federals usually used her earlier name.

12. Du Pont to Sophie Du Pont, March 4, 1863, *Du Pont Letters*, 2:467.

13. Du Pont to Henry Winter Davis, April 1, 1863, *Du Pont Letters*, 2:533.

14. Du Pont to Sophie Du Pont, June 22, 1862, in Journal Letter 65, June 19–22, 1862, *Du Pont Letters*, 2:119–37; Du Pont to Fox, March 2, 1863, ibid., 464 (Du Pont's emphasis).

15. Welles to Du Pont, January 31, 1863, ORN, 13:571.

16. Du Pont to Fox, March 2, 1863, *Du Pont Letters*, 2:463; Welles, *Diary*, entry for March 12, 1863, 1:247. Du Pont felt that his reports of the monitors' offensive deficiencies should have been sufficient to dissuade the Navy Department. Besides Du Pont's lack of "directness," however, Fox appears not to have made Welles aware of the tenor of his private correspondence with Du Pont. Browning, *Success Is All That Was Required*, 185–213.

17. Du Pont to Fox, August 13, 1862, Thompson and Wainwright, *Correspondence of Fox*, 1:149.

18. Henry Villard to Murat Halstead, February 12, 1863, Cincinnati Museum Center, Cincinnati, Ohio, MSS VF 3325.

19. Du Pont to Henry Winter Davis, April 1, 1863, *Du Pont Letters*, 2:534, and his letters to his wife preceding the attack.

20. Du Pont to William Whetten, March 17/18, 1863, *Du Pont Letters*, 2:490.

21. Stimers to Fox, February 4, 1863, Fox Papers, box 7; Stimers to Welles, telegram, March 11, 1863, ORN, 13:729.

22. Du Pont to Sophie Du Pont, March 4, 1863, in Journal Letter 39, March 4–7, 1863, *Du Pont Letters*, 2:467; Du Pont to Sophie Du Pont, March 27, 1863, ibid., 518–19.

23. Roswell S. Ripley to Thomas Jordan, April 13, 1863, OR, ser. 1, 14:259. Beauregard later called the Confederate ships a "total failure," observing, "they did not fire one shot in the defense of Fort Sumter" during Du Pont's attack. Beauregard to Porcher Miles, November 14, 1863, ibid., ser. 1, 28, part 2: 503.

24. First report of Rear Admiral Du Pont, April 8, 1863, ORN, 14:3.

25. Du Pont to Maj. Gen. David Hunter, April 8, 1863, ibid., 30–31; Du Pont to Henry Winter Davis, May 3, 1863, *Du Pont Letters*, 3:78. John Ericsson agreed that the slow-firing monitors could not deal with fortifications. In April 1863 Ericsson told Fox, "A hundred rounds cannot silence a fort," and opined that if the Charleston attack succeeded, Fox would be "marvelously fortunate." In September 1863 he wrote, "To silence, destroy, take or hold mud forts is not work that the Monitors are suited for." Ericsson to Fox, April 10, 1863, reel 3, Ericsson Papers; Ericsson to Fox, September 13, 1863, ibid.

26. "The Foe," *Charleston Daily Courier*, April 10, 1863, 2.

27. Beauregard needed no more inspiration; he wrote that the "Abolitionists" would conclude that the monitors were "great humbugs; more terrible in imagination than in reality." Beauregard to Francis W. Pickens, April 18, 1863, OR, ser. 1, 14:901.

28. Stimers soon established a semipermanent Port Royal Working Party, the forerunner of today's mobile repair teams.

29. Reports and correspondence dealing with the action are in ORN, 14:263–92; the description of the *Atlanta*'s injuries are in W. A. Webb to Mallory, October 19, 1864, ibid., 290–92.

30. Fox to Du Pont, March 11, 1863, Thompson and Wainwright, *Correspondence of Fox*, 1:192.

31. Welles, *Diary*, entry for May 20, 1863, 1:307.

32. Stimers to Fox, June 14, 1863, Fox Papers, box 7. Stimers was more concerned than his letter to Fox indicates; his superior characterized him as "braced up . . . as stiff as a frozen eel." Francis H. Gregory to Fox, June 15, 1863, Private, Fox Papers, box 6.

33. Du Pont to Henry Winter Davis, May 3, 1863, *Du Pont Letters*, 3:75.

34. Du Pont to Sophie Du Pont, May 17, 1863, in Journal Letter 66, May 17–19, 1863, *Du Pont Letters*, 3:120; Du Pont to Percival Drayton, May 19, 1863, ibid., 131.

35. Du Pont to Fox, October 8, 1862, *Du Pont Letters*, 2:243; Welles, *Diary*, entry for 27 May 1863, 1:315.

36. Beauregard observed in 1877 that had the ships attacked at night, he could not have repaired the damage and Sumter would have been "disabled and silenced in a few days." Quoted in William Conant Church, *The Life of John Ericsson*, 2 vols. (New York: Charles Scribner's Sons, 1891), 2:46–47. Beauregard also feared that the Federals might send a monitor close to Cummings Point under cover of darkness. Beauregard to Roswell S. Ripley, February 8, 1863, OR, ser. 1, 14:769.

37. *New Ironsides* "creat[ed] a general stampede for the bomb-proof." Lawrence M. Keitt to W. F. Nance, September 5, 1863, OR, ser. 1, 28, part 1: 482.

38. For example, Dahlgren to Charles Koepler et al., November 21, 1863, Papers of John A. B. Dahlgren, Library of Congress, Manuscript Division, Washington DC, box 8, Letter Book E, 169; Dahlgren to Rowan, December 3, 1863, ibid., 314; Dahlgren to Koepler et al., June 13, 1864, ibid., box 10, Book I, 562.

39. Browning, *Success Is All That Was Expected*, 355, 358; Welles, *Diary*, entry for June 23, 1863, 1:341.

40. Quincy A. Gillmore, *Engineer and Artillery Operations against the Defenses of Charleston Harbor in 1863* (New York: D. Van Nostrand, 1865), 16–17.

41. Browning, *Success Is All That Was Expected*, 217, 266–67, 351, 355–56, 358.

42. A. S. Gardner to Dahlgren, August 6, 1864, NARG 45, subject file, PL (Labor and Civil Personnel), box 536; Dahlgren to Maj. Gen. J. G. Foster, August 6, 1864; Foster to Dahlgren, August 7, 1864. Gardner to Dahlgren, August 8, 1864, NARG 45, subject file, PB (Naval Bases and Stations), box 498; Dahlgren to Foster, August 13, 14, and 24, 1864; Foster to Dahlgren, August 17 and August 30, 1864.

43. Gillmore, *Engineer and Artillery Operations*, 63, 65–66, 131–33, 343, 347–48.

44. Dahlgren, *Memoir*, 507. The feeling was apparently mutual: two of Gillmore's officers visited Welles to denounce Dahlgren as "incompetent, imbecile,

and insane." Welles, *Diary*, entry for October 24, 1863, 1:474–75. "Gillmore's book" was the aforementioned *Engineer and Artillery Operations*.

45. Thomas H. Stevens, "The Boat Attack on Sumter," in Robert Underwood Johnson and Clarence C. Buel, eds. *Battles and Leaders of the Civil War*, vol. 4, *The Way to Appomattox* (1887; repr., New York: Castle, 1956), 49–50. The correspondence is in *ORN*, 14:606–10; Union reports are in ibid., 610–36; Confederate accounts are in ibid., 636–40 and *OR*, ser. 1, 28, part 1: 125–26, 403, 724–28. The Confederates had been reading Union signals since April. Beauregard to Seddon, April 13, 1863, *ORN*, 14:689.

46. George E. Belknap, "Reminiscent of the Siege of Charleston," in *Naval Actions and History, 1799–1898*, 190.

47. Stephen R. Wise, *Lifeline of the Confederacy: Blockade Running during the Civil War* (Columbia: University of South Carolina Press, 1988), 251–59.

48. Welles to Dahlgren, October 9, 1863, *ORN*, 15:26–27.

49. Fox to Gregory, October 23, 1863, Private, Fox Papers, box 5A. An engineer who served in the Confederate Army observed, "In no single instance . . . did a naval attack succeed where the channel had been obstructed; and in no single instance did it fail where the channel had remained open." Viktor Ernest Rudolph von Scheliha, *A Treatise on Coast-Defence* (1868; repr., Westport CT: Greenwood, 1971), 178.

50. "Enlisting articles, C. S. Naval Submarine Battery Service," from John S. Barnes to Samuel P. Lee, May 10, 1864, *ORN*, 10:11.

51. Perry, *Infernal Machines*, 8.

52. William T. Glassel, "Reminiscences of Torpedo Service in Charleston Harbor by W. T. Glassell [*sic*], Commander Confederate States Navy," *Southern Historical Society Papers* 4, no. 5 (November 1877): 227–30; R. O. Crowley, "The Confederate Torpedo Service," *Century Illustrated Monthly Magazine* 66:290.

53. Underwater damage depends on brisance (shattering effect), and black powder has a brisance only 1.5 to 17 percent of that of TNT. Paul W. Cooper and Stanley R. Kurowski, *Introduction to the Technology of Explosives* (New York: Wiley-VCH, 1996), 76–77.

54. For example, Mallory ordered 25 miles of "good insulated wire, suitable for submarine batteries." Mallory to Bulloch, April 16, 1864, *ORN*, ser. 2, 2:627–28. Salvaged Federal cable was also used. At the beginning of the Torpedo Service, "we had only about four miles of insulated copper wire in the entire Confederacy," and battery material was "very scarce." Crowley, "Confederate Torpedo Service," 291.

55. Chauncey G. De Lisle to Beauregard, May 25, 1863, *OR*, ser. 1, 14:948–52; John S. Barnes, *Submarine Warfare, Offensive and Defensive* (New York: D. Van Nostrand, 1869), 69–70, 77, 123–24.

56. *Confederate Statutes*, 1st Cong., 1st sess., chapter 71, April 21, 1862.

57. Act of October 13, 1862, from W. W. Lester and Wm. J. Bromwell, *A Digest*

of the Military and Naval Laws of the Confederate States (Columbia [SC]: Evans and Cogswell, 1864) at http://docsouth.unc.edu/imls/confdocs.html. W. W. Mackall to Leonidas K. Polk, October 17, 1861, *OR*, ser. 1, 4:456; Brooke journal, entry for July 25, 1861, Brooke, *Ironclads and Big Guns*, 27; William A. Tidwell, *April '65: Confederate Covert Action in the American Civil War* (Kent OH: Kent State University Press, 1995), 81, 90–91.

58. Barnes, *Submarine Warfare*, 65, 120–21.

59. The secretary of war referred Lee's first proposal to Mallory as a navy matter, but Mallory would do nothing because Lee was not a naval officer. Pierre G. T. Beauregard, "Torpedo Service in the Water Defences of Charleston," *Southern Historical Society Papers* 5, no. 4 (April 1878): 150.

60. Lee to Thomas Jordan, October 22, 1862, *OR*, ser. 1, 14:648; Lee to Jordan, November 8, 1862, ibid., 670.

61. Lee to Jordan, November 22, 1862, *OR*, ser. 1, 14:687.

62. Duncan N. Ingraham to Lee, November 8, 1862, *OR*, ser. 1, 14:671–72; Lee to D. B. Harris, February 3, 1863, ibid., 761.

63. Lee to Jordan, March 19, 1863, *OR*, ser. 1, 14:837; Beauregard to Seddon, March 26, 1863, ibid., 844.

64. Beauregard to Porcher Miles, May 2, 1863, *OR*, ser. 1, 14:923.

65. John Fraser & Co. to Lee, June 6, 1863, with endorsements, *ORN*, ser. 1, 14:965–66.

66. Browning, *Success Is All That Was Expected*, 269–70; Lee to Beauregard, July 25, 1863, *OR*, ser. 1, 28, part 1: 229–30; Perry, *Infernal Machines*, 77–78; Lee to Jordan, July 11, 1863, *OR*, ser. 1, 28, part 2: 191; Lee to A. N. Toutant Beauregard, July 25, 1863, ibid., 229; Lee to Jordan, August 2, 1863, ibid., 251–52.

67. Carlin to Beauregard, August 22, 1863, with Beauregard's endorsement, *OR*, ser. 1, 28, part 1: 680–82.

68. Glassel, "Reminiscences of Torpedo Service," 230–33; William S. Wells to James H. Tomb, December 1, 1913, University of North Carolina, Chapel Hill, Southern Historical Collection, Tomb Papers #723. For a detailed discussion, see Roberts, *USS New Ironsides*, 80–83. Perry (*Infernal Machines*, 82–85) and Luraghi (*A History of the Confederate Navy*, 261–62) are incorrect when they state that *New Ironsides* was seriously damaged. Luraghi's fanciful assertions that the ship had to be placed immediately in drydock "lest she sink" and that she was out of service for more than a year disregard readily available sources.

69. *ORN*, 15:148, 226.

70. William F. Keeler, *Aboard the USS Florida, 1863–65: The Letters of Paymaster William Frederick Keeler, U.S. Navy, to His Wife, Anna*, ed. Robert W. Daly (Annapolis: Naval Institute Press, 1968), 73 (July 24, 1863); Post, "A Diary on the Blockade," 2339; Hunter, *A Year on a Monitor*, 97.

71. *Report of the Secretary of the Navy, 1864–65*, 391.

72. Stimers to Elisha Davis, M.D., March 7, 1864, NARG 19, entry 1252, Letters

sent to Contractors and Local Inspectors Concerning Harbor and River Monitors, May 1863–February 1864, vol. 2.

73. *Report of the Secretary of the Navy, 1864–65*, 389–92.

74. Dahlgren to Welles, August 9, 1863, ORN, 14:431–32. Welles stated, however, that the order permitting periodic rotation of men from the monitors to wooden vessels "was not availed of by their officers and crews." *Report of the Secretary of the Navy, 1864–65*, 392. The 25 percent extra pay granted to enlisted men for service aboard the monitors may have been influential in this regard.

75. Royce Shingleton, "Seamen, Landsmen, Firemen, and Coal Heavers," in *Confederate Navy*, ed. Still, 142. The James River squadron suffered even more. John M. Coski, *Capital Navy: The Men, Ships, and Operations of the James River Squadron* (Campbell CA: Savas, 1996), 180–81.

76. H. B. Littlepage to Catesby ap R. Jones, February 16, 1863, ORN, 13:820.

77. John Rodgers to Du Pont, March 19, 1863, ORN, 13:767.

78. Thornton A. Jenkins et al. to Farragut, August 13, 1864, ORN, 21:548; Still, *Iron Afloat*, 101.

79. Harold D. Langley, "Shipboard Life," in *Confederate Navy*, ed. Still, 183; Shingleton, "Seamen, Landsmen, Firemen, and Coal Heavers," in ibid., 142; Still, *Iron Afloat*, 100–101.

80. Still, *Iron Afloat*, 88–89.

81. Beauregard to Porcher Miles, November 14, 1863, OR, ser. 1, 28, part 2: 503–4.

82. Miles to Beauregard, December 30, 1863, enclosing Mallory to Miles, December 19, 1863, OR, ser. 1, 28, part 2: 595–97.

83. Beauregard to Miles, January 5, 1864, OR, ser. 1, 28, part 2: 605–6.

84. Beauregard, "Torpedo Service," 150, 154.

85. Wise, *Lifeline*, 265–68.

5. IRONCLADS IN STRENGTH

1. Wells, *Confederate Navy*, 105–6; Investigation of the Navy Department, testimony of Chief Engineer William P. Williamson, ORN, ser. 2, 1:638.

2. Wells, *Confederate Navy*, 132–33; Bulloch, *Secret Service*, 467–68. When the Confederates did try to build engines overseas, the drawings sent to Bulloch were contradictory and the engines were ill-fitted for their purposes. Bulloch to Mallory, October 24, 1864, ORN, ser. 2, 2:739, and January 26, 1865, ibid., 790–91.

3. Still, *Iron Afloat*, 94, 96, 101–4.

4. The Union ironclad program is discussed at greater length in William H. Roberts, *Civil War Ironclads: Industrial Mobilization for the Union Navy* (Baltimore: Johns Hopkins University Press, 2002).

5. Gregory testimony, *Report of the Joint Committee on the Conduct of the War*, 38th Cong., 2d sess., "Light Draught Monitors," 74; Deposition of Alban C.

Stimers, August 11, 18, and 19, 1873, NARG 123, Records of the Court of Claims, entry 1, cases 6326/6327, *Swift v. U.S.*

6. Church, *Life of John Ericsson*, 2:4.

7. The 15-inch guns could not be manufactured in time, so all the Passaics except *Camanche* received one 15-inch Dahlgren and either an 11-inch Dahlgren or a 150-pounder Parrott rifle. U.S. Navy Department, Naval History Division, *Monitors of the U.S. Navy, 1861–1937* (Washington: Government Printing Office, 1969), 10.

8. Fox to J. Hayden, April 3, 1862, Thompson and Wainwright, *Correspondence of Fox*, 2:285. A preprinted contract for the Passaic class is in NARG 45, subject file, AC (Construction), box 22.

9. Percival Drayton to Samuel F. Du Pont, November 24, 1862, *Du Pont Letters*, 2:293. Fox asked Ericsson to inspect the battle-tested *Monitor*, but he declined. David A. Mindell, *War, Technology, and Experience Aboard the USS Monitor* (Baltimore: Johns Hopkins University Press, 2000), 90.

10. Fox to Harrison Loring, April 14, 1862, NARG 45, entry M209, roll 24, 68:63.

11. Ericsson to Welles, February 5, 1863, NARG 45, entry M124, roll 433, 67; Church, *Life of John Ericsson*, 2:5; Harrison Loring to Welles, February 10, 1862, NARG 45, entry M124, roll 398:171.

12. The tenth vessel was *Camanche*, built for West Coast service. *Camanche*'s design had unique features, so references herein to the Passaic class apply to the nine East Coast ships.

13. George Michael O'Har, "Shipbuilding, Markets, and Technological Change in East Boston" (Ph.D. diss., Massachusetts Institute of Technology, 1994), 160.

14. Welles to John P. Hale and Charles B. Sedgwick, March 25, 1862, NARG 45, entry 5, Letters to Congress, vol. 11, labeled on spine "No. 13 Jan. 3, 1855 to May 12, 1862."

15. Ericsson to Fox, August 6, 1862, NARG 45, entry M124, roll 415:155.

16. Fox to Stimers, September 5, 15, and 25, 1862, Fox Papers, box 5.

17. Composite Consumer Price Index 1860–1866 from John J. McCusker, *How Much Is That in Real Money? A Historical Price Index for Use as a Deflator of Money Values in the Economy of the United States* (Worcester MA: American Antiquarian Society, 1992), 328.

18. From N. G. Thom's Record of Prices Paid by Miles Greenwood, NARG 123, entry 1, case 6326, *Swift v. U.S.*

19. Church, *Life of John Ericsson*, 1:270. The unstable economy made fixed price contracts unsuitable even for such simple items as clothing. *Report of the Secretary of the Navy, 1862–63*, 1033. Civilian specialty producers such as the Baldwin Locomotive Works turned to cost-plus contracts.

20. Henry Putney Beers, *The Confederacy: A Guide to the Archives of the Confederate States of America* (Washington DC: National Archives and Records Admin-

istration, 1998), 374, 375, 382, 383; Still, *Iron Afloat*, 9. The facilities mentioned were begun in mid- to late 1861.

21. Beers, *The Confederacy*, 374–76, 377–78, 383, 385; Coski, *Capital Navy*, 68, 71–72, 81–82. Maurice Melton, "Major Military Industries of the Confederate Government," Ph.D. diss., Emory University, 1978, 165–294, describes the Selma works in detail.

22. Coski, *Capital Navy*, 75.

23. "I was assigned to the *Chicora*, a little ironclad that was being built between two wharves which served as a navy yard." James Morris Morgan, *Recollections of a Rebel Reefer* (Boston: Houghton Mifflin, 1917) (electronic edition at http://docsouth.unc.edu/morganjames/morgan.html#morgan89), 90.

24. Deposition of Alexander Swift, November 10–11, 1876, NARG 123, entry 1, case 7157, *Greenwood v. U.S.* Deposition of James F. Secor Sr., in Evidence for Claimants, NARG 123, entry 1, cases 29,939, 29,943, and 29,944, *James F. Secor and Anna A. Secor, Executors of the Will of James F. Secor, Deceased, Survivor of Zeno Secor and Charles A. Secor, v. U.S.* (hereafter "Secor cases"); Secor & Co. to Welles, June 1, 1867, NARG 19, entry 186, s.v. Claim of Secor & Company.

25. Deposition of Nathaniel G. Thom, December 29–30, 1876, January 2, 1877, July 9–10, 1877, NARG 123, entry 1, case 7157, *Greenwood v. U.S.*

26. Jones to John M. Brooke, November 30, 1863, *Ironclads and Big Guns*, 156; Melton, "Major Military Industries," 197, 213, 215.

27. Du Pont to Benjamin Gerhard, January 31, 1863, *Du Pont Letters*, 2:395–96.

28. Mallory to Davis, ORN, ser. 2, 2:154.

29. Still, *Confederate Navy*, 74.

30. Mallory to S. S. Lee, March 26, 1862, ORN, 7:751–52.

31. Mallory to S. S. Lee, May 1 and 3, 1862, ORN, 7:779–80, 783.

32. Ralph W. Donnelly, "The Charlotte, North Carolina, Navy Yard, C.S.N." *Civil War History* 5 (March 1959): 73–74.

33. Coski, *Capital Navy*, 65, 67, 81.

34. Luraghi, *History of the Confederate Navy*, 346, 189–90.

35. Mallory to North, May 17, 1861, ORN, ser. 2, 2:70–72.

36. Bulloch to Mallory, July 21, 1862, ORN, ser. 2, 2:223. This iron-hulled vessel was built by James & George Thompson, Clydebank. At 4,670 tons she was smaller than contemporary British ironclads but still very ambitious for the day. William E. Geoghegan et al., "The South's Scottish Sea Monster," *American Neptune* 29, no. 1 (January 1969): 5–29.

37. Mallory to Bulloch, January 14, 1862, ORN, ser. 2, 2:131.

38. Bulloch, *Secret Service*, 264–67; Bulloch to Mallory, July 21, 1862, ORN, ser. 2, 2:223.

39. Mallory to Bulloch, April 30, 1862, ORN, ser. 2, 2:187.

40. Bulloch to Mallory, July 21, 1862, ORN, ser. 2, 2:224–26. The Laird vessels

were nearly identical in length and draft to the Union's *New Ironsides,* also an ironclad designed for shallow draft, although their beam was narrower.

41. *The Case of the United States, to Be Laid before the Tribunal of Arbitration,* Senate Executive Document 31, 42d Cong., 2d sess., 73.

42. Bulloch, *Secret Service,* 47–48, 67–68.

43. Bulloch, *Secret Service,* 267–68, 270.

44. Richard I. Lester, *Confederate Finance and Purchasing in Great Britain* (Charlottesville: University Press of Virginia, 1975), 10, 12, 17–18. At par in May 1861, by December 1861 Confederate remittances to England were at 25 percent premium, and by May 1862 the premium was 100 percent. Treasury Report of Funds Remitted to England, ORN, ser. 2, 2:262.

45. Geoghegan et al., "The South's Scottish Sea Monster," 17–19.

46. Lester, *Confederate Finance,* 19–20, 34, 38–44; Samuel Bernard Thompson, *Confederate Purchasing Operations Abroad* (Chapel Hill: University of North Carolina Press, 1935), 52–56.

47. Roberts, *Civil War Ironclads,* 49–51.

48. Ericsson to Fox, March 19, 1862, Fox Papers, box 3. By July 1863 the Union would be building forty-two coastal ironclads totaling over 98,000 tons.

49. Deposition of Charles A. Secor, April 24, 1876, NARG 123, entry 1, case 7157, *Greenwood v. U.S.*

50. The quest for technical perfection did not affect the Passaics as much as it did the later monitors, because the Passaic design was more mature when the contracts were let and because Ericsson himself was more involved. Unlike later monitors, the Passaics suffered from construction delays rather than from design delays.

51. Deposition of Alban C. Stimers, August 11, 18, 19, 1873, NARG 123, entry 1, case 6326/6327, *Swift v. U.S.*

52. Exhibit H, Evidence for Claimants, NARG 123, entry 1, Secor cases, 152–55.

53. Exhibit H, Evidence for Claimants, NARG 123, entry 1, Secor cases, 152–55; Deposition of Charles A. Secor, April 24, 1876, NARG 123, entry 1, case 7157, *Greenwood v. U.S.*; Deposition of James F. Secor [Sr.] in Evidence for Claimants, ibid., Secor cases.

54. Roberts, *Civil War Ironclads,* 108.

55. Fox to Ericsson, February 21, 1863, Fox Papers, box 5A; Ericsson to Welles, February 24, 1863, NARG 45, entry M124, roll 435:67.

56. Nathaniel McKay testimony, *Report of the Joint Committee on the Conduct of the War,* 38th Cong., 2d sess., "Light Draught Monitors," 31.

57. For the ships already awarded, the changes were extra work. For the later ships, however, "we require those who are now offering to build to take the new specifications at the same price or decline as they choose." Fox to Stimers, May 2, 1863, Fox Papers, box 5A.

58. Wilbur Devereux Jones, *The Confederate Rams at Birkenhead: A Chapter in*

Anglo-American Relations (Tuscaloosa AL: Confederate, 1961), 42–51. Jones provides a comprehensive discussion of the legal aspects of the case.

59. Bulloch, *Secret Service*, 245; Bulloch to Mallory, September 1, 1863, ORN, ser. 2, 2:488.

60. Warren F. Spencer, *The Confederate Navy in Europe* (Tuscaloosa: University of Alabama Press, 1983), 99, 102. Bulloch, convinced of the sympathy of the "great majority of the people of England," forgot the adage that Great Britain has no permanent friends, only permanent interests. Bulloch, *Secret Service*, 319–20.

61. David Hepburn Milton, *Lincoln's Spymaster: Thomas Haines Dudley and the Liverpool Network* (Mechanicsburg PA: Stackpole, 2003), 79–80, 90–91. Yonge was working for U.S. Consul Thomas Dudley even before the *Alabama* sailed. Ibid., 47.

62. Barron to Mallory, January 11, 1864, ORN, ser. 2, 2:572.

63. Bulloch, *Secret Service*, 331–32.

64. Bulloch, *Secret Service*, 334, 342.

65. Lynn M. Case and Warren F. Spencer, *The United States and France: Civil War Diplomacy* (Philadelphia: University of Pennsylvania Press, 1970), 429–34.

66. M. Arman to Minister of the Marine, June 1, 1863, ORN, ser. 2, 2:432–32, and reply, M. Chasseloup-Laubat to M. L. Arman, June 6, 1863, ibid., 433.

67. Mallory to Bulloch, March 27, 1863, enclosing Mallory to Slidell, March 27, 1863, ORN, ser. 2, 2:395–96.

68. Bulloch, *Secret Service*, 277; Jones, *Confederate Rams at Birkenhead*, 60–61.

69. Mallory to Bulloch, May 26, 1863, ORN, ser. 2, 2:428–29.

70. Bulloch to Mallory, August 7, 1863, ibid., 476–78; Bulloch, *Secret Service*, 336–38, 339–40. The contract is at ORN, ser. 2, 2:464–66.

71. Mallory to Davis, February 27, 1862, ORN, ser. 2, 2:152.

72. Spencer, *Confederate Navy*, 111–12.

73. Spencer, *Confederate Navy*, 102. Bulloch's sense of righteous indignation at Britain's changing the rules in midgame is frequently evident in his writing, but there were material differences between the rams and the *Alexandra*, and the British government's case against the rams was legally much stronger. Jones, *Confederate Rams at Birkenhead*, 96–97.

6. RUNNERS AND BLOCKADERS

1. *Annual Report of the Secretary of the Navy, 1860–61*, 5.

2. Thomas E. Taylor, *Running the Blockade: A Personal Narrative of Adventures, Risks, and Escapes during the American Civil War* (1896; repr., Annapolis: Naval Institute Press, 1995), 12–13.

3. Hobart Pasha [Charles A. Hobart-Hampton], *Sketches from My Life* (New York: D. Appleton, 1887), 173.

4. Lebergott, "Through the Blockade," 870–72, 876–77.

5. Sailmaker Nicholas Lynch, whose ship was used mostly as the station vessel

at Ship Island, noted that other ships took care not to capture any prizes within signal distance. Oxley, "Civil War Gulf Blockade," entry dated April 10, 1862.

6. *Report of the Secretary of the Navy, 1864–65*, December 4, 1865, 511, 517. Lee clearly intended to get his share; he insisted that prize lists "state not only the name of the vessel but that she belongs to the North Atlantic Blockading Squadron, commanded by Acting Rear-Admiral S. P. Lee." ORN, 9:188.

7. For example, ORN, 14:670–71; Wise, *Lifeline*, 119. This policy changed in early 1864 when the Confederate government took ownership of the runners. In January 1864 Welles directed, "British blockade violators will be henceforth detained," but by May he had again loosened the policy. Welles's endorsement on Seward to Welles, January 11, 1864, ORN, 9:285; Welles to S. P. Lee, May 16, 1864, ibid., 10:61–62.

8. Welles directed that a "fair proportion" of prizes be sent to Boston. Welles to Stringham, June 28, 1861, ORN, 5:751. Prizes were sent to New York, Boston, Philadelphia, Baltimore, Washington DC, Providence RI, and Key West. As courts reopened in Union-occupied areas, prizes were also sent to New Orleans (from 1863) and St. Augustine, Florida (from 1864).

9. Eighteen percent of attempts to run to and from Carolina ports in 1861 were made by steam runners. The steamers' share grew to 33 percent in 1862 and 84 percent in 1863. Lebergott, "Through the Blockade," 873.

10. Taylor, *Running the Blockade*, 12.

11. *Case of the United States*, Senate Executive Document 31, 42d Cong., 2d sess., 95, 115.

12. Frank E. Vandiver, ed., *Confederate Blockade Running through Bermuda, 1861–1865* (Austin: University of Texas Press, 1947), xxxv.

13. Courtemanche, *No Need of Glory*, 96.

14. One captain described his 1864 blockade-runner as "just strong enough to stand the heavy cross sea in the Gulf Stream." Hobart Pasha, *Sketches from My Life*, 160. As late as January 1865, the new blockade-runner *Lelia* foundered off England. *Naval Chronology*, V-16.

15. "The blockade-runner had always full speed at command, her steam being at all times well up and every one on board on the look-out; whereas the man-of-war must be steaming with some degree of economy and ease, and her look-out men had not the excitement to keep them always on the *qui vive* that we had." Hobart Pasha, *Sketches from My Life*, 136–37.

16. The letter, found in the *Kate*'s engineer's log book, is enclosed in S. P. Lee to Isherwood, July 28, 1863, NARG 19, entry 972, no. 32.

17. William Watson, *Adventures of a Blockade Runner; or, Trade in Time of War* (New York: Macmillan, 1892), 293–94. Welles denied requests to export anthracite in, e.g., Welles to Merrick & Sons, January 21, 1863, NARG 45, entry M209, roll 25, 70:282.

18. Wise, *Lifeline*, 110–11.

19. Taylor, *Running the Blockade*, 41; Hobart Pasha, *Sketches from My Life*, 89–90.

20. Du Pont to Sophie Du Pont, Journal Letter 85, August 31, 1862, *Du Pont Letters*, 2:209.

21. Off Wilmington, the Federals placed launches close in; when they saw Confederate navigation lights, "they signalled to the blockaders, who immediately commenced shelling the bar." Taylor, *Running the Blockade*, 72. The blockaders might send launches into the shallows, or leave a gap between two anchored ships and then plug it after nightfall with another vessel. Watson, *Adventures*, 165, 202; Hobart Pasha, *Sketches from My Life*, 94–95. 202.

22. S. P. Lee to B. F. Sands, September 1, 1864, ORN, 10:414.

23. Lebergott, "Through the Blockade," 873.

24. General Instructions, December 16, 1863, ORN, 9:355–58; Lee to O. S. Glisson, July 18, 1864, ibid., 10:286–87. Hobart-Hampton recorded the result: "We went on all right till half-past eight o'clock, when the weather cleared up, and there was a large paddle-wheel cruiser . . . about six miles astern of us." Hobart Pasha, *Sketches from My Life*, 113.

25. This example does not correct the local time of dawn (civil twilight) for the easting the outbound runner would make during the night. Astronomical data from the U.S. Naval Observatory, http://aa.usno.navy.mil/data/docs/RS_OneDay.html.

26. Watson noted the "understanding" among blockade-running captains "that if they sighted each other at sea they should stand away from each other, so as to lessen the danger of both being captured should one be sighted by a cruiser." Watson, *Adventures*, 204.

27. Order no. 80, September 23, 1864, Directions and Signals, NARG 45, entry 395, subseries E-95, Correspondence of CDR William Reynolds, vol. 4.

28. The Federals captured Lamb's guns in August 1863. Pearce Crosby to S. P. Lee, September 8, 1863, ORN, 9:171; W. H. C. Whiting to James Seddon, August 24, 1863, ibid., 173–74. The sight of a beached vessel "surrounded by Confederate troops" was "not uncommon." Watson, *Adventures*, 165. Hobart-Hampton noted the propensity of runner crews to burn their ships. Hobart Pasha, *Sketches from My Life*, 94.

29. Michael J. Bennett asserts that greed "often" led ships to use nondestructive tactics that allowed blockade-runners to escape and that runners would jettison cotton to cause pursuers to turn aside to pick it up. Bennett, "Union Jacks," 124–26. This makes little sense. If the pursuer were holding his own or gaining, he would not stop to pick up a bale or two of cotton and risk losing the greater prize. If the pursuer were losing ground, the runner would not need to throw money away. The technological context is critical, and Bennett does not consider it. Paddlewheel propulsion systems are very sensitive to immersion—paddles that are too deeply immersed create more drag and transmit less power to move the

ship, a condition that applied even to the feathering paddlewheels used on many runners. Several tons of cotton thrown overboard could significantly lighten the draft of a slim, shallow hull, moving the paddles up from an inefficient to a more efficient depth. Robert Murray, *Rudimentary Treatise on Marine Engines and Steam Vessels*, 3d ed. (London: John Weale, 1858), 142–43.

30. Taylor, *Running the Blockade*, 68–69. For similar tactics, see Hobart Pasha, *Sketches from My Life*, 114–15.

31. J. R. M. Mullany to Du Pont, May 24, 1862, ORN, 13:29–30; K. Jack Bauer and Stephen S. Roberts, *Register of Ships of the U.S. Navy, 1775–1990: Major Combatants* (New York: Greenwood, 1991), 92; *Lloyd's Register of British and Foreign Shipping. From 1st July, 1862, to the 30th June, 1863* (London: Cox & Wyman, 1862), s.v. *Stettin*.

32. Wise, *Lifeline*, 94–98; ORN, 9:284.

33. Lester, *Confederate Finance*, 33, 189; Wise, *Lifeline*, 142, 145. The edict required time to become effective because it was difficult to provide enough government-owned cotton to fill the space.

34. Wise, *Lifeline*, 144–47; Wilson, *Confederate Industry*, 97. The legislation, approved February 6, 1864, gave the president the power to regulate exports and the authority to use military or naval force to prevent violations. *Confederate Statutes*, 1st Cong., 4th sess., chapter 24. Hobart-Hampton complained that the Confederate government had arbitrarily pressed the runners into service, reducing the owners' profits so that "the ventures hardly paid." Hobart Pasha, *Sketches from My Life*, 172.

35. In December 1863 the Erlanger bonds had slipped to 35 percent of their face value, after being issued at 90. By February 1864 they were again in the 50s, and in early September 1864 they peaked in the 80s. By late September they had fallen to the 60s. Lester, *Confederate Finance*, 49–50, 53–54, 204–6.

36. Keeler, *Aboard the USS Florida*, 109 (November 3, 1863).

37. Keeler claimed the canned fruits provided for their antiscorbutic properties were "hardly enough like the original to claim relationship." Keeler, *Aboard the USS Florida*, 75 (August 1, 1863). Butler's diary noted gleefully the arrival of fresh meat on February 28, 1863, and Keeler told his wife, "You can imagine how eagerly we look for [the supply ship] about the time she becomes due." Keeler, *Aboard the USS Florida*, 41 (May 24, 1863). Each supply ship carried an officially appointed sutler, who was required to report what goods he sold and the prices he charged. Representative accounts may be found at NARG 45, entry M124, roll 402:83, 410:130, 412:160, 414:245.

38. Bennett, "Union Jacks," v–vi, 8, 11, 19. Officers wrote more, as might be expected. The author's wife has pointedly noted the tendency of modern naval officers to exchange "professional" gossip, and that tendency was equally evident in the 1860s.

39. George E. Belknap, "Reminiscent of the 'New Ironsides' Off Charleston," *United Service Magazine*, o.s., 1 (January 1879): 70.

40. Alvah Folsom Hunter, *A Year on a Monitor and the Destruction of Fort Sumter*, ed. Craig L. Symonds (Columbia: University of South Carolina Press, 1987), 89–90, 105, 157–58.

41. Keeler, *Aboard the* USS *Florida*, 25 (April 23, 1863).

42. NARG 24, Records of the Bureau of Personnel, log of USS *Stettin*, entries for March 28, April 29, August 9, December 8, 1864.

43. Stephen C. Rowan to Welles, November 22, 1863, ORN, 15:134.

44. Thomas Griffin to Stimers, March 24, 1864, NARG 19, entry 186, Records Relating to Claims, box 65, envelope 619, Port Royal Working Party.

45. Keeler, *Aboard the* USS *Florida*, 66–67 (July 12, 1863).

46. B. F. Sands to S. P. Lee, October 13, 1863, ORN, 9:235.

47. Federal reports of the *Raleigh* action are in ORN, 10:18–24; J. B. Breck to S. P. Lee, May 26, 1864, ibid., 10:94; W. B. Cushing to S. P. Lee, ibid., 203; E. N. Semon to O. S. Glisson, September 28, 1864, ibid., 509.

48. NARG 24, log of *Stettin*, entries for September 23–28, 1863; Butler Diary, entries for September 23–27, 1863; Van Alstine to Welles, September 24, 1863, ORN, 14:670–71.

49. Butler Diary, dates mentioned.

50. Frank Lawrence Owsley, *King Cotton Diplomacy: Foreign Relations of the Confederate States of America*, 2d ed., rev. by Harriet Chappell Owsley (Chicago: University of Chicago Press, 1959), 23–24, 37–41.

51. Wise, *Lifeline*, 226; William N. Still Jr. "A Naval Sieve: The Union Blockade in the Civil War," in Still et al., *Raiders and Blockaders: The American Civil War Afloat* (Washington DC: Brassey's, 1998), 138–39.

52. Surdam, *Northern Naval Superiority*, 73–84, 88–90.

53. Du Pont to Sophie Du Pont, November 21, 1861, in Journal Letter 8, November 18–25, 1861, *Du Pont Letters*, 1:255.

54. Owsley, *King Cotton Diplomacy*, 23–24, 30, 39, 42.

55. Surdam, *Northern Naval Superiority*, 1–8, 139–41.

56. Surdam, *Northern Naval Superiority*, 160–61, 206–9; Watson, *Adventures*, 305.

57. Runner figures from Wise, *Lifeline*, 233–59; Robert H. Newell, *Orpheus C. Kerr Papers* (New York: Blakeman & Mason, 1862), 1:205.

7. PRIVATEERS, "PIRATES," AND RAIDERS

1. *Report of the Secretary of the Navy, 1860–61*, 5. For the distinction between the belligerent rights of contraband and blockade, C. John Colombos, *A Treatise on the Law of Prize*, 3d ed. (London: Longmans Green, 1949), 253.

2. E. G. Parrott to Stringham, June 5, 1861, ORN, 1:29, and Stringham to Welles, June 6, 1861, ibid., 28. Parrott, the lieutenant commanding the *Perry*, referred to

the *Savannah* as a privateer; Stringham, more in tune with official Washington, characterized her as "piratical."

3. Robinson, *Confederate Privateers*, 133–34, 148–50. The Mexican War afforded precedent, in that the United States threatened to treat any foreigner serving in a Mexican privateer as a pirate. Bauer, *Mexican War*, 112.

4. Du Pont to Henry Winter Davis, July 18, 1861, *Du Pont Letters*, 1:106; Robinson, *Confederate Privateers*, 291–93.

5. Legally, a captured ship belonged to her original owners until she was condemned by a competent court. Not until then did she become the captors' property. If the captors destroyed her before condemnation, they would be illegally harming someone else's property. As the representative of a sovereign power, a warship's commander had the option of destroying a captured vessel as he could destroy other private property (such as a salt works or grist mill) used to benefit the enemy.

6. Semmes, *Memoirs of Service Afloat*, 141–42, 232–33.

7. James S. Palmer to Welles, November 23, 1861, ORN, 1:212–13; Palmer to Welles, November 25, 1861, ibid., 213–14; Palmer to Welles, December 5, 1861, enclosing H. A. Anandale to Palmer, December 3, 1861, ibid., 216–17; Semmes, *Memoirs of Service Afloat*, 252–64.

8. Semmes described his tribulations in Gibraltar in *Memoirs of Service Afloat*, 329–45. Despite his autobiographical comments regarding the difficulty of leaving the vessel, he had decided as early as February that laying her up would be the best course. Semmes to J. M. Mason and Semmes to Mallory, February 24, 1862, ORN, 1:663–66. The *Sumter*, which Bulloch described as his "bête noire," was eventually sold into the merchant service.

9. R. B. Pegram to Mallory, March 10, 1862, ORN, 745–49. After two successful trips through the blockade, she was again sold. She became the privateer *Rattlesnake*, but the blockade kept her pinned in Georgia's Ogeechee River until Union ships destroyed her in February 1863.

10. Bulloch *Secret Service*, 189–90. Semmes lamented that the *Sumter* was "always anchored . . . by her propeller, whenever she was out of coal." Semmes, *Memoirs of Service Afloat*, 342.

11. Fraser, Trenholm & Co. was the Liverpool branch of George A. Trenholm's interlocking companies, which also included John Fraser & Co., Trenholm Brothers, and Adderly & Co. Fraser, Trenholm became the official "depository" for Confederate funds in Europe and frequently advanced money for the Confederacy's purposes. Wise, *Lifeline*, 46–47; Bulloch, *Secret Service*, 593; Ethel S. Nepveux, *George Alfred Trenholm: The Company That Went to War, 1861–1865* (Anderson SC: Electric City, 1994), 21–22.

12. Bulloch, *Secret Service*, 48.

13. Fraser, Trenholm & Co. to North, February 5, 1862, ORN, ser. 2, 2:142–43.

14. North to J. M. Mason, February 6, 1862, ORN, ser. 2, 2:144.

15. Bulloch, *Secret Service*, 107–11.

16. Bulloch to Maffitt and Bulloch to John Low, March 21, 1862, ORN, 1:755–57.

17. Extracts from the Journal of Lt. J. N. Maffitt, CSN, commanding CSS *Florida*, ORN, 1:763–65.

18. Cdr. George H. Preble to Farragut, September 4, September 6, October 10, 1862, ORN, 1:432, 433–34, 436–40.

19. Welles, *Diary*, entry for September 19, 1862, 1:140; Welles to Preble, September 20, 1862, ORN, 1:434. Preble was reinstated in 1863, but the degree of his culpability was not finally settled until a court of inquiry was held in 1872. Abraham Lincoln to U.S. Senate, February 12, 1863, ibid., 459.

20. Bulloch, *Secret Service*, 161–71, 173–74.

21. Bulloch, *Secret Service*, 165–67, 168–69; Mallory to Bulloch, July 12, 1862, ORN, ser. 2, 2:215–17.

22. Bulloch, *Secret Service*, 168. Bulloch attributed the British action to false affidavits procured by the Federals, but later scholarship indicates that the British government had identified the deficiencies of the Foreign Enlistment Act and had decided to meet its international obligations "regardless of domestic law." Ibid., 177–78, 183–84; Spencer, *Confederate Navy*, 31.

23. Bulloch to Mallory, August 11, 1862, ORN, ser. 2, 2:235–36; Bulloch to Mallory, September 10, 1862, ibid., 263–65.

24. Welles, *Diary*, entry for September 4, 1862, 1:109; entry for September 16, 1862, 1:134; Welles to Wilkes, September 8, 1862, ORN, 1:470–71.

25. Fox to Du Pont, November 7, 1862, Thompson and Wainwright, *Correspondence of Fox*, 1:165. As one author has pointed out, the Union Navy had very few ships (the 1858 and 1862 classes of screw sloops and a few others) with the endurance, seakeeping qualities, and armament to seek out a Confederate raider and give battle on equal terms. James Murray Ruppert, "Hurry All to Sea: Union Naval Strategy to Counter Confederate Commerce Raiding," research report, U.S. Naval War College, 1992.

26. Semmes, *Memoirs of Service Afloat*, 514–16; William Ronckendorff to Welles, November 21, 1863, ORN, 1:549–50.

27. Semmes to Mallory, January 4, 1863, ORN, 1:480.

28. The Federal description of the action and its aftermath appears at ORN, 2:18–23; Semmes's official report is Semmes to Mallory, May 12, 1863, ibid., 683–84, and his unofficial recounting appears in *Memoirs of Service Afloat*, 541–50.

29. Extracts from the journal of Lt. J. N. Maffitt, entry for December 1, 1862, ORN, 1:768–69.

30. Read to Maffitt, May 6, 1863, ORN, 2:644; Maffitt to Mallory, May 11, 1863, ibid., 649.

31. Edmund A. Souder & Co. to Welles, June 13, 1863, ORN, 2:273–74; Welles, *Diary*, entry for June 13, 1863, 1:327.

32. Read to Mallory, July 30, 1863, ORN, 2:654–55; Read to Mallory, October 19, 1864, ibid., 655–57.

33. Jedediah Jewett, Collector of Customs, to Salmon P. Chase, June 27, 1863, ORN, 2:322–25; Robert H. Woods, "The Cruise of the Clarence-Tacony-Archer," *Proceedings of the United States Naval Institute* 35, no. 3 (September 1909): 675–84.

34. Farragut to Welles, June 23, 1863, ORN, 19:535–36.

35. Welles, *Diary*, entry for May 12, 1863, 1:299; ibid., entry for June 4, 1863, 1:322–23. Welles later wrote Wilkes, "You prevented the orders of the Department from being carried into execution. . . . You took the responsibility . . . and failed." Welles to Wilkes, December 15, 1863, ORN, 2:569–71.

36. Welles, *Diary*, entry for May 12, 1863, 1:299.

37. Mallory to Bulloch, September 20, 1862, ORN, ser. 2, 2:270; Bulloch, *Secret Service*, 488.

38. Bulloch, *Secret Service*, 488–92.

39. Bulloch, *Secret Service*, 490–93.

40. Douglas H. Maynard, "The Confederacy's Super *Alabama*," *Civil War History* 5 (March 1959), 80–95.

41. *Naval Chronology*, VI-314, 188, 240–41, 190; David M. Sullivan, "Phantom Fleet: The Confederacy's Unclaimed European-Built Warships," *Warship International* 24, no. 1 (1987): 18, 26–27, 32. The cover names for the four latter ships were *Ajax, Hercules, Enterprise,* and *Adventure*.

42. Semmes, *Memoirs of Service Afloat*, 626–28, 662–63, 738–43. The British later determined that the *Tuscaloosa* had been lawfully commissioned, but the Confederates could not resume possession of her before the war ended. Ibid., 745.

43. Semmes to Barron, June 14, 1864, ORN, 4:651.

44. Semmes, *Memoirs of Service Afloat*, 753–58. Arthur Sinclair, *Alabama*'s fifth lieutenant, asserted that Semmes "knew all about [the chain-armor], and could have adopted the same scheme." Arthur Sinclair, *Two Years on the Alabama* (1895; repr., Annapolis: Naval Institute Press, 1989), 234.

45. The Confederate agent at Cherbourg asked Slidell to prevent Semmes from engaging the *Kearsarge*, writing that it would be "greater service" if Semmes and his crew would "reserve their energies and their valor to continue the work" of commerce destruction. Slidell refused, since even if the *Alabama* lost, "the honor of her flag will be maintained." Ad. Bonfils to Slidell, June 18, 1864, ORN, 4:662; Slidell to Bonfils, June 19, 1864, ibid.

46. Bulloch, *Secret Service*, 192, 194; Semmes, *Service Afloat*, 628–30. In December 1862 the New York Chamber of Commerce asked Welles to dispatch ships "to cruise about the Equator and on the coast of Brazil." Welles endorsed their letter, "Done already." Chamber of Commerce to Welles, December 6, 1862, NARG 45, entry M124, roll 427:132, 132½.

47. A lookout posted 100 feet up could theoretically see the tip of a 100-foot

masthead 22.8 miles away. Two ships each making 6 knots (a relative speed of 12 knots) could cover this distance in under two hours. Smoke was more visible (our lookout could theoretically see a plume 400 feet high from 34 miles away), but a cruising ship with fires banked would not be making much smoke.

48. Welles to T. M. Brashear, August 28, 1861, ORN, 1:73; Welles to "Agent of the California Mail Steamers," June 5, 1862, ibid., 393; Welles to George M. Ransom, April 25, 1863, ibid., 2:166–67; Welles to J. M. Lardner, June 1, 1863, ibid., 2:251; Lewis McMurray & Co. to Welles, December 31, 1862, with endorsements, NARG 45, entry M124, roll 429:142. Convoy operations continued through May 1865. A special escort was provided for the *Aquila*, which carried the disassembled monitor *Camanche* to the Pacific coast for reassembly.

49. "Captain" to Welles, undated (received about December 31, 1862), NARG 45, entry M124, roll 429:148. Ironically, "Captain" wanted Welles to "send a man like Wilkes," who was already (and unsuccessfully) pursuing the "pirate."

50. For representative schemes, see Charles P. Clark to Fox, November 5, 1862, NARG 45, entry M124, roll 424:85; A. J. Bishop to Welles, January 6, 1863, ibid., roll 430:73; Fox to Edward G. Flynn, October 30, 1862, Thompson and Wainwright, *Correspondence of Fox*, 2:420–21; Welles, *Diary*, entry for August 15, 1863, 1:405.

51. Welles, *Diary*, entry for December 26, 1863, 1:497.

52. Among many examples, see A. A. Low to Welles, February 21, 1863, Welles Papers, reel 6, container 7, 148; R. B. Forbes to Fox, November 19, 1862, Fox Papers, box 5; Welles to Louis Blodget, July 22, 1861, NARG 45, entry M209, roll 23, 65:44; Welles to E. D. Morgan, September 17, 1862, ibid., roll 24, 69:341; Welles, *Diary*, entries for June 27, July 18 and July 22, 1863, 1:347, 375, 380.

53. E. D. Morgan to Welles, telegram, March 19, 1862, NARG 45, entry M124, roll 401:259; J. A. Andrew to Welles, telegram, February 2, 1863, ibid., roll 433:19; George W. Blunt to Fox, September 10, 1862, Fox Papers, box 3; Fox to Blunt, September 11, 1862, Thompson and Wainwright, *Correspondence of Fox*, 2:374.

54. Du Pont, *Report on the National Defences*, 9.

55. Welles, *Diary*, entry for September 11, 1862, 1:123.

56. Fox to R. B. Forbes, November 22, 1862, Fox Papers, box 5.

57. For example, see Welles to John A. Andrew, February 3, 1863, Welles Papers, reel 6, container 7, Letterbook February 2–May 22, 1863, 69, among many others.

58. Fox to George W. Blunt, September 11, 1862, Thompson and Wainwright, *Correspondence of Fox*, 2:374.

59. Welles to John Andrew, February 3, 1863, NARG 45, entry M209, roll 25, 70:315.

60. For example, see E. D. Morgan to Welles, November 17, 1862, NARG 45, entry M124, roll 425:109; Welles to Morgan, November 22, 1862, Welles Papers, reel 5, container 7, Letterbook October 4, 1862–February 2, 1863, 213.

61. R. B. Forbes to Fox, November 19, 1862, Fox Papers, box 5.

62. U.S. Department of Commerce, *Historical Statistics of the United States, Colonial Times to 1970* (Washington: Government Printing Office, 1976), 899, 890.

63. *Report of the Secretary of the Navy, 1882*, House Executive Document 1, 47th Cong., 2d sess., part 1: 33.

64. The plan is discussed in Tidwell, *April '65*, 105–6. Its existence is corroborated by Mallory's endorsement on Uriel Wright to Jefferson Davis, August 11, 1864. Wright forwarded a proposal to put "incendiary devices or torpedoes" on merchant vessels in foreign ports; Mallory referred it to the secretary of war because "it is the plan of operations upon which Mr. Courtney, under [War Department] authority, is believed to be engaged." *OR*, ser. 4, 3:580–83.

65. T. E. Courtney to H. E. Clark, January 19, 1864, and Porter to Welles, March 20, 1864, *ORN*, 26:186, describe the "coal torpedo" from the Confederate and Union points of view.

66. Grant to H. W. Halleck, August 11, 1864, *OR*, ser. 1, 42, pt 1: 17. Details, from the Confederate who planted the device, are in John Maxwell to Z. McDaniel, December 16, 1864, ibid., 954. McDaniel is identified as "Captain, Company A, Secret Service."

67. Ramsdell, *Laws and Joint Resolutions*, 170. A companion act made a secret appropriation of $5 million for "secret service, to be expended under the direction of the President."

68. A. L. Rives to E. Kirby Smith, September 15, 1863, *ORN*, 26:191.

69. Porter to Welles, March 20, 1864, *ORN*, 26:186.

70. Barnes, *Submarine Warfare*, 77. Butler and Porter narrowly escaped with their lives.

71. Hogg and six of his "desperate men" were captured aboard the ss *Salvador*, and the plot fell apart. *ORN*, 4:352–67.

72. Bulloch, *Secret Service*, 399–415. Mallory had ordered him to "supply [the *Alabama*'s] place if possible." Mallory to Bulloch, July 18, 1864, *ORN*, ser. 2, 2:687.

73. George W. Dalzell, *The Flight from the Flag: The Continuing Effect of the Civil War upon the American Carrying Trade* (Chapel Hill: University of North Carolina Press, 1940), 247.

74. Dalzell, *Flight from the Flag*, 257, 249–56; for a more nuanced treatment, see Thomas R. Heinrich, *Ships for the Seven Seas: Philadelphia Shipbuilding in the Age of Industrial Capitalism* (Baltimore: Johns Hopkins University Press, 1997).

75. Luraghi, *History of the Confederate Navy*, 232.

8. THE NAVAL WAR, 1864–65

1. Dahlgren to Welles, February 19, 1864, *ORN*, 15:329.

2. Lee to Jordan, May 27, 1863, with endorsements, *OR*, ser. 1, 14:1023–24; Lee to D. B. Harris, with endorsements, December 20, 1863, ibid., 28, part 2: 566–67; Lee to Harris, with endorsements, December 23, 1863, ibid., 573–75.

3. A. L. Rives to Lee, January 22, 1864, *OR*, ser. 1, 35, part 1: 537; Rives to Lee,

ibid., 548; Special Orders 23, Adjutant and Inspector General's Office, January 28, 1864, ibid., 53, 306; Beauregard, "Torpedo Service," 155.

4. B. E. Chassaing to Dahlgren, March 29, 1865, ORN, 16:378–79; E. J. Dichman to Dahlgren, March 25, 1865, ibid., 406–7; Peter Pry and Richard Zeitlin, "Torpedo Boats: Secret Weapons of the South," *Warship International* 21, no. 4 (1984): 391.

5. Bulloch to Mallory, September 16 and October 24, 1864, and January 26, 1865, ORN, ser. 2, 2:724–25, 738–39, 790–91.

6. Francis D. Lee to Jordan, March 8, 1864, with enclosures, ORN, 15:358–59. The sinkings occurred on April 1 and 16 and May 10, 1864.

7. S. P. Lee to Welles, April 15, 1864, with enclosures, ibid., 9:592–600; Davidson to Mallory, April 11, 1864, ibid., 604; Pry and Zeitlin, "Torpedo Boats," 385, 391–92.

8. Bulloch, *Secret Service*, 296.

9. Grant to Meade, April 9, 1864, OR, ser. 1, 33:828.

10. Grant to H. W. Halleck, March 25, 1864, OR, ser. 1, 34, part 2: 721.

11. Figures from Wise, *Lifeline*, 233–59.

12. Welles to Stanton, January 2, 1864, OR, ser. 1, 33:326.

13. Welles to Dahlgren, October 9, 1863, ORN, 15:26–27.

14. Still, *Iron Afloat*, 89–92.

15. Ericsson to Fox, October 5, 1862, Fox Papers, box 3.

16. Fox to Stimers, February 25, 1864, Private, Fox Papers, box 8.

17. Stimers to Fox, February 29, 1864, Private, Fox Papers, box 9.

18. Fox to Ericsson, April 22, 23, 24, and 28, 1864, Welles Papers, container 8, Letterbook March 17–June 27, 1864, 109, 117, 119, 135. It is an example of Fox's enthusiasms, quickly developed, urgently pressed, and quickly fading.

19. Ericsson's biographer wrote that Stimers was "confronted" by a plate proclaiming that *Tunxis* was built from Stimers's designs. "Mr. Stimers was evidently not proud of this record, for he was discovered at work one day with a cold chisel cutting his name out of the plate." Church, *Life of Ericsson*, 2:30.

20. Welles, *Diary*, entry for March 23, 1864, 1:546. Welles had written in 1863 that the navy had great difficulty obtaining seamen and that "at times" ships had been "unable to proceed to sea for the want of crews." *Report of the Secretary of the Navy, 1862–63*, xxvi.

21. ORN, 15:324.

22. Rowan's men had been twenty-three months aboard ship without liberty. Dahlgren to Rowan, June 9, 1864, quoted in NARG 125, entry M273, roll 128, case 3606, 173–77; NARG 24, log of *New Ironsides*, June 12–15, 1864. Charles Mervine reported, "The one years men goes to mast to day again with the old cry, (our time is out) but they are handsomely repulsed by Barney our 1st Luff [first lieutenant] he giving them a broadside in plain English, telling them to wait untill relief comes from north." Charles K. Mervine, "Jottings by the Way: A Sailor's Log, 1862–

1864," in Kent Packard, ed., *Pennsylvania Magazine of History and Biography* 71, no. 2 (April 1947): 121–51; no. 3 (July 1947): 242–82 (quote on 139).

23. Farragut, for example, told Welles he was "very much in want" of men. Farragut to Welles, July 9, 1864, *ORN*, 21:367–68; *Report of the Secretary of the Navy, 1862–1863*, xxv.

24. The provost marshal general asserted that it had been "the practice" to discharge men who were actually in the navy. James B. Fry to Stanton, December 12, 1863, *OR*, ser. 3, 3:1166. Stanton made the most of his power to exempt enlisted sailors. Welles, *Diary*, entry for August 19, 1863, 1:407.

25. Welles noted "vicious legislation" that he had supposed was inadvertent, "but which I begin to think was not wholly without design." Welles, *Diary*, entry for December 29, 1863, 1:498.

26. Bennett, "Union Jacks," 310–47, discusses the cultural dynamics and the rise of segregation and white racial hatred. NARG 24, entry 138, muster rolls of *New Ironsides*, January 1863 and January 1865.

27. Muster roll of *New Ironsides*, January 1, 1863, and October 6, 1864.

28. War Department General Orders 91, March 4, 1864, *OR*, ser. 3, 4:151–52.

29. Welles to John P. Hale, February 9 and June 20, 1864, NARG 45, entry 5.

30. Welles, *Diary*, entry for August 26, 1864, 2:121; *Report of the Secretary of the Navy, 1863–64*, xxxiv–xxxv, 909. The chief of the Bureau of Equipment and Recruiting noted that due to the "great preponderance of landsmen, the department was compelled to confine their enlistments to 15 per cent." Michael Bennett discusses the enlistment motivations of Union sailors in "Union Jacks," 7–13, 23–26.

31. Harlan & Hollingsworth to Welles, August 9, 1862, NARG 45, entry M124, roll 415:262; Ericsson to Fox, August 9, 1862, Fox Papers, box 3.

32. Welles to Merrick & Sons, July 29, 1863, NARG 45, entry M209, roll 25, 71:577.

33. *Confederate Statutes*, 1st Cong., 3d sess., chapter 48, May 1, 1863.

34. Mallory to James A. Seddon, August 11, 1863, *OR*, ser. 4, 2:705–6.

35. In April 1864 the Confederate Bureau of Conscription revoked its recognition of the navy's exemption certificates, and the navy workshops fell even farther behind. Bureau of Conscription Circular 16, April 15, 1864, *OR*, ser. 4, 3:305; Durkin, *Steven R. Mallory*, 302–4.

36. From Mallory's diary, August 15, 1862, quoted in Coski, *Capital Navy*, 69.

37. Mallory to Davis, July 1, 1864, with enclosures, *OR*, ser. 4, 3:520–23.

38. Bulloch, *Secret Service*, 302–3; Jones, *Confederate Rams at Birkenhead*, 108–11. The Laird vessels served the Royal Navy as HMS *Scorpion* and *Wivern*.

39. Geoghegan, "The South's Scottish Sea Monster," 25–27.

40. Welles, *Diary*, entry for July 6, 1864, 2:67. The event appears to have been more important in the North than in the South. Jones, easily depressed by Con-

federate defeats on land, tossed off the loss of the *Alabama*. Jones, *Rebel War Clerk's Diary*, entry for July 9, 1864, 2:246.

41. Bulloch to Mallory, June 10, 1864, ORN, ser. 2, 2:667; Bulloch to Mallory, July 27, 1864, ibid., 689–91; Bulloch, *Secret Service*, 348–50.

42. Wise, *Lifeline*, 144–46; Spencer, *Confederate Navy*, 195.

43. Figures from Wise, *Lifeline*, 265–68.

44. Special Orders 145, August 3, 1863, OR, ser. 1, 26, part 2: 136; Special Orders 38, February 15, 1864, ibid., 32, part 2: 738; Samuel Cooper to D. H. Maury, May 10, 1864, ibid., 36, part 2: 988.

45. Farragut to Porter, January 17, 1864, ORN, 21:39.

46. Grant to Henry W. Halleck, March 25, 1864, OR, ser. 1, 34, part 2: 721; Grant to David Hunter, April 17, 1864, enclosing Grant to Banks, April 17, 1864, ibid., 190–92; Canby to Halleck, June 18, 1864, ORN, 21:339; Canby to Farragut, July 1, 1864, ibid., 357; Farragut to J. S. Palmer, July 18, 1864, ibid., 378–79; Canby to Farragut, July 18, 1864, ibid., 279; Canby to Sherman, July 20, 1864, ibid., 280.

47. Percival Drayton to Thornton A. Jenkins, August 3, 1864, ORN, 21:403; Farragut to Jenkins, August 3, 1864, ibid., 404.

48. Farragut to Welles, August 12, 1864, ORN, 21:416.

49. General Orders no. 10, July 12, 1864, ORN, 21:397–98, and General Orders no. 11, July 29, 1864, ibid., 398; Farragut to T. H. Stevens, August 4, 1864, ibid., 404.

50. Farragut to Fox, June 14, 1864, ORN, 21:335; memorandum forwarded by Col. A. J. Myer, July 7, 1864, ibid., 361–64; Myer to Farragut, July 13, 1864, ibid., 371–74; Farragut to Welles, August 12, 1864, ibid., 417; T. H. Stevens to Farragut, July 23, 1864, with enclosures, ibid., 21:382–84.

51. *Naval Chronology*, IV-90, 92, 93.

52. Drayton to Jenkins, August 1, 1864, ORN, 21:394–95.

53. Rains later wrote that he had "sixty-seven torpedoes planted where this one acted." The installations he had planned to use to close the main channel were not completed after he left Mobile, and "the place [was] left open and the enemy made use of it." Rains to James A. Seddon, August 15, 1864, OR, ser. 1, 39, part 1: 433.

54. Texas ports had three runs in 1863, forty-one in 1864, and forty-eight between January and May 1865.

55. Wm. H. Ludlow to "Secretary Navy," August 12, 1864, ORN, 3:137; John Taylor Wood to Mallory, August 31, 1864, ibid., 701–3.

56. Welles to Hiram Paulding, August 14, 1864, ORN, 3:144; A. Ludlow Case to Welles, August 18, 1864, ibid., 152.

57. Welles to George A. Stevens, August 18, 1864, ORN, 3:153; Stevens to Welles, August 30, 1864, ibid., 176–77; Welles, *Diary*, entry for August 20, 1864, 2:113–14.

58. Jones, *Rebel War Clerk's Diary*, entries for September 7, 1864 (2:278) and September 24, 1864 (2:291–92).

59. W. H. C. Whiting to Mallory, September 27, 1864, *ORN*, 10:751–52; Lee to James A. Seddon, September 22, 1864, ibid., 747.

60. *Chickamauga* took seven prizes between October 28 and November 19 and *Tallahassee*, by then renamed *Olustee*, took six between October 29 and November 7. *ORN*, 3:710–14, 836.

61. Fox to Goldsborough, May 17, 1862, Thompson and Wainwright, *Correspondence of Fox*, 1:269, Goldsborough to Fox, May 21, 1862, ibid., 1:273. Fox to Lee, December 15, 1862, ibid., 2:244–45; Fox to Du Pont, January 6, 1863, ibid., 1:173; Fox to Du Pont, March 11, 1863, ibid., 1:191–92. Examples of other schemes include Fox to Goldsborough, June 3, 1862, ibid., 1:281–82; Fox to Du Pont, February 26, 1863, ibid., 1:184–85; Fox to Lee, March 26, 1863, ibid., 2:250–51; Lee to Fox, July 18, 1863, ibid., 2:264; Lee to Fox, December 14, 1863, ibid., 2:273–74.

62. Welles, *Diary*, entry for August 30, 1864, 2:127; Ulysses S. Grant, *Personal Memoirs of U. S. Grant* (New York: Charles L. Webster, 1885), 2:385.

63. William Lamb, "The Defense of Fort Fisher," in Johnson and Buel, eds., *Battles and Leaders of the Civil War*, 4:642.

64. Collins to Wilkes, December 1, 1864, *ORN*, 4:264.

65. Collins to Welles, December 16, 1864, *ORN*, 4:266; Extracts from Court-Martial of Commander Collins, U.S. Navy, *ORN*, 4:269. Collins pled and was found guilty, but Welles disapproved the verdict in 1866.

66. Lee to Welles, July 10, 1864, *ORN*, 10:247–48.

67. Reports of the expedition are at *ORN*, 10:610–22.

68. Bulloch to Mallory, September 16, 1864, *ORN*, ser. 2, 2:723–24. *Shenandoah* took her first prizes in early November 1864, but it took so long for the word to reach the United States that the hunt for her did not begin until January 1865.

69. Waddell later boasted, "I made New England suffer." Quoted in *Naval Chronology*, V-126. Targeting New Englanders was clearly important to the Confederates, since Bulloch had earlier suggested that the new cruiser "[lay] toll upon the exposed villages along the coast of New England." Bulloch to Mallory, September 16, 1864, *ORN*, ser. 2, 2:724.

70. Lamb, "Defense of Fort Fisher," 642–43; Rod Gragg, *Confederate Goliath: The Battle of Fort Fisher* (New York: HarperCollins, 1991), 19–20.

71. Grant, *Personal Memoirs*, 2:388–90; Thomas O. Selfridge, "The Navy at Fort Fisher," in Johnson and Buel, eds., *Battles and Leaders of the Civil War*, 4:655.

72. Porter to Welles, January 11, 1865, *ORN*, 11:228; Gragg, *Confederate Goliath*, 59–60.

73. "Blowed Up," *Wilmington Daily Journal*, December 24, 1864, 2.

74. Porter to Welles, December 27, 1864, *ORN*, 11:261–62; Grant, *Personal Memoirs*, 394–95.

75. Lamb, "Defense of Fort Fisher," 648–49, 654; Whiting to Lee, February 19, 1865, *OR*, ser. 1, 46, part 1: 441.

76. Charles M. Robinson III, *Hurricane of Fire: The Union Assault on Fort Fisher* (Annapolis: Naval Institute Press, 1998), 165–78.

77. Lamb, "Defense of Fort Fisher," 652.

78. Mallory to Hunter, December 14, 1864, ORN, 16:480; S. S. Lee to Hunter, December 17, 1864, ibid., 16:481.

79. Wells, *Confederate Navy*, 150.

80. Page describes the voyage and commissioning with sometimes grating coyness. Thomas Jefferson Page, "The Career of the Confederate Cruiser *Stonewall*," SHS *Papers* 7 (1879): 265–68.

81. Bulloch noted that by June 1864, the "increasing stringency" of the blockade meant that money "came forward with less and less rapidity and regularity." Bulloch, *Secret Service*, 399.

82. *Naval Chronology*, VI-191, 250; Bulloch to John Low, January 8, 1865, ORN, ser. 2, 2:787–88.

83. Sullivan, "Phantom Fleet," 29–31; Lester, *Confederate Finance*, 110–12.

84. Jones, *Rebel War Clerk's Diary*, entries for January 10 and February 8, 1865, 2:382 and 412–13.

85. Bulloch, *Secret Service*, 495–96; Mallory to Bulloch, December 2, 1864, ORN, ser. 2, 2:776–77.

86. Joint Resolution 44, approved January 27, 1865, in Ramsdell, *Laws and Joint Resolutions*, 28; Mallory to Bulloch, January 31, 1865, ORN, ser. 2, 2:793–94.

87. Bulloch to Mallory, April 12, 1865, ibid., 810.

88. Still, *Iron Afloat*, 183–86; Scharf, *Confederate States Navy*, 740–42; William Harwar Parker, *Recollections of a Naval Officer, 1841–1865* (New York: Scribner, 1883; repr., Annapolis: Naval Institute Press, 1985), 365–66.

89. Grant to Parker, January 24, 1865, OR, ser. 1, 46, part 2: 225.

90. Grant to Fox and Grant to Welles, January 24, 1865, ORN, 11:635; Grant to Fox, January 24, 1865, OR, ser. 1, 46, part 2: 218 and 221; Fox to Grant, January 24, 1865, ibid., 221–24.

91. Welles to Parker and Parker to Welles, January 24, 1865, OR, ser. 1, 46, part 2: 224; Welles to J. M. Berrian, January 24, 1865, ibid., 226.

92. Sherman and Dahlgren had apparently agreed on a feint at Charleston or Bull's Bay, but Sherman told Dahlgren to "run no risk at all," probably not what Dahlgren wanted to hear. Sherman to Dahlgren, January 17, 1865, ORN, 16:181.

93. Bulloch, *Secret Service*, 594.

94. Bulloch, *Secret Service*, 381.

95. Page commented repeatedly on the *Stonewall*'s poor seagoing and fighting qualities and saw an engagement with the "superior force" of two wooden Federal cruisers as a "momentous ordeal." Page, "Career of the Confederate Cruiser *Stonewall*," SHS *Papers* 7:273–74.

96. Bulloch, *Secret Service*, 381–82. Welles court-martialed Commodore Thomas T. Craven of the *Niagara* for his failure to engage the ironclad. Found

guilty, he was sentenced only to suspension from duty with pay—evidence that his contemporaries fully agreed with his decision not to engage an ironclad with his wooden cruiser. Welles saw the sentence as a two-year vacation and disapproved it; Craven retired as a rear admiral in 1869.

97. Jones to R. Taylor, March 15, 1865, *OR*, 49, part 1: 1060.

98. Secret Act 17, 2d Cong., 1st sess., approved May 27, 1864. Ramsdell, *Laws and Joint Resolutions*, 172.

99. Parker, *Recollections*, 374–89. This began a month-long odyssey that included escorting President and Mrs. Davis before the midshipmen were disbanded on May 2, 1865. E. F. Winslow to E. B. Beaumont, April 9, 1865, *OR*, 49, part 1: 483–84. The Columbus works were destroyed soon thereafter. Winslow to Beaumont, April 18, 1865, ibid., 485–87.

100. *Report of the Secretary of the Navy, 1865*, ix.

101. *Stettin* was sold out of the service in June 1865. As a merchant ship under the name *Sheridan*, she was lost in 1866.

102. Some volunteer officers received regular commissions under a law, enacted in July 1866, that capped their number at 150 and their rank at lieutenant commander. Chisholm, *Waiting for Dead Men's Shoes*, 326, 328. John M. Butler applied for a permanent commission but failed to receive it. He was honorably discharged from the navy in June 1868.

103. Welles to commandants, April 28, 1865, *ORN*, 4:500.

104. S. Draper to Hugh McCulloch, May 12, 1865, and Welles to William Hunter, May 12, 1865, *ORN*, 4:516.

105. Boggs to Welles, May 17, 1865, with enclosures, *ORN*, 4:520–21.

106. Page to Bulloch, May 19, 1865, ibid., 4:748; Page, "The Career of the Confederate Cruiser *Stonewall*," *SHS Papers*, 7:279. The United States reimbursed the Spanish government and claimed the ship. She was sold to Japan in 1867, being renamed first *Kotetsu* and then *Adzuma*, and was discarded in 1888.

107. Wise, *Lifeline*, 222–25.

108. Surdam, *Northern Naval Superiority*, 160–61, 151.

109. The Erlanger Loan dropped from the 60s in December 1864 to the teens in April 1865 and single digits in May. British bondholders were trying to collect from the United States as late as 1944. Lester, *Confederate Finance*, 207–8, 55–56. The Union steadfastly refused to assume the debts of its former adversary, a policy enshrined in Section 4 of the Fourteenth Amendment to the U.S. Constitution.

110. Glimpses of the complex financial affairs of the various Trenholm companies may be found in Ethel Trenholm Seabrook Nepveux, *George A. Trenholm, Financial Genius of the Confederacy* (Anderson SC: Electric City, 1999), 164–66, 170–72, 178–89, 194–202, 206–11.

9. WINNERS AND LOSERS

1. Paul A. C. Koistinen, *Beating Plowshares into Swords: The Political Economy of*

AmericanWarfare,1606–1865 (Lawrence: University Press of Kansas, 1996), 178–83, 187, 265–69;Wilson, *Southern Industry*, 18.

2. The impact of family hardship on desertion rates is discussed in Jean V. Berlin, "Did Confederate Women Lose the War?" in Mark Grimsley and Brooks D. Simpson, eds.,*The Collapse of the Confederacy* (Lincoln: University of Nebraska Press, 2001), 184–86.

3. Tamara Moser Melia, *"Damn the Torpedoes":A Short History of U.S. Naval Mine Countermeasures, 1777–1991* (Washington DC: Naval Historical Center, 1991), 16.

4. Mallory to Hunter, December 14, 1864, ORN, 16:480; S. S. Lee to Hunter, December 17, 1864, ibid., 481.

5. The myth of victory of theWar of 1812 gave the U.S. Navy "an air of permanence and assurance rather surprising in an armed force of such youth." Johnson, *Rear Admiral John Rodgers*, 1. Even contemporaries noticed: Lt. Robert D. Minor told his friend Cdr. Catesby ap R. Jones, "War is the time to create a love for the service that will make it popular in peace, and I begin to fear that our opportunity has passed." Minor to Jones, March 23, 1864, ORN, 9:807.

6. Jones, *RebelWar Clerk's Diary*, entry for February 1, 1865, 2:406.

7. Welles, *Diary*, entry for June 10, 1864, 2:52–53, entry for February 21, 1865, 2:241–42.

8. Judah P. Benjamin encapsulated the issue: unable to control operations "confided by law to a distinct department," the commanders could only try "to establish concert of action through mutual understanding"—which was generally lacking. Benjamin to Mansfield Lovell, January 19, 1863, ORN, 18:286.

9. Dew, *Ironmaker to the Confederacy*, 315–19.

10. Harold and Margaret Sprout,*The Rise of American Naval Power* (Princeton NJ: Princeton University Press, 1946), 165.

11. Thomas P. Hughes, *Networks of Power: Electrification inWestern Society, 1880–1930* (Baltimore: Johns Hopkins University Press, 1983), 286.

12. Michael E. Vlahos, "The Making of an American Style (1797–1887)," in *Naval Engineering andAmerican Seapower*, ed. RandolphW. King (Baltimore: Nautical and Aviation, 1989), 19.

13. Church, *Life of Ericsson*, 2:102.Welles saw more clearly.When congressmen wanted to stop the sale of monitors to Peru, he wrote, "Simpletons, I wish we could sell all."Welles, *Diary*, entry for May 8, 1868 3:349.

14. Daniel Ammen, *The Old Navy and the New* (Philadelphia: J. B. Lippincott, 1891), 430–31, 434. The need for sail power ruled out ironclads for peacetime cruising; besides being only marginally habitable, no ironclad sailed well.

15. In 1875 Porter, then the highest ranking officer in the navy, wrote, "For fighting purposes, I prefer turreted vessels, of the monitor class, to any others." *Report of the Secretary of the Navy, 1875*, 299.

16. Figures from *Report of the Secretary of the Navy, 1882*, part 1: 33.

17. Dalzell, *Flight from the Flag*, 257.

18. Heinrich, *Ships for the Seven Seas*, 9; F. G. Fassett Jr., *The Shipbuilding Business in the United States of America* (New York: Society of Naval Architects and Marine Engineers, 1948), 44–45.

Bibliographic Essay

The naval aspects of the Civil War have received less literary attention than the war on land, and much of that literature is operationally oriented. Some studies, most of them recent, have gone beyond the ships themselves and the strategic and political aspects of the naval war to address naval administration, naval acquisition and logistics, and industrial mobilization.

For campaign history, the *Official Records of the Union and Confederate Navies in the War of the Rebellion* (commonly ORN) and *The War of the Rebellion: A Compilation of the Official Records of the Union and Confederate Armies* (commonly OR) are both indispensable. Unfortunately, the second series of the ORN, which was to include nonoperational items, was truncated after only three volumes. The correspondence in the OR helps to fill the gaps, especially in areas such as torpedo warfare and blockade-running in which Confederate army and navy interests overlapped. Many of the Confederate navy's records burned during the evacuation of Richmond in 1865, so Confederate documents are much sparser than Union.

Diaries and collections of personal and official correspondence provide important contemporary views and are especially helpful for explaining the reasoning that underlay action. Howard Beale's 1960 edition is the most accurate version of Gideon Welles's detailed diary. Stephen R. Mallory, Welles's Confederate counterpart, also kept a diary, but no published edition exists. Neither secretary's correspondence has been published, although Welles's papers are available on microfilm. Useful collections of letters include John D. Hayes's three-volume *Samuel Francis Du Pont: A Selection from His Civil War Letters* and George M. Brooke Jr.'s recent selection, *Ironclads and Big Guns of the Confederacy: The Journal and Letters of John M. Brooke*. The published collection of Assistant Secretary of the Navy Gustavus V. Fox's letters (*Confidential Correspondence of Gustavus Vasa Fox, Assistant Secretary of the Navy, 1861–1865*) is very limited and incomplete; serious researchers must consult Fox's papers at the New-York Historical Society.

Realizing that an author's recollections may be distorted by time and that every important action engendered at least two schools of thought, reminiscent works provide indispensable information. James Dunwody Bulloch's memoirs (*The Secret Service of the Confederate States in Europe; or, How the Confederate Cruisers Were Equipped*) are vital to understanding the Confederates' overseas construction program, and first-person narratives by Confederates and neutrals open a window on blockade-running and commerce raiding. In 1887, *Century Magazine* published a collection of reminiscent articles as *Battles and Leaders of the Civil War* that includes a number of naval topics. Reminiscences also appear in the papers of the Union Military Order of the Loyal Legion and in the Confederate Southern Historical Society and United Confederate Veterans magazines.

Newspapers of the period are valuable but should be used with caution, since many stories, especially those involving distant events, were more or less embellished, speculative, or inaccurate. Partisanship was rampant, so knowledge of a newspaper's political biases helps the researcher to evaluate its credibility.

Biographies of Civil War figures abound, and both Union and Confederate secretaries of the navy have been the subjects of full-length works. The "standard" biography of Welles is John Niven's 1973 *Gideon Welles: Lincoln's Secretary of the Navy*; among older works is Richard S. West Jr.'s *Gideon Welles: Lincoln's Navy Department*. The only significant work on Mallory is Joseph T. Durkin's *Confederate Navy Chief: Stephen R. Mallory*. Biographies of top uniformed leaders on both sides range from superficial hagiography to such well considered works as Robert J. Schneller Jr.'s *A Quest for Glory: A Biography of Rear Admiral John A. Dahlgren*, with a similar but smaller range for more junior navy men.

Biographies of second-tier civilians are much rarer. Fox, for example, has no full-fledged treatment; William J. Sullivan's dissertation, "Gustavus Vasa Fox and Naval Administration," is the only lengthy work on this complex figure.

Interest in enlisted sailors has increased of late with the publication of works such as Dennis J. Ringle's *Life in Mr. Lincoln's Navy* and Michael J. Bennett's recent dissertation, "Union Jacks: The Common Yankee Sailor of the American Civil War, 1861–1865." The definitive study of enlisted sailors, North or South, remains to be written.

Among secondary works, Robert M. Browning Jr.'s books on the North and South Atlantic Blockading Squadrons (*From Cape Charles to Cape Fear: The North Atlantic Blockading Squadron during the Civil War* and *Success Is All That Was Expected: The South Atlantic Blockading Squadron during the Civil War*) deserve mention not only for their operational insights but also for their treatment of logistics. Stephen R. Wise's *Lifeline of the Confederacy: Blockade Running during the Civil War* is an excellent survey, and David G. Surdam's *Northern Naval Superiority and the Economics of the American Civil War* offers a corrective to some of Wise's conclusions. Other useful works include Bern Anderson's *By Sea and by River*, dated in some respects but still sound, and a number of books on specific battles or campaigns.

At the beginning of the war, neither combatant had a naval administration equal to its circumstances. Confederate naval administration is documented in Tom Henderson Wells's *The Confederate Navy: A Study in Organization* and William N. Still's *The Confederate Navy: The Ships, Men, and Organization, 1861–65*, while Donald L. Canney's *Lincoln's Navy: The Ships, Men, and Organization, 1861–65* addresses the Union. Raimondo Luraghi's general *History of the Confederate Navy* incorporates organizational matter but occasionally errs by placing too much reliance on purely Confederate sources. A notable exception to the generally adequate historiography of the Confederate navy is the Naval Submarine Battery Service. No good history of Confederate torpedo warfare exists; the work to date (e.g., Milton F. Perry's *Infernal Machines: The Story of Confederate Submarine and Mine Warfare*) is primarily anecdotal and focused on the technology rather than on the organizations that supported the technologists.

Confederate naval activities in Europe were constrained both by statecraft and by money. Richard I. Lester's *Confederate Finance and Purchasing in Great Britain* summarizes operations in that country, while Warren F. Spencer's *The Confederate Navy in Europe* also covers France. Howard I. Jones's *Union in Peril: The Crisis over British Intervention in the Civil War* and Lynn M. Case and Warren F. Spencer's *The United States and France: Civil War Diplomacy* discuss diplomatic aspects of the conflict. Frank Lawrence Owsley's *King Cotton Diplomacy: Foreign Relations of the Confederate States of America* still has much to recommend it, although later work has tempered some of Owsley's conclusions. Wilbur Devereux Jones's *The Confederate Rams at Birkenhead: A Chapter in Anglo-American Relations* offers both an examination of British policy toward Confederate shipbuilding and a corrective to the idea that the "American War" was Great Britain's primary foreign policy concern.

Little has been done to investigate the naval mobilization of industrial resources North and South, and only the author's *Civil War Ironclads: Industrial Mobilization for the Union Navy* specifically addresses this topic. Maurice Melton's chapter in Still's *Confederate Navy* provides an overview of Confederate mobilization, but Melton's dissertation ("Major Military Industries of the Confederate Government") is an in-depth examination of three important Confederate industrial projects. Despite its broad title and important scholarship, Harold Wilson's *Confederate Industry* focuses on textiles and the Confederate army. As in other areas, the lack of Confederate navy records has inhibited detailed research, but even for the Union navy, there are few sources other than government archives—the personal and business papers of most shipbuilders have not survived.

Index

In the Great Campaigns of the Civil War series

Six Armies in Tennessee
The Chickamauga and Chattanooga Campaigns
By Steven E. Woodworth

Fredericksburg and Chancellorsville
The Dare Mark Campaign
By Daniel E. Sutherland

Banners to the Breeze
The Kentucky Campaign, Corinth, and Stones River
By Earl J. Hess

The Chessboard of War
Sherman and Hood in the Autumn Campaigns of 1864
By Anne J. Bailey

Atlanta 1864
Last Chance for the Confederacy
By Richard M. McMurry

Struggle for the Heartland
The Campaigns from Fort Henry to Corinth
Stephen D. Engle

And Keep Moving On
The Virginia Campaign, May–June 1864
Mark Grimsley

Vicksburg Is the Key
The Struggle for the Mississippi River
William L. Shea and Terrence J. Winschel

Now for the Contest
Coastal and Oceanic Naval Operations in the Civil War
William H. Roberts